LEISURE AND RECREATION
Advanced GNVQ
Optional Units

G000154721

Also available from Addison Wesley Longman

Foundation GNVQ Leisure and Tourism
Carole Jones & Margaret Radcliffe
0-582-29339-1
Covers all three mandatory units of the Foundation GNVQ

Intermediate GNVQ Leisure and Tourism 2nd edition
Verité Baker
0-582-27841-4
Covers all four mandatory units of the Intermediate GNVQ

Advanced GNVQ Leisure and Tourism 2nd edition
Ray Youell
0-582-27842-2
Covers all eight mandatory units of the Advanced GNVQ

Intermediate GNVQ Leisure and Tourism Optional Units
Katherine Kemp & Stephen Pearson
0-582-29217-4
Covers the four BTEC optional units for the Intermediate GNVQ

Advanced GNVQ Travel and Tourism Optional Units
Ray Youell
0-582-29337-5
Covers the seven BTEC optional units comprising the Travel
and Tourism stream of the Advanced GNVQ

All the above titles have been written to the latest 1995 specifications.

For further information about these and other titles, or to order a copy, please contact:

Addison Wesley Longman Customer Information Centre
PO Box 88
Harlow
Essex
CM19 5SR
Telephone: 01279 623928
Fax: 01279 414130

LEISURE AND RECREATION

Advanced GNVQ

Optional Units

Julie Gibson
Eric Macintyre
Ian Wood
Katherine Kemp
and
Stephen Pearson

 LONGMAN

Pearson Education Limited
Edinburgh Gate, Harlow,
Essex CM20 2JE, England
and associated companies throughout the world

First published 1997
Second impression 1998
Third impression 1999

British Library Cataloguing in Publication Data
A catalogue entry for this title is available from the British Library

ISBN 0-582-29338-3

Set by 36 in 10/12 pt Palatino
Printed in Malaysia, PJB

Contents

Preface

The 1995 revision of the BTEC GNVQ (Advanced) in Leisure and Tourism introduced the possibility of students following two separate optional streams, those in Travel and Tourism and those in Leisure and Recreation. The latter stream was grouped around two particular foci, the first on the *Operation of Built and Natural Facilities* and the second on *Sports, Fitness and Coaching*. This book aims to provide students following this stream with a user-friendly text which will help them in their studies over the wide-ranging subjects involved.

It has been compiled by lecturers who are actively involved in the Advanced GNVQ in Leisure and Tourism as teachers, assessors or verifiers. The material is thus provided in a manner which the course demands of students following the sport and physical recreation range of options. Each unit closely follows the elements, performance criteria and range statements. It expands upon each of them and further develops relevant issues as a prompt to students for further study.

The writing of texts for GNVQs is not an easy task as authors could simply produce material in a manner which would allow students merely to copy the information provided into their own portfolios. While this might be attractive to many students, it would not meet the aims and philosophy of the GNVQs which is to provide students with the necessary knowledge and skills about an occupational area which would allow them to enter that industry or to proceed to courses of further study. Most importantly, such a bland approach to writing a text would not stimulate students to produce imaginative work of their own and thus achieve better results. It is hoped that this book avoids this pitfall and will provide a stimulus to further, individual study of the units concerned.

This work is produced by lecturers with direct GNVQ experience, but they are also experienced in the leisure, sport and recreation industries. The ideas presented have all been tested in the business and are thus valid and current.

Our advice is to use this text wisely: understand the performance criteria and build on the information provided to do your own investigations. The activities at the end of each section are based on the Evidence Indicators of the optional units and should be used to build towards your portfolio of evidence. Is is our hope that all of this will produce interesting studies and successful outcomes for all following this optional stream.

The authors

Acknowledgements

The authors of Unit 11 would especially like to thank the following people on whose specialist skills they have drawn:

Ken Payne and Paul Cassidy, North Wales Gliding Club

Nigel Burke, Chairman of the Instructors, Longsleddale Outdoor Pursuits Centre

Katie Mac Donald, University of Stafford Canoe Club

Keith Dawson, Fell & Mountain, Accrington

Mike Quinn, Head of Sport, Leisure and Tourism, Bolton College

Rob Gale, Lecturer in Sport, Craven College, Skipton

Unit 9
SPORT AND PHYSICAL RECREATION

Element 9.1   Investigate sport and physical recreation in the UK

Element 9.2   Investigate the factors affecting participation in sport and physical recreation in the UK

Element 9.3   Explore trends and developments in sport and physical recreation

Element 9.1   Investigate sport and physical recreation in the UK

Performance criteria

1 Identify and give examples of sport and physical recreation activities in the UK.
2 Describe and give examples of the organisations involved with sport and physical recreation in the UK.
3 Describe the roles of the organisations involved with sport and physical recreation.
4 Explain how sport and physical recreation is funded in the UK.
5 Describe the scale of sport and physical recreation in the UK.

Definitions and fields of study in sport and physical recreation

In the study of the Mandatory Units it will have been observed that it is very important to be aware of the definitions of the terms and concepts under discussion. Thus Leisure is basically defined as a time-based idea, with its central focus being time which is free to the individual to use at one's discretion. In the same way, Recreation is defined as an activity-based idea, with the activities done in one's leisure time as the key concept underpinning it. It is important that we define our present fields of study.

What is sport?

Sport has a number of roles in modern society. These are

- As an outlet for competitive aggression
- As a leisure and recreational pursuit
- As part of the health and fitness industry
- As mass spectacle
- As a means of demonstrating nationalistic pride, as with national teams
- As part of the socialising process in society, for example club membership in sport
- As a business – professional sport or the equipment industry

Activity

Look up the word 'sport' in a standard dictionary and note down the meanings given for future reference.

Sport therefore involves

- An element of competition
- An emphasis on physical activity
- Activities bound by rules
- Activities with a large degree of organisation such as courts or pitches
- Activities with a distinct goal or outcome

What is physical recreation?

This concept clearly has links to the general idea of recreation and to the particular one of sport. However, it has certain particular characteristics of its own and these are

- An emphasis on participation and not performance as in sport
- More limited organisation needed than in sport
- More emphasis on relaxation than in sport
- More emphasis on the socialisation process than in sport
- The activities themselves are more important than goals or outcomes
- The pleasure comes from the experience itself rather than, as in sport, beating an opponent
- Less need for facilities or equipment than in sport
- May involve an environmental challenge, as in outdoor pursuits

Activity

1 Consider the following list of activities: aerobics, dance, hang gliding, horse racing, jogging, chess, mountaineering, snooker.

2 Put each one under a heading of either Sport or Physical Recreation. You can, if you think it fits, put an activity under both headings.
3 Discuss your choices with another student or in a small group.

Sport and physical recreation activities in the UK

Sport and physical recreation activities are made up of a vast range which people choose to take part in for different reasons and in different ways. The 1993 General Household Survey (GHS) lists the ten most popular sports for adults (aged 16 and over).

Top ten sports for women	**Top ten sports for men**
• Walking	• Walking
• Keep fit/yoga	• Snooker/pool/billiards
• Swimming	• Swimming
• Cycling	• Cycling
• Snooker/pool/billiards	• Soccer
• Tenpin bowls/skittles	• Golf
• Darts	• Weight lifting/training
• Weight lifting/training	• Darts
• Badminton	• Running (excluding track)
• Running (excluding track)	• Keep fit/yoga

Activity

List the above sports under the headings Indoor, Outdoor, Team, Individual, Organised and Casual to reflect the way in which people take part in them. They can appear under more than one heading if appropriate.

UK organisations involved with sport and physical recreation

It will be seen from the study of the Mandatory Unit on Investigating the Leisure and Tourism Industries that provision for sport and physical recreation falls under the three headings of the public, private and voluntary sectors. Each one has its own aims and objectives and sets about meeting the demand for provision in different ways. The organisations involved in provision can be classified under a number of headings.

Statutory organisations

These derive their status and authority from being established under a statute or Act of Parliament. Examples are the Department of National Heritage, the Sports Council or local authorities.

Non-statutory organisations

These are important organisations, but they do not exist under the terms of an Act of Parliament. Examples are the major governing bodies of sport, such as the All England Netball Association or the Football Association.

National organisations

These have a national status and national influence within a sport or recreational activity. Examples are the Rugby Football Union and the All England Women's Hockey Association.

Regional organisations

As the name implies, these organisations operate within a distinct regional area of authority and control. An example would be the East Midlands Regional Council for Sport and Recreation, a forum comprising a range of representatives from sporting bodies in Nottinghamshire, Derbyshire, Lincolnshire, Leicestershire and Northamptonshire.

Local organisations

The word 'local' indicates that these organisations have authority and status within a clearly defined city, town or county boundary. The best example of these is the local authority or the 'council' as it is more popularly referred to.

Regulatory organisations

These organisations exercise some power or control such as in setting laws or standards. A governing body of sport is a good example of such an organisation, as is the Health and Safety Executive which plays an important role in facility management.

Representative organisations

As the term indicates, a representative organisation exists to speak on behalf of its members. An example is the Central Council for Physical Recreation (CCPR), described sometimes as the 'parliament' of the governing bodies of sport.

Figure 9.1 shows the structure of sport in the United Kingdom in relation to the government's role in working with a range of other organisations.

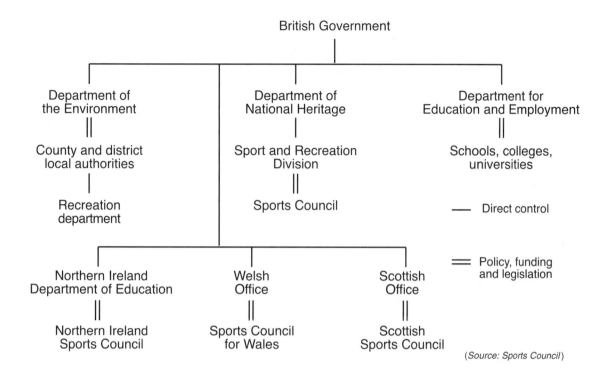

Fig. 9.1 *The structure of sport in the UK*

Roles of the organisations in sport and physical recreation

The wide variety of organisations involved in the industry means that there is a corresponding range of roles for them. This is illustrated in the case study on the Sports Council.

Sports Council

The Sports Council is an independent body, established in 1972 by Royal Charter, and funded largely through funds from the Department of National Heritage. It has a remit covering British sport as a whole although there are separate Councils for Scotland, Wales and Northern Ireland. It consists of members appointed by the Secretary of State and around 550 permanent employees.

The Sports Council has four main aims:

● To increase participation in sport and physical recreation
● To increase the quality and quantity of sports facilities
● To raise standards of performance
● To provide information for and about sport

Increasing participation

The Council has an extensive programme to increase participation by:

- Providing regional participation grants to help a range of local organisations to get local people into sport
- Running campaigns to persuade people to get involved in sport
- Funding development staff to help governing bodies to increase participation in their particular sport
- Organising programmes such as 'Action Sport' to promote sport through a wide range of formal and informal agencies

Facilities

The Council works to improve facilities by:

- Encouraging the development of new or improved sports facilities through advice and financial assistance
- Preparing standard design solutions for sports buildings and systems
- Developing innovative facilities and systems such as artificial playing surfaces
- Identifying examples of good practice in facilities and management
- Funding research into local and national sport facility requirements

Raising standards of performance

Action by the Sports Council in the area of standards of performance includes:

- Running six centres of excellence at:
  - Crystal Palace (National Sports Centre)
  - Bisham Abbey (National Sports Centre)
  - Lilleshall (National Sports Centre)
  - Holme Pierrepont (National Water Sports Centre)
  - Plas y Brenin (National Centre for Mountain Activities)
  - Manchester (National Cycling Centre)
- Offering support to governing bodies of sport
- Financing the National Coaching Foundation (NCF) to help meet the demand for trained coaches
- Encouraging sponsorship of sport by the private sector
- Running the campaign against drug abuse in sport

The council is the country's main central source of information and data about sport. It provides a national information centre and a network of nine regional centres based at its regional offices. The Sports Council researches and publishes a wide range of data on sport, briefs journalists, politicians and other interested parties and runs sport's largest annual conference 'Recreation Management'.

Changes to the Sports Council structure

On 8 July 1994, Iain Sproat, the Minister for Sport, announced a major re-shaping of the administration and focus of Government support for sport. A new United Kingdom Sports Council (UKSC) and English Sports Council was to be established in place of the current Great Britain Sports Council on 1 April 1996. The new UKSC will concentrate on helping to bring major international sporting events to the UK and to increase greatly the influence of the UK in international sport. The new English Sports Council will concentrate its resources on helping grass-roots sport and the governing bodies of sport. The costs of the new arrangements will be met within the present planned provision.

(Information courtesy of the Sports Council)

Not all the organisations in sport and physical recreation have as wide a remit as the Sports Council, but they play an important role as well. This is illustrated in the case study on the CCPR.

Central Council for Physical Recreation (CCPR)

The CCPR has been called 'the voice of British sport and recreation'. It directly represents the interest of the 22 million sportswomen and sportsmen in Britain. There is hardly a single recognised sport or physical recreation in Britain that does not come under the aegis of the CCPR. Its current membership consists of 209 British and 68 English organisations that control or represent sport and physical recreation.

How the CCPR is organised

The CCPR is a completely voluntary and independent organisation, and exists solely for the good of its members. Its 280 bodies are arranged in six divisions:

- Interested organisations
- Games and sports
- Movement and dance
- Major spectator sports
- Outdoor pursuits
- Water recreation

These divisions elect the executive committee and its officers, including the chairman and deputy chairman. The divisions, executive committee and officers are served by the CCPR secretariat, including the general secretary and team at Francis House, Francis Street, London.

The difference between the CCPR and the Sports Council

The Sports Council is a publicly funded government body whose members are appointed by the secretary of state. The CCPR is a non-governmental voluntary organisation, which is largely self-financing, and whose officers and executive committee are elected by the membership as a whole.

The link between the CCPR and the Sports Council

This is most clearly expressed in the 1972 agreement between the two bodies:

> *The Sports Council agrees that (so long as the CCPR is a body representing national organisations of sport and physical recreation as a whole) the Sports Council will make such resources and facilities available to the CCPR without cost to the CCPR, as may be reasonably required by the CCPR for the carrying out and implementation of the objects of the CCPR.*

How the CCPR is funded

- Donations from its governing body members
- Generous support from industry and commerce under the 'Sponsors of Sport' scheme
- Sponsorship by individuals or companies of particular events and projects under the auspices of the CCPR
- The sale and marketing of CCPR publications and research material
- Contracted support from the Sports Council

Mounting campaigns

Among the many problems affecting sport on which the CCPR has vigorously campaigned have been

- Sport and drugs
- The threat to sport and physical education in schools
- Sport and recreation for disabled people
- The unjust taxation of sport
- Medical aspects of sport and recreation
- Loss of playing fields and sports grounds

Fair play in sport

A celebrated success of the CCPR was the stance it took on fair play in sport. Disturbed by the trends towards indiscipline and disregard of the spirit of the game, the CCPR drew up the *Fair Play in Sport Charter*. This laid down a set of basic principles that should govern the behaviour of competitors, governing bodies, coaches and promoters. Nearly every sport in Britain committed itself without hesitation to the Charter, which was then translated into all the major world languages, and adopted by sports organisations worldwide.

Liaising with central government

Government and Parliament have become increasingly responsive to the approaches and arguments put to them by the CCPR. Government ministries and departments and individual MPs and MEPs frequently turn to the CCPR for information and advice on matters of sport. This means that the CCPR is able to put the worries and complaints of sporting bodies directly to the relevant departments and officials. For its part, the government is able to turn to the CCPR to ask for information on the likely effects of government policies on organised sport. The publication in February 1992 of its report on the grim state of sport in primary schools was a clear example of the ability of the CCPR to throw light on vital issues.

A particular success occurred in 1993 when the CCPR persuaded the government to honour its commitments, under EU financial regulations, by remitting and repaying the VAT levied on voluntary sports club subscriptions.

Liaison with local authorities

This is a vital area because local authorities are collectively the greatest providers of sporting facilities in Britain. Therefore, it is essential not only that local government be continually updated on the needs of organised sport, but also that sporting bodies be kept informed on the effect of local authority policies on sport and recreation.

Promoting sport in the community

Every year in Britain some 50 million hours are devoted freely by volunteers to the organisation of sport and recreation in the community. Without these volunteers sport as we know it in Britain would simply disappear. In recognition of this enormous contribution to the social well-being, as well as the sporting life of the nation, the CCPR has created a special *Community Sports Leaders Award* (*CSLA*) Scheme.

The aim is to develop the existing voluntary effort by recruiting from the various sports people who might care to extend their involvement by training to become leaders, organisers or coaches in their own chosen activity. The CSLA is divided into four settings: Junior, Preliminary, Basic Expedition Training and Higher. It is recognised as a qualification for the voluntary service element of the Duke of Edinburgh's Award. Since the launch of the CSLA in 1982, over 2,500 courses have been organised, producing some 35,000 qualified sports leaders annually.

The response to the award scheme has been so big that the CCPR has had to extend its own special staffing provision to cater for the demand for courses from schools, colleges and community organisations.

Here is a summary of the syllabus for the higher award in community sports leadership, known as the Hanson Leadership Award.

Hanson Leadership Award

Section A – Compulsory
A1   Preface
A2   Leadership in the Sporting Community
A3   First Aid

Section B – Community Groups
B1   Sport and People with a Disability
B2   Sport and People with a Learning Difficulty
B3   Sport and Visually Handicapped People
B4   Children's Play in a Sports Environment

Section C – Sports Specific
C1   Fitness for Sport
C2   National Governing Body Coaching/Leadership/Officiating Awards
(Those wishing to pursue the Hanson Leadership Award as a GNVQ may be required to follow a Level II National Governing Body Award)

Section D – Sports Administration

D1   Sports Club Administration
D2   Sports Information Technology
D3   Sports Sponsorship
D4   Organising an Event

Section E – Community Service
Minimum 30 hours Community Service

Course candidates
- Must have completed the CSLA (Preliminary) or have the equivalent leadership experience (at the discretion of the Course Director) prior to enrolling on a Hanson Leadership Award Course.
- Must successfully complete
  Section A   Compulsory
  Section B   Minimum – modules 1
                  Maximum – modules 2
  Section C   Minimum – module 2
                  Maximum – modules 3
  Section D   Optional

  Total requirement
  – Section A
  – Five other Modules of Work
- Must then undertake a minimum of 30 hours' voluntary community service – relevant to the areas of training completed (above).

Providing information

Governing bodies, individual sportswomen and sportsmen, students and general members of the public frequently approach the CCPR for information on sport. The value of the CCPR as a sports information bureau may be judged from the following selection from its current list of publications:
- *The Palmer Report: Amateur Status and Participation in Sport*
- *The Howell Report into Sports Sponsorship*
- *Careers in Sport and Recreation*
- *Guide to National Governing Body Coaching Award Schemes*
- *Let's Get Organised – A Guide to the Setting Up and Running of a Sports and Recreation Club*
- *The Organisation of Sport and Recreation in Britain*
- *Sport in the Primary School*
- *The Golden Plan for British Sport*
- *National Water Sports Code*

Obtaining sponsorship for sport

Without sponsorship, organised sport would find it impossible to survive, let alone develop. In 1974 sponsors contributed close on £275 million in support of sporting events and projects. The CCPR is uniquely equipped to assist its member organisations in gaining sponsors. Through its association with the Institute of Sports

Sponsorship, the CCPR set up the *Sports Sponsorship Advisory Service*. This provides a liaison and advisory service, enabling contact to be made between sporting bodies and their potential commercial partners. Clearly it is the governing bodies themselves that are the best agents for selling their sport as a product to a commercial company. This being so, the Advisory Service is geared to giving assistance in the most effective and efficient manner to governing body representatives at national and local levels in their search for commercial support. The CCPR's guide to obtaining sponsors, *The Search for Sports Sponsorship*, has proved to be extremely popular.

Governing bodies of sport

Britain can justifiably claim to have led the world in the organisation of most sports in their modern form. Governing bodies were the practical vehicles for establishing these organisational principles and the majority of these were founded in the years between 1850 and 1900. In the modern sporting environment there are around 150 governing bodies. Their membership varies considerably in size.

The ten largest governing bodies are

- English Golf Union   501,000
- National Federation of Anglers   285,000
- Scottish Golf Union   149,000
- English Bowling Association   132,000
- British Crown Green Bowling Association   128,000
- English Karate   110,000
- English Ladies' Golf Association   107,000
- British Association for Shooting & Conservation   105,000
- Scottish Bowling Association   92,000
- Badminton Association of England   90,000

These figures show the largest sports organisations in 1989 based on numbers of members, rather than numbers of clubs, because clubs vary widely in size.

(Information from Sports Council, *A Digest of Sports Statistics for the UK*, 1991.)

There are no figures available for the number of members of clubs affiliated to the Football Association, although estimates based on the average number of teams within a club and the average number of players required to run a team provide a figure of 1 million adult club players in England (Sports Council, CCPR, NPFA 1990). The Scottish Football Association estimates 75,000 registered players, with a further 79,000 players under the jurisdiction of the Scottish Amateur Football Association.

Whatever the size and scale of their operations, governing bodies share certain common roles and responsibilities:

- The direction of the general strategy and policy of the sport
- Drafting and implementing the rules and laws of the game or sport
- Organising local, national and international competitions
- Keeping players and participants informed on all relevant matters affecting that sport

- Maintaining good relations with the media
- Advancing the particular interests of the sport
- Training coaches within the sport
- Training and deploying officials within the sport

Activity

1 Select a sport of your choice.
2 Research its organisational structure – governing body, and so on.
3 Investigate how the sport is organised in your own local area – local clubs, governing bodies and competitions.

Sport for disabled people

The provision of sporting opportunities for those with disabilities, either physical or mental, has increased greatly over the years. Competition for disabled persons now extends right up to Olympic level and specialist coaching is available in most major sports. Individual governing bodies have an interest in disabled sporting provision and many play an active part in promotion. The major co-ordinating role for disabled sport is carried out by a specialist organisation.

British Sports Association for the Disabled (BSAD)

The BSAD was founded in 1961 and now includes around 500 disabled sports clubs and some 50,000 disabled sportspersons among its members. It carries out its functions in a number of ways:

- By grant-aiding individuals, projects and facilities
- By co-ordinating disabled sports provision
- By liaising with other governing bodies, the Sports Council and national government
- By undertaking education and research projects
- By public relations and promotional work on behalf of sport for disabled people
- By organising disabled sports competitions
- By training coaches and officials to work with disabled sports persons

Professional organisations

The sport and recreation industry is now regarded as being a profession in the same way as many older-established occupations. As such, there exist many organisations which seek to promote high standards within the industry and at the same time to represent the interests of their members. Two examples of these are the Institute of Sport and Recreation Management (ISRM) and the Institute of Leisure and Amenity Management (ILAM).

These organisations aim to

- Raise management standards within the industry
- Promote sport and physical recreation to the public at large
- Represent the interests of their members
- Represent the industry in dealings with government
- Provide training courses for the industry
- Publish relevant material on sport and recreation
- Offer schemes of professional qualifications
- Distribute relevant information within the industry

There are many other specialist professional organisations and associations in the sport and recreation field, for example the Physical Education Association of Great Britain and the British Association of Sports Coaches.

How sport and physical recreation is funded in the UK

Across the three sectors of provision – public, private and voluntary – there are various methods and sources used to fund sport and recreational facilities and services. Let us look at each in more detail.

Public sector

Any local authority or council can choose, under its discretionary powers, to channel some of its income towards sport and recreation. This income comes from:

- Central government
- Council tax and uniform business rate
- European Social Fund
- Charges for services
- National Lottery
- Millennium Commission

Central government

Through the taxes which it levies on citizens and businesses, the government receives a lot of income. In turn, some of this money is passed on to local authorities by the Department of the Environment and the Department of National Heritage (see Figure 9.1). This might come directly to the councils or from agencies such as the Sports Council, to whom local authorities can bid for funds for projects.

Council tax and uniform business rate

Council tax is levied on individuals living in its area by the local authority. Uniform business rate is paid by local businesses for the services which they receive from the council.

European Social Fund

The European Union has funds which it allocates to bids for special projects. A local authority could bid for some of this money for a sport and recreational project in its area.

Charges for services

Although a local authority aims to provide services for all its residents at the most reasonable charges possible, sometimes even free for certain groups, it still must raise income to keep them running and maintained. Charges for activities vary from activity to activity and from area to area. The Chartered Institute of Public Finance and Accountancy (CIPFA) produces useful statistical information on these charges. Table 9.1 summarises local authority charges for 1994–5.

Table 9.1   Local authority charges for leisure services in England and Wales, 1994–5

Facility	Non-metropolitan (£)	Metropolitan (£)	London (£)
Leisure centre (Charges per hour)			
Main hall	23.20	38.00	41.50
Small hall	12.60	14.50	25.00
Badminton	4.50	4.60	6.10
Weight training	2.10	2.0	2.70
Aerobics	2.20	2.20	3.00
Swimming pool (Charges per session)			
Adult	1.50	1.50	1.70
Junior/senior citizen	0.80	0.80	0.90
Club booking	32.00	28.70	38.30
Instruction	3.70	2.70	3.50
Sauna	3.00	3.20	4.50
Outdoor sports (Charges per hour)			
Bowls	1.40	1.00	1.60
Tennis	2.50	1.90	2.70
(Charges per pitch)			
Cricket	25.10	25.00	32.50
Football	22.00	22.20	30.50

(*Source: CIPFA [Chartered Institute of Public Finance and Accountancy]*, Charges for Leisure Services Statistics, *London*)

National Lottery

The National Lottery started in 1994 and aims to channel some of the money raised into sport. The Sports Council is responsible for deciding on Lottery bids with a sporting emphasis; the guidelines state that they should be 'capital projects which have a significant element of partnership'. This can be a combination of local authorities, private companies and the voluntary sector working together.

Sport and the National Lottery

The Sports Council welcomes applications from

- Voluntary sports clubs, charitable trusts, playing fields associations, youth clubs, community associations, etc. – as long as one of the sports is an aim within your constitution and you are open to all
- Area sports associations – provided you are made up of local sports clubs
- National governing bodies of sport recognised by the Sports Council
- Local Authorities and other public bodies

Can commercial bodies apply?

Only if the project is not primarily oriented towards individual personal gain or shareholders' dividends, if it helps resolve a real shortage of facilities, if the project delivers significant community benefit, with significant guaranteed public access – through a Community Use Agreement. That applies to professional sports clubs, too.

And schools, universities, colleges?

Not solely for curricular activities – and, again, there must be a shortage of facilities helped by significant guaranteed public access through a Community Use Agreement. Only independent and grant-maintained schools can apply directly to us; the others must go through the local education authority.

What sort of projects are eligible?

The range of projects is very wide, but there is one important condition: they must be capital projects, that is, construction, buying land, upgrading, etc. So that means things like pitches, sports halls, swimming pools, bowling greens, jetties and slipways … the list is endless. Revenue costs – salaries, maintenance, insurance, etc. – are not normally eligible for Lottery grants, unless you have a capital project we want to support. If you do, then we may be able to help with revenue costs, if:

- The only way you can get help with certain elements of the start-up costs (e.g. development officer, coach) is from us – and even then, we have to judge the project high priority, and you will not get revenue money for more than three years
- Equipment is eligible only where it is a necessary part of a capital project being supported by the Lottery, or is a substantial item with a lifespan of at least five years, based at a permanent site.

One thing a project must have to attract Lottery funding is organisation: it must be well worked out, carefully planned, financially viable and realistically managed. It must be well on the way to being ready to start. It may need to have outline planning permission before we can approve it. We cannot support pipe dreams.

Table 9.2 on the following page gives examples of successful Lottery funding bids in the West Midlands region. They show the range of projects which received grant-aid.

Table 9.2 Lottery funding awards in the West Midlands

Applicant	Project	Sport	Location		Overall cost (£)	Award (£)
All England Netball Association	Purchase 3 'Tetraflex' floors (portable) for use at World Championships (NIA, July 1995) and then at future events	Netball	n/a	n/a	50,000	32,500
Betley Cricket Club	Extend and refurbish changing rooms	Cricket	Newcastle under-Lyme	Staffs	9,744	6,244
Birmingham LEA (Arthur Terry School)	Dual use facilities	Multi-sports	Birmingham	W.Midlands	1,426,000	752,600
Bomere Heath Cricket Club	Clubhouse/pavilion on new ground	Cricket	Shrewsbury	Shropshire	93,900	28,000
British Amateur Gymnastics Assoc.	Equipment for European competitions	Gymnastics	Birmingham	W.Midlands	69,874	45,418
Church Eaton Tennis Club	Upgrading of 2 all-weather courts	Tennis	Stafford	Staffordshire	12,000	6,750
Halesowen Athletic and Cycling Club	All-weather synthetic athletics track (4-lane suitable for training, juniors & low-level competition)	Athletics	Dudley	W.Midlands	125,000	71,350
Ilmington Tennis Club	Floodlit multi-use games area	Multi-sports	Shipston-on	Warks	67,714	44,014
Prince Henry's High School	Construct sports hall, Centre of Excellence for cricket	Cricket	Worcester	Worcs	500,000	250,000
Rugby Gymnastics Club	Equipment and new roof	Gymnastics	Rugby	Warks	55,998	36,258
Shobdon Cricket Club	New ground – new pavilion and maintenance equipment	Cricket	Leominster	Herefordshire	42,212	27,438
Shropshire County Council (Sir John Talbot Upper School)	New sports facilities and modification to existing buildings to include sports hall, changing rooms	Multi-sports	Shrewsbury	Shropshire	846,700	331,000
South Shropshire District Council	Ludlow Swimming Pool	Swimming	Ludlow	Shropshire	3,065,000	1,432,500
St Peter's Urban Village Trust	Multi-purpose fitness/aerobics centre	Movement & Dance	Birmingham	W.Midlands	124,126	124,126
Stoke-on-Trent Rugby Club	Extension to include medical room, indoor training area and extra changing facilities	Rugby Union	Stoke-on-Trent	Staffs	55,000	33,000
Tamworth Athletic Club	Installation of new 400 metre 8-lane all-weather track inc. renewal of field event areas and new floodlighting	Athletics	Tamworth	Staffs	371,355	178,372
The Muzzle Loaders Association	Toilets and enclosure of firing points	Shooting	Warwick	Warks	39,000	25,000
Wellington Playing Field	New pitches, courts, changing	Football	Hereford	Herefordshire	206,276	113,276
West Midlands Amateur Gymnastics Association	Equipment for regional development	Gymnastics	Various	West Midlands	26,335	17,178

West Midlands Region: 19 projects TOTAL £3,554,964

(*Source: Lottery Link* newspaper, June 1995)

Millennium Commission

The Millennium Commission is also an off-shoot of the National Lottery and it aims to help projects which mark the year 2000 and the beginning of the third millennium. The Commission envisages that it will help around a dozen major projects, a larger number of smaller projects, a millennium festival and a bursary scheme. An example from the sporting world is the project to build a major national stadium to take on officially a role which the ageing Wembley Stadium has filled in the popular imagination since 1923.

Private sector

Unlike the public sector, the private sector in sport does not receive guaranteed income from central government or local taxes. Its operations are funded in various ways:

- Sole traders
- Public limited companies
- Leasing and hire purchase
- Income from sales and services
- Grants

Sole traders

Sole traders are generally small-scale businesses and may be funded from private savings or capital. If additional funding is needed, this will be raised by approaching a bank to borrow funds at commercial rates of interest.

Public limited companies

These can range in scale from small local businesses to large multinational companies like the Rank Organisation. Major companies can raise capital by having their shares quoted and traded on the Stock Exchange, with shareholders receiving a return on their investment, known as a dividend. The money raised form its shareholders can be used by the company to fund new projects.

Leasing and hire purchase

It can require a lot of initial capital for a company to set up a sports business such as a health club. Therefore, the option of leasing equipment or having it on a hire purchase arrangement can be attractive in that it spreads the repayments and allows the company to retain some of its capital to use for other purposes within the business.

Income from sales and services

By their nature, private sector companies rely heavily on the income received directly from customers. This can come from direct admission charges or from membership fees. Membership schemes are very common in the private sector where, for example, a health club wishes to promote a high quality image and service and feels that a membership scheme can best provide this, as well as giving it a guaranteed cash flow.

Grants

As has been discussed in relation to the public sector, private companies can bid for grants from funding agencies. These might include

- Sports Council
- National Lottery
- Millennium Commission
- Department of Trade and Industry (enterprise schemes)
- Football Trust
- Foundation for Sport and Arts

If such bids include the element of a partnership with other sectors or organisations, then the greater is the chance of their being successful.

Voluntary sector

This sector is vital to the provision of sport and recreation in Britain, yet its diverse nature makes it hard to define and to describe fully and accurately. Its prime objectives are

- The provision of a service for a group sharing mutual interests such as playing a particular sport
- The desire to help other people with similar interests and to contribute to the mutual funding of these activities

With no guaranteed sources of income, voluntary sector clubs and organisations need to fund their operations in a variety of ways:

- Membership fees
- Match fees
- Grants
- Loans
- Sponsorship

Membership fees

Anyone joining a sports club can expect to pay an annual membership fee or 'subs'. This will vary according to the number of members in the club, the extent of its activities and the upkeep necessary on any premises owned by the club.

Match fees

In addition to the annual 'subs', sports club members usually pay match fees every time they play. This may help to cover the cost of refreshments, transport, referee's fees or washing the club kit.

Grants

A voluntary sector sports club can apply to any of the grant-awarding bodies mentioned above. A particular source might be the governing body of the sport concerned. Not all governing bodies are large enough, wealthy enough or willing to grant-aid clubs, but many are and can be a vital source of club income.

Loans

Any voluntary sector club can take out a bank or other loan to fund its operations. This will usually relate to ground or clubhouse improvements and will use these as collateral to guarantee the loan. The club must then ensure that it can meet the repayments; this means that the role of club treasurer is a vital one.

Sponsorship

Any organisation in any of the sectors of the sport and recreation business can seek out commercial sponsorship. Indeed, the largest deals are to be found in the world of professional sport with companies sponsoring teams, prize money or whole events. Sponsorship can be vital to a local voluntary sector sports club where a company might provide the team's kit or give help towards transport costs.

Activity

Investigate a local voluntary sports club of which you or someone whom you know is a member.
1 How does it fund its operations?
2 If it receives any commercial sponsorship, list the benefits and the drawbacks of this as a source of funding.

Conclusion

The funding of sport and physical recreation in the United Kingdom is not done in any single way with, for example, all the money coming from one central government department. There are differences and similarities between the public, private and voluntary sectors; on occasions, they come together to form partnerships. This can often be the best way to fund a project, but it is not always possible to operate in this way and the three sectors have their own special factors and arrangements.

The scale of sport and physical recreation in the UK

Sport and physical recreation are important aspects of life in modern Britain. Many people take part in activities and, in turn, this generates a lot of economic activity and creates employment.

Participation

Surveys have shown that over 30 million adults (aged 16 and over) take part in sport and recreation at least one a month; this represents around two-thirds of the adult population. With children added on, the figure rises to over 36 million people or two-thirds of the entire British population. The General Household Survey (GHS) is a report produced by the Office of Population Censuses and Surveys. Every three years it includes questions in its survey questionnaire on sport and recreation. A summary of the findings from a vast range of activities tells us a lot about the scale of sport and recreation.

This list gives the average number of times per adult during 1993 for participation in the following activities:

Walking	40.8	Self-defence	0.6
Keep fit/yoga	12.8	Cricket	0.4
Cycling	12.7	Basketball	0.4
Swimming	8.8	Field sports	0.3
Snooker/pool/billiards	7.4	Water sports (exc. sailing,	
Weight lifting/training	5.5	canoeing, windsurfing)	0.3
Running (jogging, etc.)	3.9	Motor sports	0.3
Darts	3.0	Rugby	0.3
Soccer	2.8	Athletics (track and field)	0.3
Golf	2.7	Climbing	0.2
Bowls	1.6	Sailing	0.2
Badminton	1.2	Hockey	0.2
Tenpin bowling/skittles	1.0	Netball	0.2
Tennis	1.0	Skiing	0.2
Squash	0.9	Ice skating	0.1
Horse riding	0.9	Canoeing	0.1
Fishing	0.8	Windsurfing, boardsailing	0.1
Table tennis	0.7	Boxing/wrestling	0.1

Participation rates in at least one kind of sporting or physical activity (including any not listed above) were 82 per cent of all people aged 16 and over in the UK (*General Household Survey* 1993).

Element 9.2 will examine more closely some of the factors underlying participation in sport and recreation.

Spectating

People become involved with sports other than as players themselves; live spectating is still hugely popular in spite of the increasing extent and range of television coverage. Table 9.3 gives attendances at football matches between 1961-62 and 1991-92.

Table 9.3 Average attendances at football matches

	Football League (England and Wales)				Scottish Football League		
	Division 1	Division 2	Division 3	Division 4	Premier Division	Division 1	Division 2
1961/62	26,106	16,132	9,419	6,060		11,147	1,686
1966/67	30,829	15,701	8,009	5,407		9,270	1,068
1971/72	31,352	14,652	8,510	4,981		10,236	1,416
1976/77	29,540	13,529	7,522	3,863	11,844	2,331	765
1980/81	24,660	11,202	6,590	3,082	9,777	2,202	609
1986/87	19,800	9,000	4,300	3,100	11,720	1,524	662
1987/88	19,300	10,600	5,000	3,200	13,949	1,339	745
1988/89	20,600	10,600	5,500	3,200	15,708	2,455	504
1989/90	20,800	12,500	5,000	3,400	15,576	2,064	761
1990/91	22,681	11,457	5,208	3,253	14,424	2,369	489
1991/92	21,662	10,525	5,423	3,404	11,970	2,334	643

(*Source: Social Trends 23*, 1993)

Attendances at selected events

	1981	1993
Wimbledon	358,000	393,000
Grand National	56,000	50,000
The Derby	50,000	27,000
Varsity Rugby Match	28,000	66,000
Open Golf Championship	112,000	140,000
Royal Tournament	280,000	235,000
Edinburgh Military Tattoo	205,000	210,000
National Eisteddfod	n.a.	132,000
Biggin Hill Air Fair	57,000	64,000
London International Boat Show	243,000	185,000
Southampton International Boat Show	n.a.	104,000
London Motor Show	229,000	363,000
Ideal Home Plus	871,000	551,000
Crufts	74,000	79,000
Chelsea Flower Show	n.a.	180,000

Between 1981 and 1993, the numbers of spectators increased for some events and fell, sometimes dramatically, for others. Attendances at some national events are limited by the number of seats, for example the FA Cup Final has a capacity crowd of 80,000 every year at Wembley. (Information from *Social Trends 24*, 1994.)

Numbers employed

There is now a sport and recreation industry in Britain. This is a relatively new phenomenon, having its origins in such developments as the jogging boom of the 1970s and the health and fitness boom since the 1980s. Taken with the range of new facilities which have opened up, this led to a situation in which sport and recreation is now a significant employer. In the UK tourism and leisure industry as a whole, it is estimated that there are around 1.5 million employees and about 180,000 self-employed people. In sport and recreation this provides interesting comparisons with other sectors of employment. Here is a summary of the numbers of people employed in various industries in the UK in 1990:

Mechanical engineering	765,000
Banking and finance	634,000
Food, drink and tobacco	557,000
Paper, printing and publishing	496,000
Sport-related economic activity (including commercial non-sport sector)	467,000
Postal services and telecommunications	441,000
Chemical industry	329,000
Agriculture, forestry and fishing	305,000
Footwear and clothing	301,000
Sport-related economic activity (excluding commercial non-sport sector)	262,000
Timber and wooden industries	254,000
Textiles	214,000

(Source: Sports Council, *The Economic Impact of Sport in the United Kingdom in 1990*, 1992)

Financial turnover

Sport is now a significant factor in the UK economy. The term 'value added' is used by economists to measure the value of the output of an economy or a particular sector of it. The Sports Council report *The Economic Impact of Sport in the United Kingdom in 1990* (1992) measured the figure for sport to be £8.27 billion at that year's prices. To put this in context, here is a summary of 'value added in' in various sectors of the UK economy in 1990.

	£ billion
Electrical and instrument engineering	14.02
Mechanical engineering	12.73
Paper, printing and packaging	11.66
Chemicals and man-made fibres	11.40
Food	9.49
Sport-related economic activity (including commercial non-sport sector)	8.27
Motor vehicles and parts	6.37

Metal manufacturing	4.09
Drink and tobacco	3.54
Clothing, footwear and leather	3.30
Sport-related economic activity (excluding commercial non-sport sector)	3.28
Textiles	2.83

(Source: Sports Council, 1992)

The Sports Council report provides data on the income generated by various sectors of the sport and physical recreation industry, which illustrate its importance to the UK economy.

Summary of commercial non-sport income in 1990

	£ million
Receipts net of tax from consumer spending:	
Travel	95
Gambling	2,324
Skiing	183
Public schools	26
TV rental	52
Sales of current inputs to:	
Central government	31
Local government	164
Commercial sport	2,558
Voluntary sector	485
Interest from voluntary sector	24
Sales of capital inputs to:	
Local government	338
Commercial sport	132
Voluntary	238
Promotion expenditure for sponsorship (intra-sectoral flow)	(226)
Total income	6,650

(*Source:* Sports Council, *The Economic Impact of Sport in the United Kingdom in 1990*, 1992)

Assignment 9.1

Title: Sport and physical recreation in the UK
Performance criteria satisfied: 9.1.1, 9.1.2, 9.1.3, 9.1.4, 9.1.5
Core skills satisfied at level 3: Communication 3.1, 3.2, 3.3, 3.4
                                   Information technology 3.1, 3.2, 3.3
                                   Application of number 3.1, 3.2, 3.3

Situation

Your college group is taking part in an exchange visit with a group of students from a similar college in France. Your tutor wants your group to provide the French students with as much information as possible on sport and physical recreation in the UK for when they come to Britain. You have been asked to prepare some suitable material.

Tasks

1 Prepare a summary report on sport and physical recreation in the United Kingdom. You should discuss the range of activities undertaken in the country and give examples of popular ones.
2 Give examples of the role and purpose of the important organisations providing facilities and services
3 Discuss the scale of sport and recreation in the UK economy and from where it draws its major funding.
4 Prepare a written, word-processed report and also a presentation for the French students when they visit.

Investigate the factors affecting participation in sport and physical recreation in the UK

Performance criteria

1 Describe the benefits to the individual from participation in sport and physical recreation.
2 Explain factors affecting participation in sport and physical recreation.
3 Describe types of participation.
4 Describe ways of increasing individual participation in sport and physical recreation activities.
5 Carry out and summarise a questionnaire based survey of participation in a locality.

Benefits from participation in sport and physical recreation

In figures published by the World Health Organisation in the 1980s, Scotland and Northern Ireland recorded an annual death rate from coronary heart disease among 55–64 year olds of over 1,000 persons per 100,000 head of population. The corresponding rate in Japan was 100 persons. There could be no more dramatic illustration of the fact that Britain has a major health problem brought on by lifestyles, too much smoking and drinking, eating an unhealthy diet and lack of exercise. Sport and physical recreation can play a large part in this battle. The health issue has given a big impetus to schemes to increase participation and to promote an active lifestyle.

National Fitness Survey

In 1992 the Sports Council and the Health Education Authority published the Allied Dunbar National Fitness Survey. It had a great number of lessons on the benefits of active participation and its messages were plain for all:

- We are not physically active enough in Britain
- We are not as fit as we think we are
- We should aim to exercise regularly a minimum of three times a week
- It does not have to hurt in order to get fit
- Fitness levels should be built up gradually

- We should take long walks more often
- An active lifestyle should become a way of life
- Exercise should not be looked upon as a task, rather as a pleasure
- Sport can be a pleasant and healthy way to take exercise
- Physical activity can help delay the onset of the ageing process
- Don't let inactivity become a way of life
- Physical activity can reduce stress and high blood pressure
- An active lifestyle should begin in childhood

If the above points were acted upon, then an individual would clearly derive great benefits and have a better chance of a longer, healthier life. In turn, society would benefit with reduced costs for some social services and medical services seeking to deal with the problems of an unhealthy lifestyle. Since the 1960s there has been an increasing emphasis on the role of sport and physical recreation in this health battle, with the jogging boom and the rise in the number of health clubs being prime examples.

The role of education

The National Fitness Survey stressed the importance of good attitudes and practices being encouraged in childhood. As schools and the education system are where many of these attitudes are formed, the government, through its educational policies, takes the matter very seriously. Since 1988 schools have operated under the direction of the National Curriculum, with all pupils aged 5–16 coming under its jurisdiction. Physical education is a foundation subject in the National Curriculum and has clear aims, as shown in the case study.

CASE STUDY

The aims of physical education

Physical education in schools aims to develop control, co-ordination and mastery of the body. It is primarily concerned with a way of learning through action, sensation and observation. It is possible to gain knowledge of physical activities in a theoretical way but skills can be acquired only by personal experience of movement. Such experience, which requires thought as well as effort, leads to improved performance, personal achievement, understanding and increased knowledge. Satisfaction and enjoyment arise from working with a sense of purpose and practising hard enough and long enough to overcome the challenges represented by the practical work.

The aims of physical education are to

- Develop a range of psycho-motor skills
- Maintain and increase physical mobility and flexibility
- Develop stamina and strength
- Develop understanding and appreciation of the purposes, forms and conventions of a selection of physical activities
- Develop the capacity to express ideas in dance forms

- Develop the appreciation of the concepts of fair play, honest competition and good sportsmanship
- Develop the ability to appreciate the aesthetic qualities of movement
- Develop the capacity to maintain interest and to persevere to achieve success
- Foster self-esteem through the acquisition of physical competence and poise
- Develop self-confidence through understanding the capabilities and limitations of oneself and others

(*Source*: Department for Education, *Physical Education 5–19*, 1989)

Competitive sport in schools

There is a debate going on about the role of competitive sport in schools and the benefits which it can bring to children and young people. Many feel that there has been a decline in the range of sports on offer in schools and this will have a detrimental effect on individuals and their fitness and, of course, Britain's success in the international sporting arena. In 1995, the Prime Minster, John Major, launched a major government initiative on the matter entitled *Sport: Raising the Game* in which he set out his vision for our sporting future:

Sport: Raising the Game

My ambition is simply stated. It is to put sport back at the heart of weekly life in *every* school. To re-establish sport as one of the great pillars of education alongside the academic, the vocational and the moral. It should never have been relegated to be just one part of one subject in the curriculum. For complete education we need all of those four pillars of school life to be strong.

We are setting out today a detailed blueprint for the future of sport in schools. It will ensure career and training opportunities for teachers, better chances for children, and public recognition for those schools that offer those chances. We want to sustain the place of minor sports that bring much enjoyment. But I am determined to see that our great traditional sports – cricket, hockey, swimming, athletics, football, netball, rugby, tennis and the like – are put firmly at the centre of the stage.

Sports education is only the first step to a lifetime's enjoyment of sport. Sporting opportunities must continue after school. So we shall be looking to colleges and universities to do more to promote sport among their students. At present, too many teenagers find it difficult to transfer their sporting interests to the world outside school. So we will also aim to improve links between school and club sport. In that way we can improve access to high quality coaching and promote sensible arrangements to share facilities and equipment. There is much to gain in this, both for clubs and for schools.

Finally, I want to help our best sports men and women make the very best of their talents. I take as much pride as anyone in seeing them lead the world. I do not want to see them having to go abroad to learn how to exploit their talents. That is why our new proposals include ideas to improve talent spotting and talent support right here at home. With the help of the National Lottery we will create a new British Academy of Sport with worldclass facilities, to help sporting stars, and we will support it by a developing network of regional and sports academies to bring on the best.

I hope that no one will underestimate the significance and the seriousness of our aims. I believe the targets we are setting – for schools, for young people, for the best – will be shared by millions and we will work with everyone who can help us to make them a reality.

John Major

(*Source:* Department of National Heritage, *Sport: Raising the Game*, 1995)

Activity

1 List some of the benefits which an individual can derive from participating in sport and physical recreation.
2 What benefits can society gain from high levels of participation?

Factors affecting participation sport and physical recreation

People choose to take part in sport, or not to take part, for a variety of reasons. Money or the lack of it is a basic factor preventing participation in certain activities, but there are many more influences at work. A very powerful one in today's society is the effect which the mass media can have on our desire to become involved in sport. It is natural for young people to wish to follow in the footsteps of their sporting heroes and the media can do a lot to make or break careers and reputations. The influence of the mass media on levels of participation must, however, be considered in a wider context. Not everyone can succeed and become a professional sports performer, but most people can take part at their own level.

Activity

1 Monitor media coverage of sport over a few days in newspapers, on radio and on television.
2 How well does the mass media help in efforts to promote a positive image of sport and of the benefits of taking part?
3 What problems are there in media coverage and what improvements can you suggest?

The *General Household Survey* has already been mentioned as providing a lot of useful information on sport and physical recreation. The survey found that 72 per cent of men took part in sport on a regular basis compared with 57 per cent of women. These rates decreased with age from 86 per cent among 16–29 year olds to 64 per cent in the 45–59 age group and 33 per cent for those over 70. Socio-economic status was also a factor, with rates being higher for those in non-manual groups and those in employment and lower for those in homes with a child under the age of 5.

Here is a list of the top six sports for women and men in various age groups (*General Household Survey* 1993).

Women 16–19
Walking
Keep fit/yoga
Swimming
Snooker/pool/billiards
Cycling
Running

Men 16–19
Snooker/pool/billiards
Walking
Soccer
Cycling
Weight lifting/training
Swimming

Women 25–29
Walking
Keep fit/yoga
Swimming
Cycling
Snooker/pool/billiards
Tenpin bowls/skittles

Men 25–29
Walking
Snooker/pool/billiards
Cycling
Swimming
Weight lifting/training
Soccer

Women 45–59
Walking
Swimming
Keep fit/yoga
Cycling
Golf
Darts

Men 45–50
Walking
Snooker/pool/billiards
Swimming
Cycling
Golf
Darts

Women 70 plus
Walking
Keep fit/yoga
Swimming
Cycling
Bowls
Golf

Men 70 plus
Walking
Cycling
Bowls
Golf
Keep fit/yoga
Snooker/pool/billiard

Many other factors can play a part in rates of participation among the British people. Those suffering from disabilities may face special problems over lack of mobility or transport or they may wish to enter sports buildings which have not been adapted for those in wheelchairs. Few sports or leisure centres now fall into this category, but disabled people may still have other problems:

- A lack of volunteer helpers to run a disabled sports club which may require one-to-one supervision
- A problem over being able to book special slots for disabled sessions in sports centres
- The difficulty of overcoming feelings that they may stand out if taking part alongside able-bodied sportspersons

Investigate the factors affecting participation in sport and physical education in the UK   **29**

Persons from some ethnic backgrounds may face cultural barriers to participating in sport. For example, women may have problems or religious barriers about exposing their bodies while swimming. If there are no special sessions available for them, then their chance to participate in sport is limited.

Sometimes the reasons why people do not take part in sport can be very simple indeed, though none the less important. Many may be simply unaware of the joys and benefits of taking part or not know where a sport can be played. Similarly, many may be put off by an impression of sport being only for the best and 'not for the likes of us'. The Sports Council and other agencies work hard to overcome such wrong impressions and stress that sport really is 'for all'.

Types of participation

People participate in sport and physical recreation for a variety of reasons such as health and fitness or the challenge of competition. They can do so in activities ranging from a lone walk to being one of over 20,000 in the London Marathon. They can do so in the warmth of an indoor setting or on the frozen top of a mountain. They can be very relaxed or casual about taking part or they can be facing a three foot putt to win the Ryder Cup or the British Open Golf Championship. Figure 9.2 represents some of the linked factors in this complicated process.

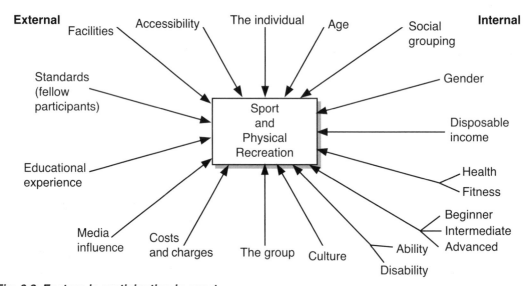

Fig. 9.2 Factors in participation in sport

Activity

1 Take one of the factors from Figure 9.2, for example beginner.
2 Draw up a flow diagram to represent how a person in this category can take part in sport and progress on to the next stages.
3 Insert factors which are barriers to the person's participation and progress.

Ways of increasing individual participation

Many organisations involved in sport and physical recreation wish to see more people taking part. This will, of course, vary with their own objectives and place in the sporting environment. This could be summarised as follows:

- Agencies such as the Health Education Authority seeking to promote exercise as a way of improving health and preventing illness by mounting public awareness campaigns.
- Sports clubs mounting a recruitment drive to attract more players and members
- A governing body of sport running training courses to increase the number of coaches or officials in its sport
- A private health club offering a special membership rate to new members in order to boost income and cash flow
- The government launching its *Sport: Raising the Game* document as an attempt to focus attention on the importance of sport and get more young people involved in it
- The Sports Council mounting campaigns to stress the benefits of sporting participation. These have included *What's your sport?*, *Sport for all Disabled People* and *50+ All to Play For*.
- The vital role of education as a factor in sporting participation

Lots of people in their fifties are missing out by not enjoying any physical activity. Maybe you've never thought of it, hated sport at school, feel you're too old, flabby or unfit, are frightened of making a fool of yourself, don't have the time or money, don't know how to go about it, or just can't be bothered.

Stop making excuses and have a go! The choice is vast, from angling to yoga, cycling, 'keep fit', rambling, snooker, swimming and many more. All ages and abilities are welcome. It doesn't have to be too expensive or energetic. Fancy yourself as a coach, referee, club secretary or team manager?

Above all, taking part is fun and helps you to keep fit and active. Join our campaign; you've got *all to play for*.

When you get to 50 it's a good time to take stock. Many people's circumstances change': you may be without work, preparing for retirement, holding down a stressful job, free for the first time from family ties, feeling lonely or bored and looking for a chance to get involved in something interesting. You may even be putting on weight, feeling stiff at the joints, getting breathless too easily and worried about your heart.

It's got lots to offer including … activity, enjoyment, involvement, interest, exercise, relaxation, recreation, social contacts. There's something for everyone and you'll feel much fitter as a result.

Before you start - a word about health …

Get involved even if you haven't taken much physical exercise for years. There's plenty of evidence to show that getting a little puffed and increasing your heart rate is good for you. Doctors agree that there are no risks in regular exercise, as long as you start gently and gradually build up to the more strenuous activities. After all, bones, joints and muscles were made to be used! Keeping trim, i.e. toning up your muscles and preventing flab, reduces stress and makes life easier. If you're reasonably fit and start exercising gently then there's no need to worry. But if you have any doubts, for example, if you get overtired, feel uncomfortably out of breath or have a pain in your chest when you exercise, or if you are under medical attention or treatment, then check with your doctor. Just be sensible and avoid activities involving sudden exertion or straining. You may feel stiff afterwards but you'll feel much fitter too, and you'll enjoy it.

Sport needs you

If you've a sporting skill, pass it on! Put something back into the game. There's plenty to do and you'll enjoy lending a hand.

Go on! Find your local club and offer your services. You don't have to compete to be more complete! There are lots of jobs that need doing and you'll enjoy getting involved.

Here's a checklist of things you might do ...

- become treasurer of the local sports club
- serve on a club committee
- run a jumble sale for a disabled sports group
- be a bartender in a club
- manage the mini hockey team
- transport the junior rugby team to matches
- run a club tennis tournament
- type agendas
- help at a swimming club for disabled people
- mark out the football pitch
- be a secretary of a county sports federation
- be a representative on a local sports advisory council
- prepare teas for cricket matches
- play the piano for a 'keep fit' class and plenty more

(*Source:* Sports Council)

Survey of participation

If the various providers and organisations in sport and recreation are to make sound decisions on funding, campaigns or new activities, then it is vital that they are in possession of reliable information on which to base their decisions. This can come from:
- Published data such as the *General Household Survey* or *Social Trends*
- Information from Sports Council or other surveys

- Data from surveys commissioned from consultants
- User surveys conducted in facilities or in the local area
- Inviting suggestions from customers in suggestion boxes placed in facilities

Any of the above methods or publications will yield information which the management will then process and use in decision making. Some common aspects of this information include:

- Age and gender profiles of current customers or participants
- Data on groups currently not participating in sport and physical recreation
- Social grouping and financial factors
- Reasons for participating
- Reasons for not participating
- Rates of frequency of participation
- The range of activities enjoyed
- Suggestions for new activities which would be popular

Surveys or questionnaires are frequently used in this type of work. Figure 9.3 lists questions asked of respondents to the *General Household Survey*.

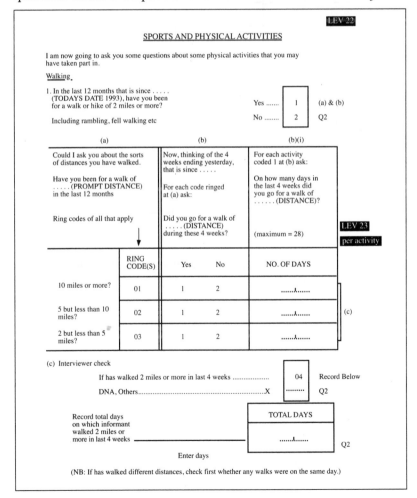

Fig. 9.3 continues overleaf

2. In the last 12 months have you been swimming or played soccer or bowls?

LEV 24

Yes .... 1 — Record details at (a) below then ask (b)

No .... 2 — Q3

(a)	(b)	(b)(i)
If took part in 12 months ending yesterday	Now, thinking of the 4 weeks ending yesterday	For each activity coded 1 at (b) ask:
Including training, coaching and refereeing	For each activity coded at (a) ask:	On how many days in the last 4 weeks did you . . . . (ACTIVITY)?
Prompt outdoors/indoors and ring codes of all that apply ↓	Did you . . . . (ACTIVITY) in these 4 weeks?	(maximum = 28)

LEV 25 per activity

	RING CODE(S)	Yes	No	NO. OF DAYS
Outdoor swimming or diving	11	1	2	......↓......
Indoor swimming or diving	12	1	2	......↓......
Soccer outdoors (mainly 11 a side)	13	1	2	......↓......
Soccer indoors (mainly 5 a side)	14	1	2	......↓......
Outdoor (lawn) bowls	15	1	2	......↓......
Indoor/carpet bowls	16	1	2	......↓......

(c) Interviewer check

swam both indoors and outdoors in last 4 weeks .... 17 (c)(i)

DNA, Others...X Q3

NO. OF DAYS
......↓......

(c)(i) (Can I just check) on how many days in the last 4 weeks have you done any swimming at all either indoors or outdoors?

Enter days

Fig. 9.3 Sport and physical activities questions in General Household Survey (*Source: General Household Survey* 1993)

Assignment 9.2

Title: Surveying sporting participation
Performance criteria satisfied: 9.2.1, 9.2.2, 9.2.3, 9.2.4, 9.2.5
Core skills satisfied at level 3:   Communication 3.1, 3.2, 3.3, 3.4
                                    Information technology 3.1, 3.2, 3.3
                                    Application of number 3.1, 3.2, 3.3

Situation

Your local council is considering building an all-weather sports pitch for use by local sports clubs and organisations. Before proceeding with the project, the council requires a lot of information upon which to base its decisions. The Director of Leisure has approached the local college to ask for help in conducting a survey on local sporting participation. Your group has been given the task to take on as a project.

Tasks

Working in teams, you are required to produce a background report on

- Factors which influence participation in sport and physical recreation
- The benefits to the individual and the community of taking part in sport and physical recreation
- The different ways in which people choose to participate
- Ways in which participation can be increased in different sports

This background report will be used by the Director of Leisure to prepare papers for presentation to the council members.

However, the council will make a final decision on the all-weather facility only if it has specific data on which to base it. Your team has now to

- Devise a questionnaire on sporting participation in your area
- Run the questionnaire with a random sample of local residents
- Analyse the data to be found in the responses received
- Present your findings in a suitable format

The completed tasks should then be available for presentation to the Director of Leisure for use in considering the all-weather pitch project.

Explore trends and developments in sport and physical recreation

Performance criteria

1 Identify and give examples of technological developments affecting sport and physical recreation.
2 Explain trends in sport and physical recreation.
3 Discuss current issues in sport and physical recreation and summarise the discussion.
4 Describe the trends in sport and physical recreation activities in a locality over the last twenty years

Technological developments in sport and physical recreation

When people first began to take part in activities that were the origins of modern sports, there was little need for any help which could be described as technological. A race to the top of the nearest hill or a bare-knuckle fight may seem to have little connection with modern athletics or professional boxing. This is mainly because we are accustomed to the present-day forms having close links with technology and all the sophistication which it brings to the sport. The most highly developed modern technological sport is grand prix motor racing. Millions of dollars depend on the car going that split second faster than a rival's and, most vital of all, having all possible safety aids. Sadly, as the death of Ayrton Senna in 1994 showed, even a world champion can be let down by technology or human error.

There are many examples of how technology has come to influence sport and physical recreation. We shall now examine a few of these:

Transport

The coming of the railways in the nineteenth century and the motor car in the twentieth have given people the freedom and mobility to enjoy sport and physical recreation in the widest sense, whether as direct participants or travelling away as spectators. With widespread availability of affordable air travel, foreign opportunities also present themselves.

Equipment

The earliest sporting equipment was primitive, heavy and difficult to use. Wooden-shafted golf clubs and feather-stuffed balls could not give the accuracy or distance of their modern equivalents. Footballs were once heavy and had laces, thus making them very unappealing to head on a wet day when they also absorbed a lot of water! Many more examples could be given of the way technology has influenced and helped to improve modern sports.

Activity

List as many examples as you can of sports which have benefited from technology and the ways in which this has happened.

Clothing and footwear

Modern mass production has made sports and leisure clothes and shoes available to millions of people. Similarly, the top performers rely on the technical back-up available to them to produce, for example, new forms of running spikes which will shave hundredths of a second from their performance.

Sports surfaces

Grass, the traditional surface for many outdoor games, is subject to extremes of weather which can either cause fixtures to be cancelled or have an adverse effect on the conduct of the game. With the advent of artificial surfaces in the 1960s, this situation changed for many sports. Hockey, for example, is now almost universally played at international level on artificial pitches. This provides a setting with no difficult or dangerous bounces. At the level of community sport, artificial surfaces mean that a facility can be open 24 hours a day, 7 days a week and 52 weeks a year whatever the weather.

Sports science

There are many courses on this topic as it has become important to have highly trained staff to undertake the detailed research necessary in modern sport. At basic levels of performance, health club attendants need scientific knowledge to advise clients on individual exercise and fitness programmes. In professional sport, scientists can advise on such topics as diet and nutrition, correct technique and mental preparation, all vital elements in achieving the ultimate performance. All of these aspects demonstrate the recent importance given to the role of the sports scientist.

Technology

A recent development is the 'Third Eye' umpire whereby a video playback can now provide objective evidence for sports decisions such as run outs in cricket. Rugby League was the first contact sport to vote to use it in matches.

Sports medicine

Since the mid-1970s sport and the medical profession have come together for the good of the performer at all levels. Many hospitals now run clinics devoted to sports injuries and there are many physiotherapists, both private and operating within the National Health Service, who specialise in sports-related problems. The subject of GP referral schemes in partnership with leisure centres will be discussed in Unit 10.

Sport on the verge of the Third Eye era

Sport on the edge of the Third Eye era

Rugby league is to leave crucial decisions to the TV camera; will soccer follow?

John Duncan, Martin Thorpe and Paul Fitzpatrick

Rugby league became the first British contact sport to introduce the "spy in the stands" yesterday with the announcement that for all televised matches an official in a monitor booth will have the final say on controversial incidents.

Soccer may be the next. It is understood that there are moves within the Football Association to create a working party to look into the whole question of using technology to help decide issues during games. The group could be in place by the summer.

There is a growing feeling at Lancaster Gate that this area must soon be addressed. Issues for consideration would include a radio link from referees to colleagues with television facilities in the stands, and a standardised form of time-keeping to end disputes about the amount of injury time played.

However, a working party would enter a minefield of tough decisions. Who would be allowed to call for a replay? What issues would be referred for a decision? How could the flow of the game be maintained? Would it undermine referees? How long would the change extend a normal game beyond 90 minutes?

David Davies, the FA's director of communications, would not comment last night on the working party proposal. "These matters are under continuing consideration here and we don't discount anything in the future," he said.

The Rugby Football League, though, was enthusiastic yesterday about the value of a TV official. Super League, which starts in March, will use slow-motion replays to decide on controversial incidents, particularly the validity of tries.

In matches televised by Sky, referees will be able to call for assistance over touchdowns just as cricket umpires can call for a ruling on run-outs.

The clock will be stopped while the ruling is awaited but Greg McCallum, the Rugby League's controller of referees, is confident that a decision will be reached within 30 to 45 seconds. Spectators will be able to judge some of these incidents for themselves, for it is intended that giant TV screens, complete with explanatory graphics, will be used at Sky matches.

"Other sports have benefited from this kind of facility and rugby league should take advantage of all the technological advances available," said the League's chief executive Maurice Lindsay.

The move marks the latest TV encroachment into sport. In Scottish soccer, video evidence will next season be used retrospectively for disciplinary purposes. In rugby union the France centre Richard Dourthe faces a two-match ban after admitting, after TV evidence, to kicking England's Ben Clarke.

Racing has used photo-finishes since 1947 and has filmed races for the benefit of race stewards since 1960 at Newmarket, four cameras now being used to offer officials every angle on controversial incidents.

It is also common now for leading English soccer referees to study match videos before submitting their reports to the FA. Last week Gerald Ashby, having watched televised footage, voluntarily reversed the booking of Newcastle's David Ginola for diving at Arsenal. Last night, however, Ashby rejected the use of TV during a game, arguing that it would cause more problems than it solved.

"Where would it start and where would it end?" he asked. "It is time people recognised that everyone, including referees, makes mistakes, but the game is all about talking points and opinions."

Tim Crabbe, chairman of the Football Supporters' Association, agreed. "I know we all shout at referees, but the human element is all part of the game."

"The third eye was tried in American football in 1966, when an instant reply official was introduced and both teams were allowed a limited number of appeals to the official. But the replay booth was abandoned in 1991. "It was mainly because of the time it took," an NFL spokesman said last night, "but also because it questioned the referee's integrity. It implied that his decisions weren't good enough, begging the question of what he was doing on the field."

■

(*Source: The Guardian*, 24 January 1996)

Activity

1 Consider the use of the 'Third Eye' in decisions.
2 Write down the benefits and drawbacks of using it.

Trends in sport and physical recreation

Sport is subject to fluctuations like any other activity in society. These can be internal ones within a sport itself, for example rule changes or innovations such as the tie-break in tennis or the 'golden goal' in soccer. They can be external influences such as a varying population or changing attitudes to health and fitness. Both types of influence can have a major impact on sporting and recreational activities. Let us examine some of these effects:

• New activities becoming popular, e.g. the aerobics boom since the 1980s
• Established activities reaching peaks in participation or even seeing a decrease such as squash which rose rapidly in the 1960s and 1970s and has now declined
• An activity becoming popular as a result of media exposure, snooker's rise in the 1970s being an example
• Changes in facility design and services altering an activity, the building of 'leisure pools' of varying shapes being an instance of this trend

Figure 9.4 illustrates trends in participation in the eight most popular activities, apart from walking, for the years 1987, 1990 and 1993 in Britain.

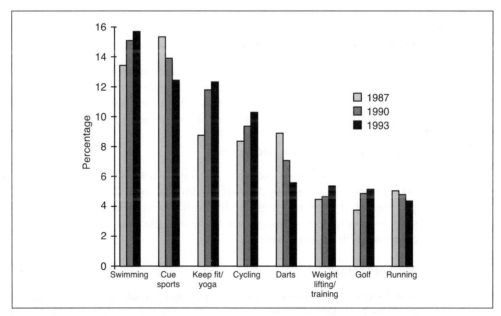

Fig. 9.4 Trends in participation rates for selected activities: 1987, 1990 and 1993

(*Source: General Household Survey* 1993)

Activity

1 Look at Figure 9.4.
2 Give three reasons why keep fit/yoga has shown a steady rise.
3 Give three reasons why cue sports have dropped in popularity.

As we have seen earlier in this section, there are significant differences in participation rates according to age, gender and socio-economic factors.

Participant expectations and changing markets

Since the 1960s it has been possible to speak of a sport and leisure 'revolution' as new activities have become popular and the customer has come to expect improving services and products. Sport is now very big business indeed and is a significant factor in the national economy. It is possible to look at both the demands of people and market changes to see how these have combined to cause major trends in sport and physical recreation.

Demographic and social factors

Britain has a population which is living longer and is also staying involved in sport longer than in the past. Women over 35 and men over 40 years old now have the opportunity to compete as 'veterans' right up to world championship level. There has been a major drive by such bodies as the Sports Council to encourage more women of all ages to become active in sport and physical recreation. The rise in sporting participation by disabled persons is another notable trend.

Multi-purpose leisure centres

Anyone born after 1970 has been able, as a member of the first generation to do so, to take part in sport in a multi-purpose leisure centre. Most of these facilities have been built since the mid-1970s and they have responded well to customer needs, so leisure centres have put on more aerobics classes or installed fitness suites.

Standards of facilities and service

In the leisure 'boom' of recent years the customer has become more sophisticated and discerning, as facility providers compete for a share of the 'leisure pound'. The paying public demands high quality facilities, equipment and standards of customer service. If a facility cannot meet these expectations, then a rival one will and the customer will go elsewhere.

Market factors

It is clearly in the private sector of provision that investors in sports facilities and services have to have a particular regard for the marketplace. If their investment is to succeed and deliver a return, then it must hold its place in a highly competitive sports market. The growth in health clubs and pools in hotels would be a good example of this trend. However, the public sector too can no longer ignore market forces, as the advent of Compulsory Competitive Tendering (CCT) has ensured that local authority facilities and services must also compete for customers with their commercial sector rivals. Finally, it is clear that the cash injections to sport offered by the National Lottery will have a profound effect on the sport and physical recreation market in the twenty-first century.

Activity

1 List three trends which you feel will be significant in sport and physical recreation over the next decade
2 How do you feel that the possibility of National Lottery funding might influence these trends?

Current issues in sport and physical recreation

This section has constantly sought to emphasise the point that sport and physical recreation play a significant part in modern society. As such, they can become controversial in a number of ways:

- There can be disagreement on their key roles, for example the controversy over competitive sport in schools
- There can be problems over the link between sport and politics
- There can be concerns expressed about the role of the mass media in sport
- There can be a feeling among some people that sport is now too commercialised, with a danger that it might become too elitist
- There is much concern about cheating in sport, especially the use of drugs to enhance performance
- There is a concern among many people that sport is too reliant on commercial sponsorship, especially tobacco money
- There are constant debates over violence in sport, both on and off the field
- There are concerns expressed that not enough is done to attract minority groups into sport, for example persons from ethnic backgrounds, disabled people and so on
- There are concerns expressed about whether enough is being done to encourage and attract children into sport. This leads on to a wider debate about diet and the taking of enough active exercise in the week to promote good health
- There is a lot of concern about ethics and fair play in sport at all levels. This leads on to questions about the punishment of offenders and the conduct and responsibilities of professional performers as role models for children

All of the above key issues can be refined into a series of questions:

1 What is the purpose and role of sport in our society?
2 What problems does this role bring with it?

3 What can be done to improve the situation?

4 What are the lessons for the future of sport in society?

Drugs in sport

Drug taking in both sport and society receives a lot of media attention. Each new performer caught by the testers or teenage death from Ecstasy provokes a massive debate and calls for action which usually boils down in both cases to

- A call by some for tougher penalties for offenders
- A call by others for drugs to be legalised and bring them out of their present 'underground' status

It has to be said that drug taking in both sport and society at large is not a recent development. What is new in the case of sport, however, is the sophistication of both the testing process and the ability of performers, using scientific help, to avoid detection. The 1988 Olympic 100m champion, Ben Johnson, was the most famous athlete ever to be caught, but the extract from the *Guardian* shows that he was not alone in seeking to improve performance through the use of drugs.

How the problem of drugs has made itself felt in other sports

Football

Soccer's testing programme has thrown up a number of high-profile cases of drug taking. Diego Maradona tested positive for cocaine in March 1991 and was banned for 15 months. This year he was thrown out of the World Cup after taking five different forms of the stimulant ephedrine to help with a weight loss programme.

His Argentinean international colleague, Claudio Caniggia, was banned in 1992 for 13 months following a positive test for cocaine.

In this country, the Football Association started drug testing in 1979. Since 1991, there have been four stimulant findings – three of them in Wales – including one positive test for amphetamines.

Golf

Mac O'Grady, former UK tour player and coach to Seve Ballesteros, earlier this year accused seven of the world's top 30 players of taking beta-blockers.

The drug, used in the treatment of heart complaints, suppresses adrenaline flows and could help

players cope with pressure of putting, he claimed.

Nick Price, winner of this year's Open, later admitted he had taken beta-blockers for a congenital heart complaint but gave them up after they had an adverse effect on his game.

In July, former USPGA winner John Daly claimed some golfers on the US tour took cocaine but withdrew the allegation after he was criticised by his fellow professionals.

Rugby

Richie Griffiths, the former Wales B Rugby Union centre, became the first player in the world to be banned when he tested positive for anabolic steroids after a match in which he scored a try.

In Rugby League, Bradford Northern player Simon Tuffs was banned for two years after traces of amphetamine were found in his urine sample.

Since 1991, four players have tested positive for a range of drugs, including the analgesic dihydrocodeine which helps participants extend painful training sessions.

Snooker

Canadian player Kirk Stevens admitted taking cocaine in the late 1980s, but no action was taken by the sport's governing body as his drug-taking did not take place during competition.

Stevens' countryman, Bill Werbeniuk, was fined £2,000 and suspended in 1988 after he admitted taking the beta-blocker Inderal. He suffered from a tremor in his cueing arm, and claimed he needed to consume copious amounts of lager to control the tremor and that Inderal was necessary to control the stress on his heart caused by his drinking.

Racing

Dope testing has long been a feature of racing and has uncovered a number of instances of fancied horses being "stopped", usually by sedatives such as detomidine.

From October 1, jockeys will be subject to the same degree of scrutiny with random testing for a range of narcotics, including cannabis, cocaine, alcohol (above the legal limit for driving), and LSD. However, the list does not

include the stimulant ephedrine or diuretics – known in the trade as "pee pills" – which help overweight riders to shed precious pounds.

Other sports

The taking of banned substances is not the preserve of highly paid athletes, as the recent case of a 73-year-old Scottish grandmother illustrated. She was forced to pull out of this year's Scottish national bowling championships because tablets she was prescribed after a heart bypass were on the sport's list of banned substances.

A Sports Council report published earlier this year reveals that drug abuse takes place in a wide range of sports: beta-blockers in archery; steroids in cycling; painkillers in boxing; even netball has thrown up two positive tests for banned stimulants.

More predictably, 44 powerlifters tested positive for steroids in the last six years, while there have been six cases of cannabis abuse in surfing.

Lawrence Donegan

▶

Hitting the drugs barrier

Sport's most popular drugs and what they do.

Anabolic steroids

Synthetic versions of the male hormone testosterone. Steroids increase weight and muscle bulk enabling athletes to train harder and for longer periods as well as helping recovery from heavy training. Large doses have dangerous side effects: cancer, liver damage and 'road rages' – increased aggression. Severe acne, impotence in men and facial hair and voice deepening in women.

Stimulants

These drugs increase movement, mental activity and usually elevate mood. Best known are amphetamines ('speed'). Main benefit to the athlete is to delay the onset of fatigue, or at least, the perception of fatigue. Ephedrines are very similar to amphetamines. They widen the lung airways and are used in asthma and bronchitis treatment leading to confusion when testing. Unfortunately they also crop up in natural products such as ginseng and it was ginseng tea that caused Linford Christie to test positive in the 1988 Olympics. Caffeine is a banned stimulant, but more than six large cups of strong coffee would need to be drunk to test positive.

Beta blockers

Slow the heart rate. Occasionally used by rifle and pistol marksmen and archers to calm a pounding heart and so increase accuracy. Very common in the treatment of high blood pressure, angina and heart beat irregularities.

Narcotic analgesics

Drugs which relieve pain, including morphine and codeine. They reduce the athlete's perception of fatigue. Very common in pain-killers and cough medicines and so sports coaches have to be scrupulous in the use of 'safe' alternatives.

Diuretics

Drugs which increase the body's excretion of water. Used to treat high blood pressure, they are misused by jockeys and boxers to lose weight.

Testing

A urine sample is divided into two, put in sealed containers and taken to an international Olympic Committee-approved laboratory. One of the samples is tested; if negative, both samples are destroyed.

If the first test is positive, the British Athletic Federation is notified and then the athlete is informed by letter and invited to attend the testing of the second sample or send a representative. If this test is negative, no further action is taken. If positive, then disciplinary action will be taken against the individual. The athlete has the right of appeal on a number of grounds including medication, level not sufficient for a ban or unintentional use. The BAF can decide to take no further action as in the Linford Christie ginseng tea incident.

Disciplinary action

Individual sports federations decide on the penalty. This could be a ban from further competitions for a number of years or life. ■

(*Source: Guardian* 26 August 1994)

Activity

In small groups consider the following questions:

1 Should drugs in sport be legalised in order to get back to a 'level playing field' for all?
2 Should 'random' testing be introduced in all sports?
3 Should life bans be automatic for those caught taking drugs?

Summarise the various views expressed by group members under each question.

Sport and the media

This section has already shown some of the ways in which the mass media are important to sport and physical recreation. An activity can become popular as a result of media exposure. Tabloid newspapers sell millions of copies per day and top sports stars are constantly on their pages, either for success on the field of play or an off-court incident in their private lives. Millions of people enjoy television coverage of major sporting events and until recent years, this was mainly available on BBC or ITV without the viewer having to pay directly for viewing the event. That situation has changed with the coming of satellite television and the large sums of money which the companies bid to cover sports events. At present there are eight 'listed' events which cannot be exclusively shown on pay-per-view television stations.

These are

- Cricket Test matches at home involving England
- The Derby
- FIFA World Cup Finals
- FA Cup Final
- Grand National
- Olympic Games
- Finals week of Wimbledon
- Scottish FA Cup Final

In 1993 the BBC spent £90 million on sports coverage, ITV £37 million, Channel 4 £14.4 million and BSkyB £59 million. The hours of coverage by the four terrestrial channels are listed in Table 9.4

Table 9.4 Viewing of sport on terrestrial TV channels, 1993

	Hours and minutes	BBC1	BBC2	ITV	Ch4
Football	421.35	31	4	37	28
Horse racing	306.45	23	11	—	66
Cricket	285.5	36	63	—	—
Snooker	269.25	17	58	26	—
Golf	180.25	28	58	7	7
Tennis	175.55	8	68	—	4
Rugby union	135.25	40	29	31	—
Athletics	88.35	28	35	29	8
American football	71.30	—	—	—	100
Boxing	58	27	—	72	1
Motor sport	56.25	25	49	21	5
Wrestling	39	—	3	97	—
Basketball	31.30	2	7	84	7
Skiing	20.20	15	77	3	5

(*Source:* Sportscan/Sports Marketing Surveys 1993, in *The Independent*, 7 July 1994)

However, there is still a long way to go in this debate, as the satellite channels have many millions of pounds at their disposal and are hungry to extend their sports coverage.

Activity

In a small group consider the following questions:

1 How well does television cover sport and physical recreation?
2 What improvements in coverage can you suggest?
3 Should the 'listed' events always be available only on terrestrial and not satellite television?

Trends in sport and physical recreation

This element has examined the key roles which sport and physical recreation play in modern British society. These roles are complex and involve a vast range of organisations, sometimes co-operating with each other, while at other times being in an intense competition for customers. We have seen that the reasons why people take part in these activities are manifold and are subject to constant change. These changes and trends are, in fact, the key dynamics of sport and physical recreation in modern society and promote a great deal of debate on the issues arising. There is no reason to suppose that the pace of these trends will slacken or that the issues will become any less controversial in the twenty-first century.

Assignment 9.3

Title: Sport and physical recreation in a local area
Performance criteria satisfied: 9.3.1, 9.3.2, 9.3.3, 9.3.4
Core skills satisfied at level 3: Information technology 3.1, 3.2, 3.3
                                                    Communication 3.1, 3.2, 3.3, 3.4
                                                    Application of number 3.1, 3.2, 3.3

Situation

Your local leisure centre is twenty years old. The council wants to attract as much publicity as possible to this occasion. It has approached the local college to ask advice on publicity through newspaper or other coverage. Your tutor has given you this as a project.

Tasks

Prepare a newspaper article on trends and developments in sport and physical recreation over the last twenty years.

The article should highlight such aspects as:

- Technological developments which have affected sport, especially in your own local area
- Activities which have become popular in the area over the last twenty years
- Current issues which have an impact on sport and recreation and their place in society

You should include as many relevant examples as possible under each heading or category discussed.

Unit 10
LEISURE CENTRE OPERATIONS

Element 10.1   Investigate a programme for a selected leisure centre

Element 10.2   Investigate the key operational requirements for running a leisure centre

Element 10.3   Investigate the products, services and pricing policies of a selected leisure centre

Element 10.1   Investigate a programme for a selected leisure centre

Performance criteria

1   Explain the objectives of a selected leisure centre.
2   Describe the policies related to the selected leisure centre.
3   Describe the programme of the selected leisure centre.
4   Evaluate the extent to which the leisure centre programme meets the objectives of the leisure centre.

Introduction

We have seen in Unit 9 that the sport and physical recreation operating environment is wide-ranging and complex. Providers of facilities and services have to cater for people with a vast spectrum of needs and abilities who want an ever-improving product at a price which reflects the level of service given. In the modern sport and leisure industry, the customer is a consumer with many alternative choices available and competition is growing all the time for a share of the 'leisure pound' component of one's disposable income. It is thus vital that managers set very high standards in operating their facilities if the customer is to be attracted in the first place and motivated to make return visits. Figure 10.1 gives an overview of the customer's contact with a typical sports centre and usefully sets the scene for the content of this unit.

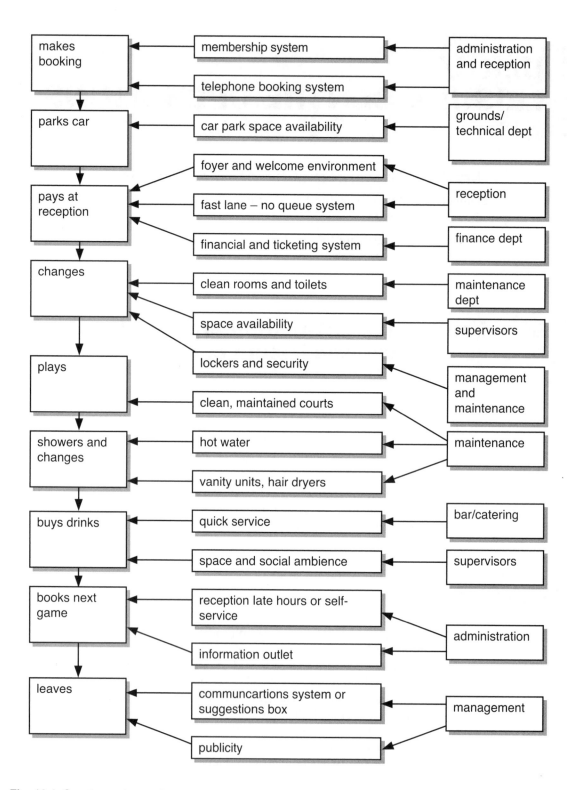

Fig. 10.1 Sports centre customer

The modern leisure centre

Public swimming pools have existed for over a hundred years as have sports halls and gymnasia. For much of that time they have operated as separate facilities in distinct segments of the market. It is only since the 1960s that planners have developed the concept of the 'leisure' centre offering an integrated facility for wet and dry sports and ancillary services such as catering or vending. In addition such buildings can be used for social events such as weddings or for craft fairs and exhibitions. A modern all-purpose leisure centre can be found in most towns or areas serving reasonable-sized populations. They vary in size according to the density of that population. At one end of the scale there is the *Small Community Recreation Centre* (SCRC), a concept devised by the Sports Council to meet the needs of a local community for a limited sports and social facility. Figure 10.2 shows the scale of this type of facility built at Markfield, Leicestershire.

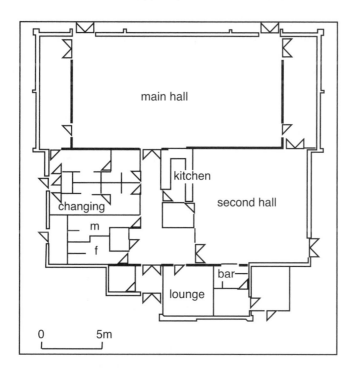

Fig.10.2 Small Community Recreation Centre, Markfield, Leicestershire

At the other end of the scale can be found the Ponds Forge International Sports Centre in Sheffield. This facility aims to provide wet and dry sports venues for the citizens of Sheffield, but the swimming pool in the centre is of Olympic standard and is used for major events as well as for community swimming. Whatever the size or complexity of the leisure centre, the aim is always the same: to provide the best possible service to the customer through the widest possible programme being offered.

Aims and objectives of leisure centres

When using the terms aims and objectives, we often tend to speak of them as almost being one and the same thing. In reality, however, they are very different. Aims are the general operational principles which the owners have laid down for a particular facility. They will vary according to which sector of the industry the facility operates within, but in all sectors they will be general statements of intent. They could be stated thus:

- To provide a leisure service to all customers wishing to use the facility, irrespective of sex, age, race, colour, creed, ability or disability
- To provide levels of service and activities to satisfy the maximum number of client needs
- To use all facility resources in the most appropriate manner
- To evaluate services on a regular and systematic basis

Having established the general operating principles in line with the philosophy of the managing organisation, the management of a leisure centre will then go on to list its objectives. While aims are long term, objectives are short term and attainable. They are laid down in line with the overall aims and serve to meet these aims. Above all, the objectives must be measurable and have a definite timescale. They are linked to the targets which management will set out and are often framed alongside questions such as What? When? How? How much? They might be phrased in this manner:

- To stage a five-a-side football competition for primary school children in the town
- To bid for the staging of five craft fairs in the next year
- To maximise income from the bar and cafeteria and to re-invest the profits in new equipment

Specific objectives

All leisure centres will have their own objectives to be met through offering services to customers. Let us examine some possible examples.

- *To meet community needs* – This is an example of an objective which is expressed in qualitative, rather than quantitative terms. It is most likely to be found in a traditional local authority leisure centre which exists to meet the needs of all residents in that areas.
- *To meet individual needs* – This is similar to the first objective and is linked to theories of maximising individual potential and equal opportunities policies and practices.
- *To encourage health and fitness and to promote health education to customers* – This could be linked to GP referral schemes which are becoming very popular (see case study).
- *To cater for target groups* – These are groups of customers, or potential customers, that the management wish to attract. The effort might be linked to national

promotions by such agencies as the Sports Council. Disabled people, the 50+ age group, women and teenagers have been target groups since the mid-1980s.

- *To maximise the use of space and equipment* – A leisure centre has to generate income and by setting objectives of this type, the management can lay down targets, the achievements of which can later be measured.
- *To maximise skills of staff* – The staff represent the most costly investment which facility managers make and they must be deployed to the best possible effect. In the same way, staff must be trained in new skills and qualifications so that they be of greatest possible use to the centre.
- *To meet financial targets* – All facilities, whether in the public, private or voluntary sectors of provision will be set financial targets by their owners. If these are not met, this could lead to staff reductions or even the closure of the facility.
- *To maximise income and to generate profits* – This is clearly linked to the previous example. Even a local authority leisure centre, with substantial subsidies from the council, is still required to achieve the maximum income possible. In the case of a private facility, such as a health club, the objective might be to generate profits for the investors or shareholders.

GP referral schemes

Since the early 1990s there have been many pilot projects in which doctors have worked with leisure centres to provide an alternative form of treatment for many illnesses and medical conditions.

Outline of operation

Doctors and health workers register with the project by reading and signing a copy of the project manual. Doctors who feel that patients can benefit from the course refer them to the Liaison Officer via a prescription which specifies

- The name of the patient's doctor
- The name of the doctor referring the patient if different from above
- The nature of the exercise the doctor is recommending
- Any further information the doctor feels is necessary to assist with fitness evaluation and exercise prescription e.g. medical/physiological limitations.

The patient brings the prescription to the Leisure Centre at the time shown and meets the Liaison Officer who then

- Discusses the expectations of the patient
- Shows the patient the facilities available
- Discusses the programme in which the patient will be participating
- Arranges a fitness evaluation for the patient.

The patient then joins the scheme (price can be £1.00 for fitness training facilities and 50p for swim). The Liaison Officer monitors the patient's activity during the programme to ensure satisfactory progress, and to arrange retailoring of the course if necessary. After the patient has completed the programme he/she is referred back to the doctor for evaluation. At the doctor's discretion the patients are offered a two-month free membership of the centre. It is expected that patients become long-term users of the Leisure Centre.

Benefits of the project

In its basic form the project is a GP referral scheme which improves the fitness levels of the referred clients. However, since the scheme attracts large numbers of people who would not, in normal circumstances, enter a leisure centre, there are other secondary benefits which collectively are very important.

A number of authorities operate schemes which target specific groups which may be under-represented in leisure centres. Usually, these schemes involve some form of price reduction and often experience a reduction in the prestige of the scheme which can reflect on the participants' self-image. Additionally, these schemes tend to be 'broad-based' by their very nature, and can offer incentives to people who do not really need them, while still not targeting the individuals with the greatest need.

Compulsory Competitive Tendering (CCT)

This measure was introduced in 1988 under the terms of the Local Government Act. It required many local council-operated facilities and services to be offered out to competitive bids. By the end of 1993, all sports and leisure facilities in England and Wales had to be put out to CCT in terms of their management. This means that while a council still retains ultimate ownership of a facility, the day-to-day running and operations can now be carried out by a contractor working to a specification drawn up by the council. The government believed that CCT would lead to increased competition to run leisure centres and that this, in turn, would ensure better facilities and services for customers. Many leisure centres have had their management taken over by contractors. This change in management has inevitably led to changes in some of the operational objectives of leisure facilities and services.

Activity

Considering the examples of objectives given above:

1 Which ones do you think might be changed if a facility was contracted out under CCT?
2 Write some notes on the changes which could take place in these objectives.

Policies and charters of leisure centres

Having set out its aims and objectives for managing the facility, the management of a leisure centre is then likely to produce policy documents to cover aspects of its operations. These will cover certain key areas and they should be

- Clear and unambiguous in their wording
- Written so as to avoid possible legal challenge by customers
- Non-discriminatory either for or against any particular group or category of users
- Written in a manner which clearly sets out the rights of both customers and management.
- Set out in a way which includes time frames on such aspects as the management's response to customer complaints

In common with many other organisations, such as British Telecom or large chain stores, leisure centres might choose to frame such policy documents in the form of charters. These show a high degree of concern for the needs and rights of the customer and aim to set up a form of 'contract' between management and paying consumers.

A model customer charter

We are committed to providing a high quality service every time you visit our centre.

We promise that
- the time and availability of services will be as published in our customer information leaflet
- any foreseen change will be duly notified to our customers by the display of an appropriate notice within the centre
- any unforeseen (emergency) interruption to services which have been booked will result in refunds and/or an offer of alternative services where possible

The swimming pool will be
- maintained at a minimum of 28 °C
- balanced chemically and tested regularly to ensure customer comfort and safety
- supervised by the recommended number of qualified and trained staff
- kept in a warm, clean, safe and hygienic condition

The dry sport/activity areas will be
- clean and safe to use
- furnished with equipment which is in good working order and checked and maintained regularly
- set out in accordance with the requirements of the governing body of the sport where necessary
- ready for use within five minutes of the commencement of the booked period where equipment change-overs are necessary
- illuminated, heated and ventilated to ensure comfort, good play conditions and safety

Staff will be
- trained and appropriately qualified
- easily identifiable by wearing their uniforms at all times
- helpful, experienced and informative to ensure that your visit is safe and enjoyable

All ancillary areas, including changing rooms, showers and toilets, will be
- clean, hygienic and in good working order
- checked by staff every hour and remedial action taken where necessary
- maintained at a temperature which is comfortable and complimentary to other areas

In general, we will
- ensure the centre is clean, safe and well maintained
- listen and be responsive to comments, complaints and suggestions
- maintain a balanced programme of activities and services which cater for the needs of all sections of the community
- publish up-to-date and accurate customer information for all activities
- have clear technical standards for all important features of the service and meet them
- make prices competitive and fair to ensure value for money
- undertake regular surveys of our customers to ensure that we continue to meet their stated priorities

Of course, not all the policies of a leisure centre can, or should be, framed in charter form. Some are not for public consumption: financial and staffing policies are the key examples.

Activity

A leisure centre is staging some sessions aimed at mothers with young toddlers. Draft out a Customer Charter aimed specially at this group of customers.

Programming in the leisure centre

The programming of the centre is the key way in which all the aims, objectives and policies are put into practice and delivered to customers. It has obvious links with the marketing of the facility, an aspect examined elsewhere in this course. As well as meeting customer needs, the programming process is the way in which the management can ensure that the facility is

- Operating at its maximum possible capacity
- Operating in a planned manner, with clear guidelines which are fair and take into account competing interests for time and space
- Getting the best out of its staff members by using the full range of their expertise

- Subject to constant review and evaluation in the way in which it offers its services

Programming is a highly skilled process and, being based upon the aims and objectives of a facility, will vary from sector to sector in the leisure industry. A private sector facility is, for example, likely to offer a more restricted programme in terms of range when compared to a local authority centre. This is due to the different markets in which they are operating and the differing philosophies of use laid down by management. The programme in any facility seeks to meet the needs of its users and this can be influenced by different factors:

- *Catchment area* – Refers to the sphere of influence of a facility and how far it extends
- *Population information* – It is important that the management is aware of the make-up of the population which it seeks to serve through its programme
- *Market research* – Management will want, from time to time, to conduct surveys among existing or potential customers to evaluate current programmes and consider possible new ones
- *Target groups* – This refers to particular groups which the facility management might wish to attract to certain activities or at certain periods of the day, for example women or retired people.
- *Usage information* – Any of the above points could help to feed information into the programme planning process. All are designed to give the maximum possible insight into the needs and changing wants of current or potential customers.

It is possible to represent the programming process in a number of ways, but a useful one is to think of it as wedge-shaped as shown in Figure 10.3

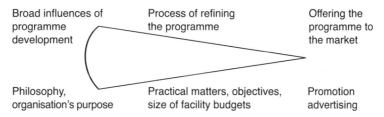

Fig. 10.3 *Schematic representation of programme development*

Once devised, the delivery of the programme to customers is the 'sharp end'. This revolves around three key factors: activities, facilities and services.

Activities

Not all leisure centres can cater for all possible sport and leisure activities, swimming being the most obvious example. It is clear that the activities available play a large part in the shape of the final programme.

Facilities

The scale of a facility clearly determines the programming possibilities, as does the availability of ancillary aspects such as catering or crèche areas.

Services

This refers to the ways in which the programme on offer is presented to customers through advertising, special price offers or transport to and from the facility.

Three sample programmes

The programme of a leisure centre will vary according to the factors listed above which will determine its place in the leisure market. Here are three sample programmes from different leisure environments.

Charnwood Leisure Centre, Loughborough

This is a facility built in 1975 and now operated by Serco as contractor in a CCT contract with Charnwood Borough Council. It could be described as a typical wet and dry leisure centre of the type to be found in a town like Loughborough with a core population of around 30,000 (see Figure 10.4).

Fig. 10.4 Swimming pool programme for Charnwood Leisure Centre, Loughborough

Ponds Forge International Sports Centre, Sheffield

This facility was built in 1991 at a cost of some £52 million. It offers a full range of sporting opportunities to the residents of Sheffield and surrounding districts, a potential catchment of around 500,000. In addition, it has world-class facilities, especially the pool, which has hosted the European Championships (see Figure 10.5).

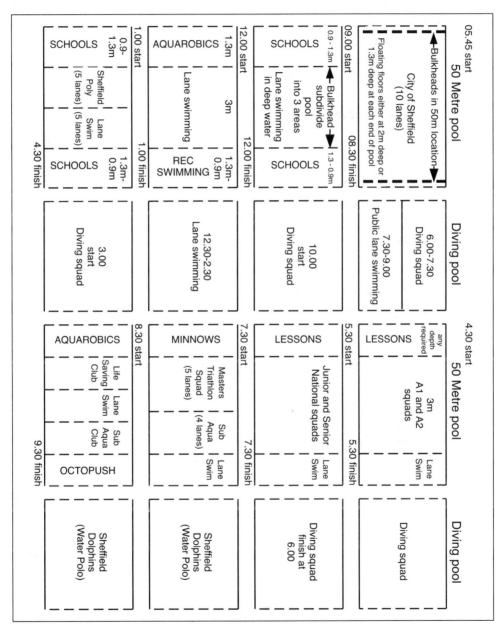

Fig. 10.5 Swimming pool programme for Ponds Forge International Sports Centre, Sheffield

The range of fitness activities offered at Ponds Forge is illustrated in the timetable.

	No card	LEISURE CARD RATE		
		Peak	Off peak	Mid peak
Aerobics and step classes				
For adults	2.50	2.25		
For juniors	1.75	1.50		
For Gold Card holders		1.50		
Circuit training				
For adults	2.50	2.25		
For juniors	1.75	1.50		
For Gold Card holders		1.50		

Aerobic bodyshop programme

	Monday		Tuesday
Beginner step	12.15 p.m. – 1.15 p.m.	Intermediate step	5.15 p.m. – 6.15 p.m.
Fit 'n' firm	5.30 p.m. – 6.30 p.m.	Beginner step	6.30 p.m. – 7.30 p.m.
Aero step	6.45 p.m. – 7.45 p.m.		
Circuit training	7.45 p.m. – 8.45 p.m.		

	Wednesday		Thursday
Intermediate step	12.15 p.m. – 1.15 p.m.	Intermediate step	12.15 p.m. – 1.15 p.m.
Beginner step	1.30 p.m. – 2.30 p.m.	Intermediate aerobics	5.30 p.m. – 6.30 p.m.
Fit 'n' firm	5.00 p.m. – 6.00 p.m.	Intermediate step	6.45 p.m. – 7.45 p.m.
Circuit training	7.15 p.m. – 8.15 p.m.		
Advanced aerobics	6.15 p.m. – 7.15 p.m.		

	Friday		Saturday
Aero step	12.15 p.m. – 1.15 p.m.	Beginner aerobics	10.30 a.m. – 11.30 a.m.
Intermediate step	5.15 p.m. – 6.15 p.m.	Intermediate step	11.45 a.m. – 12.45 p.m.

Step classes can be booked up to 7 days in advance. Bookings cannot be taken over the phone. Please retain your ticket/receipt until the day of the class.

Leisure Card times at Ponds Forge
Peak times Monday to Friday 5.00 p.m. – 10.00 p.m. All day Saturday and Sunday (except for sports hall)

Customers please note that we are closed for staff training on Wednesday mornings until 10.30 a.m.

Double up activity savings
If you choose two activities on this brochure the second activity will be at Gold Card rate, if on the same day subject to availability. Does not apply to sunbeds.

National Indoor Arena, Birmingham

This facility, well known as the venue for TV's Gladiators programme, was opened in 1991. As its name implies, it has national status and importance through Sports

Council funding and its designation as the premier British indoor venue (see Figure 10.6).

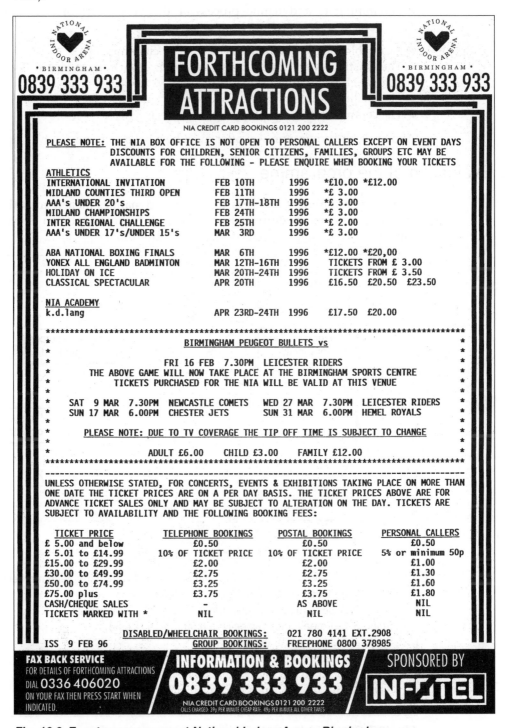

Fig. 10.6 *Events programme at National Indoor Arena, Birmingham*

Programming objectives

Programming is a dynamic process at the very heart of any leisure facility's operations. It seeks to ensure that

- A suitable range of activities is on offer to customers
- These activities are timed to suit the needs of customers and at the same time to generate the maximum possible income
- The facility's space is used to best effect
- The centre's staff are deployed to best effect

Above all, the programme on offer must be a balanced one.

Evaluation of the programme

If the programming process is to be truly dynamic, then it must be constantly evaluated for current effectiveness and possible future adaptation. The entire process can be shown in diagrammatic form (see Figure 10.7).

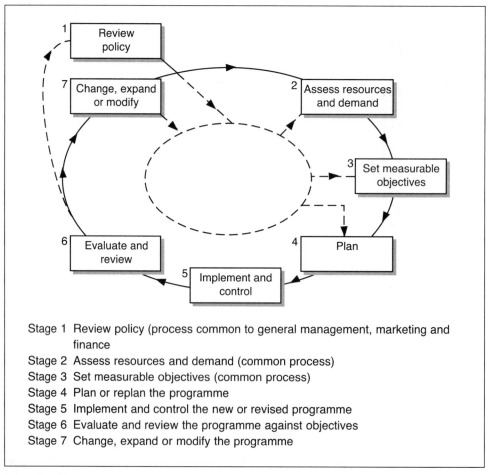

Stage 1 Review policy (process common to general management, marketing and finance
Stage 2 Assess resources and demand (common process)
Stage 3 Set measurable objectives (common process)
Stage 4 Plan or replan the programme
Stage 5 Implement and control the new or revised programme
Stage 6 Evaluate and review the programme against objectives
Stage 7 Change, expand or modify the programme

Fig. 10.7 Sequence in programming process

The programme might be evaluated in terms of

- The levels of income generated in the facility
- The achievement, or otherwise, of any financial targets set for the programme
- The number of users going through the facility in a particular time period
- The level of satisfaction among customers. This can be gauged through questionnaires or suggestion boxes
- The number of repeat visitors to the facility in a given time period

Assignment 10.1

Title: Programme evaluation
Performance criteria satisfied: 10.1.1, 10.1.2, 10.1.3, 10.1.4
Core skills satisfied at level 3: Communication 3.2, 3.3, 3.4, 3.5
                                   Information technology 3.1, 3.2, 3.3
                                   Application of number 3.1, 3.2, 3.3

Situation

On work placement or as part of your course, you have been asked to examine the programme for your local leisure centre. You should gather as much information as possible, such as leaflets on the programmes on offer in the centre.

Tasks

1 Prepare a report on the centre's aims and objectives. This should include details of ownership, philosophy of use and any relevant policies in operation.
2 Describe the key activities in the centre's programme.
3 Evaluate how the programme sets out to meet the centre's objectives and how the success or otherwise of this could be measured.

You should at all stages back up your report with relevant examples.

Investigate the key operational requirements for running a leisure centre

---

Performance criteria

1 Identify and give examples of the legal requirements relating to the operation of a leisure centre.
2 Describe the licensing requirements relating to the operation of a leisure centre.
3 Explain the maintenance requirements of a leisure centre.
4 Explain the purpose of booking systems in a leisure centre.
5 Explain the methods of payment and recording systems in a leisure centre.

Introduction

Having seen how a leisure centre sets out and runs its programmes, this section goes on to examine the many factors which ensure that the operation runs smoothly. It is a highly complicated process which must take account of the needs of customers, the demands of management and numerous legal requirements. Many systems and people need to work in harmony for the day-to-day operations in a leisure centre to take place in a pleasant, safe and well-maintained environment. In addition, this must all happen in a facility whose management wishes it to be successful, attracting a lot of customers and seeking to retain them for repeat business. The whole operation must therefore be a balance between customer needs and the necessary requirements which management must impose on staff and customers in the facility.

Legal requirements in the operation of a leisure centre

In common with all other organisations and premises, a leisure centre must operate within the law. There are many special factors applying to a leisure centre and this section will examine these.

Health and safety

Under the terms of the Health and Safety at Work, etc. Act 1974, any organisation employing five or more persons must produce and display a policy on health and safety. Virtually all the leisure centres in Britain come into this category. The Act lays down the duties of both employers and employees.

Employers' duties

- To provide and maintain plant and equipment which are not a risk to health
- To ensure safe work practices
- To undertake regular monitoring of health and safety factors in a facility
- To ensure the safe storage of any dangerous substances
- To provide a written statement of safety policy and to bring it to the attention of everyone
- To provide information and staff training on health and safety

Employee's duties

- To take reasonable care to avoid injury to themselves or others at work
- To co-operate with their employers and others to ensure that the Act is carried out
- To avoid interfering with or misusing anything provided to protect their health, safety and welfare under the Act

Legal necessities

It is clear that a multi-purpose and multi-activity leisure centre involves many aspects of the Health and Safety at Work Act and these include

- The need for floors to be clean and of a non-slip surface
- The need for strong, safe and well-maintained equipment
- The need for lights to be covered when ball games are played
- The need to avoid low-level obstructions in sports halls
- The need for adequate and safe storage facilities
- The need for correct room temperatures for safety and customer comfort reasons
- The need for safe, clear water in swimming pools
- The need to have qualified lifesavers on a poolside
- The need for pool surrounds to be clean and of non-slip surfaces
- The need to mark depth and danger areas in swimming pools
- The need to train staff in incident procedures
- The need to have trained first aiders on hand

Activity

List six possible examples in a leisure centre where failure to follow health and safety rules could lead to major problems or incidents.

Food hygiene

Most leisure centres now run some form of catering operation as an ancillary service to customers and a means of increasing income to the facility. As such, the centre must comply with the Food Hygiene Regulations under the Food Safety Act 1990. These regulations are tightly enforced by inspectors and can lead to heavy fines or, in severe cases, the closure of that facility's catering operation. The Regulations place great importance on

- Food not becoming exposed to contamination
- The need for staff at all times to observe hygienic methods
- The need for staff to cover cuts to the skin and to report certain diseases
- The banning of smoking anywhere near food
- The need for a constant supply of hot water
- The need for good washing facilities and materials
- The need for safe storage and correct temperatures of some foods

Fire precautions

Under the terms of the Fire Precautions Act 1971, later amended by the Fire Safety and Safety of Places of Sport Act 1987, all public buildings must have a Fire Certificate. If this is granted after inspection the conditions met will include:

- Fire escapes being kept clear
- The facility undertaking staff training in fire safety drills
- Regular inspection of fire extinguishers and hose reels
- Limits on the number of persons in a building at one time
- The proper storage of any flammable liquids
- The prominent displaying of warning notices
- The keeping of records on fire safety matters

Insurance

Leisure centres are places where incidents and accidents can and do occur. Many of these are the fault of the customer, either by complete accident or some action such as a foolish tackle in five-a-side football. When an accident has happened, it is vital that full details of it are recorded, as legal action could result from it if it is felt that the centre management was negligent in some way.

 ### *Charnwood Leisure Centre accident and incident forms*

Many leisure centres use standard accident report forms and standard incident report forms as shown in this case study.

Accident report form

SERCO

ACCIDENT REPORT FORM

THIS FORM IS **NOT** TO BE USED FOR
ACCIDENTS INVOLVING SERCO EMPLOYEES

| LEISURE CENTRE |

S/No.
LC 09999

PART A - About the person who had the accident

Full name & title – Mr/Mrs/Ms/Miss

Address:

Telephone No.:   Post Code:

Date of Birth: Occupation:

If a member of a party, or under group instruction, name of organisation and name of leader/supervisor:

PART B - About the accident

When did it happen (time & date):   Where did it happen (location in Leisure Centre):

How did it happen (give details of any equipment in use):

Treatment given: Injuries caused:
                                             (Indicate position & type of injury)

Further treatment:

1. No action taken	YES/NO
2. Advised to see Doctor	YES/NO
3. Advised to attend Hospital	YES/NO
4. Taken to Hospital	YES/NO

If YES –
by whom and to which Hospital:

PART C – Witnesses

Name	Address	Telephone No.

PART D – To be completed by the injured person

To the best of my knowledge and belief the details stated above are a true record of what happened to me. Signed:

PART E – About you, the person who treated the casualty

Your full name & title: Mr/Mrs/Ms/Miss   Job Title:

In your opinion is any action required to prevent further accidents of this kind: YES/NO
If YES give details:

Your Signature:

PART F – To be completed by the Duty Manager

Is the accident reportable to HSE: YES/NO   If YES attach copy of completed Form 2508 and give time, date and name of HSE contact.

Follow up action & comments:

                              Date: Signed:

Distribution: White – Southall Commercial Services.   Blue – Manager Health & Safety, Serco Resource Management.   Yellow – Retained at Leisure Centre

SX0249

Incident report form

Name:

Address:

Nature of employment (applicable to employees only) ....

School ....

Date .... Time ....

Location of incident ....

Nature of incident (i.e. accident, complaint, assault, dangerous occurrence, etc.)

Action taken: ....

Action taken by: .... Position ....

Persons notified:.................................. Position ....

.... Position ....

.... Position ....

Detailed report (with diagrams if necessary)

Remarks ....

....

....

.... Manager .... Date

ANY OTHER INFORMATION MAY BE ATTACHED ON SEPARATE SHEETS
OR OVERLEAF ON COMPLETION, PLEASE SUBMIT THIS REPORT TO THE
MANAGER

Public liability

The Occupier's Liability Act 1957 introduced the notion of 'common duty of care' which it defined as: 'a duty to take such care as in all the circumstances of the case is reasonable, to see that the visitor will be reasonably safe in using the premises for the purposes for which he is invited or permitted by the occupier to be there'. This was reinforced by the Occupier's Liability Act 1984 to include visitors, spectators and neighbours and others living nearby. There have been many cases of negligence brought against facility management for such tragic accidents as drowning in swimming pools. These legal actions can lead to costly settlements, if negligence is proved, and for this reason it is important that public liability insurance is taken out as a possible offsetting of such bills. In the same way the fabric of the building and its contents must be covered by insurance. The premiums on all these policies can be very costly indeed and must be taken into account in drawing up the annual facility budget.

Risk assessments

The legal requirements on health and safety are constantly being updated, often under pressure from the European Union. An example of this is the 1993 changes to the Health and Safety at Work Act which require management to carry out 'risk assessments' on their facilities and the activities going on within them. The aim of this self-evaluation is to draw up a list of potential risks and the steps which can be taken to prevent them turning into full accidents. A standard risk assessment form is shown here.

Risk assessment – initial review

Site name:	Risk assessment by:
People	Date: Next review date:
Location	Risk assessment for:
Activities	
Other (state)	

Description   Ref   Special hazards

(List tasks, activities equipment, machinery, location details as applicable)

Activity

1 Select a sporting activity undertaken in a leisure centre.
2 Draw up a list of the potential risks which it involves.
3 Draw up a list of the steps which could be taken to minimise these risks.

Licensing requirements in the operation of a leisure centre

In everyday use the word 'licensing' is usually taken to mean the sale of intoxicating liquor. However, in the case of leisure centre operations the term has wider applications. The multi-use leisure centre of today provides so many activities that many of these are covered by specific licensing arrangements. These include

- Liquor licences
- Public entertainment licences
- Theatre licences
- Cinema licences
- Indoor sports' licences

Liquor licences

There are eight types of permission which could be required to sell intoxicating liquor. These are obtained by applying to the local Licensing Justices and any facility wishing to sell alcoholic beverages must go through this process. There are two particular liquor licences which apply to leisure centres.

- *An on licence* – This is a full, all-year-round licence which allows the management of a facility to sell alcohol for consumption on the premises, usually in the leisure centre's bar.
- *An occasional licence* – This could be applied for to cover such events in the centre as dances, wedding receptions, dinners and fêtes where the alcohol might be being sold in a venue other than the bar or the function is extending beyond normal opening or licensing hours.

All such licences are subject to renewal and the magistrates could refuse an application, or fail to renew, if any problems had existed at the centre over alcohol sales or objections had been received. As the sale of alcoholic beverages can be such an important additional source of income, then the management of a leisure centre, like any other licensee, will take great care to protect its reputation and thus future licence applications.

Public entertainment licences

These will be needed if the facility is providing public dancing, music or any similar public entertainment. This applies to the building, but it may also extend to open air spaces on which the facility is staging any such events. These licenses are granted after a successful application to

- The local authority
- The Chief Constable
- The local Fire Officer

A leisure centre would have to hold a public entertainment licence to stage discos, roller discos, tea dances, pop concerts and pool parties (with music included).

Theatre licences

These are required for any public performance of a play. The applications are made in the same way as for Public Entertainment Licences and would, in a leisure centre context, cover plays, pantomimes and ballet performances.

Cinema licences

These licence are obtained by applying to the local authority and they cover the showing of films, videos, video juke boxes and the live broadcasting of television events to an audience. Many leisure centres can generate a lot of extra income by having a television set in the bar and putting on events for customers. With the changes to the broadcasting of live sports events, discussed in Unit 9, and with so many events being available only to satellite subscribers, this aspect of income generation for leisure centres could become even more important in future years.

Indoor sports' licences

This type of licence might seem a strange one considering the nature of the everyday activities in leisure centres. However, they apply in cases where the public is invited into sports events as spectators. These could include boxing tournaments, a snooker or darts demonstration by a celebrity, a swimming gala or a tennis match. These licences are applied for in the same way as public entertainment licences.

It is clear that there are a great many potential events and activities within a leisure centre which are covered by licensing arrangements. The management must at all times follow the correct application procedures and carry out the strict operational requirements laid down by the granting body. Failure to do so could affect the centre's income and reputation and could lead to many later problems.

Activity

A leisure centre is hosting a wedding reception which will run from 5 p.m. until 2 a.m. the next morning. It will have a disco and live performance by a music group.
List the various licences which will have to be in place for the event to go ahead.

Maintenance requirements of a leisure centre

What is maintenance?

The Institute of Sport and Recreation Management's manual on *Practical Leisure Centre Management* (vol. 2; p. 347) says that 'Maintenance has been defined as work undertaken to keep or restore an asset to an acceptable standard at an acceptable cost'. Perhaps a less subjective definition and one which fits the concept of service which must be a main objective of a leisure facility is 'keep in a proper and good condition, i.e. ensure firstly the facility is available to the public and secondly that it may be used safely'.

A leisure centre is a highly complex organisation in which many people and systems must work together to provide a service to customers. Moreover, a lot of money will have been invested in the building, in plant and in equipment to bring it up to the required standard. It would make no sense whatsoever if the management failed to do everything possible to keep these aspects of the service up to that standard. Maintenance thus affects

- The health and safety of staff and customers
- The image which the facility presents to customers
- The value of the building, plant and equipment
- The morale of the staff
- The investment policy of the management in terms of replacement and minimising this by sound maintenance
- The ability to attract paying customers and secure them as repeat business
- The income and cash flow of the centre if closures result from poor maintenance
- The facility's ability to fend off competitors for the customer's business

Good maintenance of a leisure centre proves the old cliché that 'prevention is better than cure'. This is demonstrated by the three main strands of activity within a centre: planned, corrective and preventive maintenance.

Planned maintenance

This is when schedules are drawn up for work to be undertaken at set intervals. Examples of this would be for external painting to be undertaken on a 5–7 year cycle, while internal painting is done on a 3–5 year cycle. Of course, changes found in the fabric of either or a change in policy could alter these longer-term plans.

Corrective maintenance

As the term implies, this takes place when an unexpected fault has been detected and must be repaired in order to keep a facility operating. A burst pipe or building subsidence would be examples of this work.

Preventive maintenance

This is the ideal method of maintaining a facility as fully as possible, as it is based on systems of good planning, inspection and rectifying faults as they are detected. The best example to be found in a wet leisure centre is that of the regular testing by staff of the swimming pool water and the inspection of the plant. It is essential that this is done on a planned basis for both customer health and safety reasons and for the efficient, economic and long-term operation of the pool plant room. Figure 10.8 is an example of a log (with explanations) of this vital process.

Notes:

Pumps started/stopped/running/in use
Shows rotation of pump use - assuming 3 1/2 capacity pumps.

Strainers Changed
Records strainer maintenance based on either backwashing interval or flow rate or experience of need.

Filters Inlet & Outlet
Records pressure readings and differential hence condition of bed

Backwash
Records frequency and duration of backwashing.

Circulation Flow
Monitors efficiency of pumps, pipework and filters. Variations in performance require investigation.

Test - Free/Combined/pH
Presumes 2 hourly frequency with one test prior to use at the start of each day. Similarly one test at the end of each day.

Also allows for further analysis of Combined Chlorine where they exceed required levels. Facilitates a record of the Mono' Di' chloramine readings to show the underlying form, either organic or inorganic and hence the appropriate action required.

Alkalinity/Calcium Hardness/TDS/Temperature
Probably a weekly test to give an indication of pool water balance.

Range - alkalinity 75-250 mg/l, calcium hardness 75-500 mg/l, TDS - within 1000 of source water, temperature 28-30°C, Langelier Index 0 to 0.5.

Chemical Additions
In this case presumes hypochlorite but could be other forms of disinfectant. Coagulant dosing metered throughout the daily bathing cycle. 1-2.5 mg/l or 5% solution Aluminium Sulphate. PAC (polyaluminium chloride) 0.1 ml/m3.

Clarity
A subjective assessment by the operator using a 1 to 10 scale.

Number of Bathers
In some cases estimating where necessary to ensure design loading not exceeded and to show freshwater dilution rate.

Dilution
The additions of fresh water principally by backwashing supplemented by trickle feed during bathing cycle. Necessary standard to reduce organic chloramine and TDS 30 litres/bather/day.

Additional Considerations:
* Recording one weekly/monthly - sulphate concentration recommended upper limit 360 mg/l.
* Measuring redox levels pre and post water treatment to show effectiveness.
* Recording when tests are taken by Public Health monitoring and the free chlorine combined chlorine and pH at the time.

This is an example of a requirement for just one hypothetical pool - your needs may be different!

ISRM Pool Log Sheet

ISRM, Giffard House, 36/38 Sherrard Street, Melton Mowbray, LE13 1XJ
Tel: 01664 65531 Fax: 01664 501155

Institute of Sport & Recreation Management

Name Of Pool: _____

SWIMMING POOL LOG SHEET - MONDAY / / TO SUNDAY / /

Water Pumps	MON		TUE		WED		THUR		FRI		SAT		SUN	
Pump Started Time														
Pump Stopped Time														
Hours Running														
Pump In Use No.1, 2 or 3														
Strainers Changed														

Filters		IN	OUT	IN	OUT	IN	OUT	IN	OUT	IN	OUT	IN	OUT	IN	OUT
Inlet And Outlet Pressures	No. 1														
	No. 2														
	No. 3														
	No. 4														
Backwash (Mins)	No. 1														
	No. 2														
	No. 3														
	No. 4														

Circulation Flow M³/h or l/h

Test Results		Fr	Co	pH	Fr	Co	pH	Fr	Co	pH	Fr	Co	pH	Fr	Co	pH	Fr	Co	pH	Fr	Co	pH
FREE, COMBINED CHLORINE & pH	Test 1																					
	Test 2																					
	Test 3																					
	Test 4																					
	Test 5																					
	Test 6																					
	Test 7																					
	Test 8																					

Analysis of Monochloramine Dichloramine		M	Di	M	Di	M	Di	M	Di	M	Di	M	Di	M	Di
	Test															
	Test															

Total Alkalinity								
Calcium Hardness								
Total Dissolved Solids								
Temperature								
Langelier Index								

CHEMICAL ADDITIONS	Alum/ Coagulant							
	Hypochlorite							
	CO²/Acid							
	Others							
	Others							

Clarity 10=Perfect 0=V.Poor								
Number of Bathers								
Fresh Water Dilution (Litres)								

Fig. 10.8 Pool log sheet

Leisure centre staff will follow the *Operations and Maintenance Manual* which will set out detailed schedules of the tasks to be undertaken, the timing of such inspections and the persons responsible for each aspect. This will be set out in the form of daily checklists, weekly checklists, periodic checklists and yearly checklists.

Here is a typical planned preventative maintenance schedule.

Daily checklist

* Check storage tank levels
* Check operation of ball valves

- Check valve glands for leakage
- Check pump glands for leakage
- Check heating flow and return temperatures
- Check for leaks at radiators and heater batteries
- Check heating system pressure
- Check ventilation inlets and outlets are free from obstruction
- Check for unusual machinery noise and vibration
- Check gas valves and cocks for operation and leakage
- Report and log all findings

Weekly checklist

- Repeat daily checks
- Check operation of all safety valves
- Vent air from heating system and equipment
- Check settings of thermostats
- Check flexible fan and ductwork connections for signs of deterioration
- Clean all strainers
- Report and log all findings

Importance of good maintenance

Good maintenance is vital to a leisure centre's operation, as it affects levels of business and if not properly undertaken, can lead to crippling bills for repair or replacement which were not in the facility's original annual budget. It requires

- Sound, planned systems of inspection
- Good staff training and deployment on maintenance tasks
- Good budgeting so that repairs or replacement can be accounted for without causing unexpected financial problems
- Systems, either internal or using external contractors, to rectify faults or undertake major items of planned maintenance

Activity

Draw up a flow chart to represent the main types of maintenance undertaken in a wet and dry leisure centre.

Purpose of booking systems in a leisure centre

With so many activities on offer and so many potential customers, it is essential to operate a booking system in a multi-purpose leisure centre. Bookings are closely linked to the programming of the facility and an efficient bookings system allows the management to

- Allocate the required time slots to particular activities, for example squash court bookings
- Operate a fair policy on use by customers by, for instance, allowing bookings for a maximum of only six days in advance
- Set a balance between casual and club use of facilities
- Set a balance between casual and block bookings
- Simultaneously record equipment hire by customers
- Gather information on patterns of use which can be used to modify the centre's programme
- Programme special events which have an impact on the routine programme of the centre

Computerised booking systems

Most leisure centres will now be using computerised booking systems which are quicker and more efficient than the former, paper-based systems. Figure 10.9 shows a typical booking sheet.

```
666 CHARNWOOD LEISURE CE    100 BADMINTON        TUE  5 MAR 96 Your move   11:34
       SPORTS HAL
         1     2     3     4     5     6     7     8
0900:    .     .     .     .    BAD   →     →     →
1000:    .    Kea   Pow   Hud   ↳     →     →     →
1100:    .     .     .     .     .     .     .     .
1200:   Mc    -->   -->   -->   Rob   -->   -->   -->
1300:    .    Moo   Jac   Wil   Ell   -->   -->   -->
1400:   BAD    →     →     →   >BAD<   →     →     →
1500:    .    Boy   Loh    .    Isl   -->   -->   -->
1600:    .     .    Loh    .    Bar   -->   -->   -->
1700    Rog   -->   -->   -->   Far   -->   -->   -->
1800    Kay    .    GYM    →    Hay   Caf   Caf   BAD
1900    Bel   Har   ↳      →    Bal   BAD    →     →
2000    Hod   -->   -->   -->   Har   BAD    →    Cam
2100:   Kin   -->   -->   -->   Har   Per   Tuc   Wil
2200:    .     .     .     .    Gre   -->   -->   -->
```

Fig. 10.9 Computerised booking sheet

At the start of a working day, the daily booking sheet will be checked by centre staff and thus allow for

- The required equipment to be set up at various stages of the day
- The necessary staff to be deployed
- Minor programme changes to be made where, for example, a club booking has been cancelled due to illness

Methods of payment and recording systems in a leisure centre

When a booking has been made and paid for, the receptionist will issue the customer with a ticket. This acts as both a receipt and a confirmation of the booking and has important resulting implications for control and accounting in the centre's operations. A ticket should include

- The name of the centre
- The activity or item involved – either by name or coded number
- The unit price of each activity or item such as equipment hire or purchase
- The total amount paid by the customer
- The method of payment – cash, cheque or credit card
- The time and date of issue
- A code to denote the staff member issuing the ticket
- A receipt number

Method of payment

The main method of customer payment in a leisure centre will usually be

- Bank notes and coins
- Cheques or postal orders
- Credit cards such as Visa or Access
- Debit cards such as Switch or Delta

All methods have their advantages and disadvantages to the centre. For example, large amounts of cash can pose security and transport problems, yet they represent an immediate and guaranteed way of getting money into the organisation's bank account. Cheques and debit cards are safe and secure, yet abuse such as stolen cheques can be a problem and a receptionist must carefully check all details when processing them. Credit cards offer similar advantages and disadvantages to cheques, with an additional one being that a commission may have to be paid by the centre to the card-holding agency.

Charnwood Leisure Centre: cash and stock procedures

The processes of booking and payment are closely inter-linked and, being subject to both internal and external audit, must be carried out according to very strict rules. Figure 10.10 illustrates the payments process.

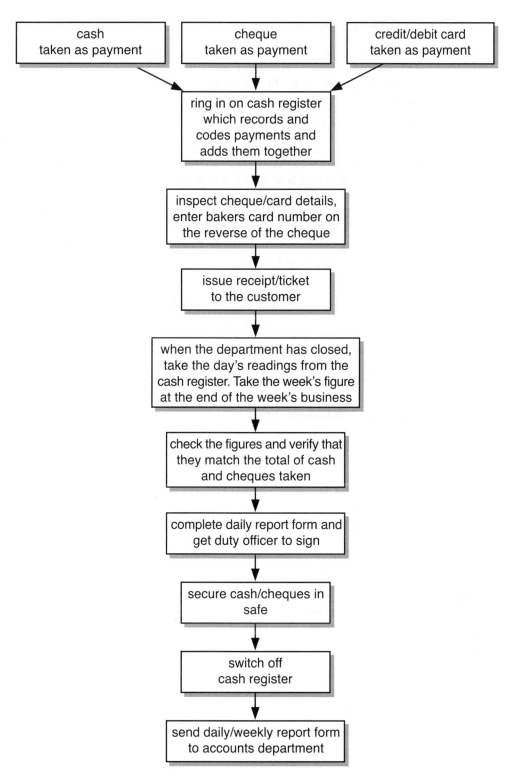

Fig. 10.10 Payments process

Guidelines for receptionists

Always remember that we are the first contact the public has with our centre, and they carry that impression away with them
Always be pleasant, polite and above all cheerful
Uniform should always look clean, tidy and correct

Daily procedure to be followed

Start of shift

1   Collect float of £75, keys and walkie talkie from Duty Officer.
2   Check and weigh float and if necessary get change, then sign the float out.
3   Read diary and information board
4   Check date and general information on computer and check ticket roll
5   Deposit float into cash box and sign on at PC Station to be used
6   Make sure office and particularly desk is clean and as tidy as possible. Always have pen and scrap-pad handy.

End of shift

1   Cashier carry out 'end of shift' routine. DO NOT FORGET.
2   Check £75 float and hand over to staff replacement or Duty Officer and sign float master recording book.
3   Complete cash reconciliation form
4   Complete slip listing monies being paid over.
5   Call Duty Manager to be cashed up.

Reception cashing up sheet

Cash analysis	£	p
£50		
£20		
£10		
£5		
£1		
50p		
Silver		
Copper		
Total		
Cheques		
Access		
Visa		
Total		

Difference:

Signed   Receptionist

         Duty Manager

Date: Time:

Assignment 10.2

Title: Operating a leisure centre
Performance criteria satisfied: 10.2.1, 10.2.2, 10.2.3, 10.2.4, 10.2.5
Core skill satisfied at level 3: Communication 3.1, 3.2, 3.3, 3.4
Information technology 3.1, 3.2, 3.3
Application of number 3.1, 3.2, 3.3

Situation

Your group has been on work placement as part of your course. Three of you have been to local leisure centres and your tutor has put you in a group to prepare a presentation on running a leisure centre.

Tasks

1   Discuss the common requirements of operating a centre. This should cover: legal requirements, licensing requirements, maintenance requirements.
2   Discuss the systems used for: bookings, payments and recording.
3   Prepare and deliver the presentation.

You should give as many relevant examples as possible to reflect the different facilities and services on offer in the leisure centres under discussion.

Investigate the products, services and pricing policies of a selected leisure centre

---

Performance criteria

1 Describe the products provided by a selected leisure centre.
2 Describe the services provided by a selected leisure centre.
3 Explain pricing policies for the products and services available in a selected leisure centre.

Introduction

This unit has so far examined some of the key objectives and operational requirements of running a multi-purpose leisure centre. It is clearly a complex process which requires a lot of planning and then for many persons and systems to come together to operate effectively to deliver the services and products. This is all done for the good of the customer and this section will focus on that aspect in terms of services, products and pricing policies. It will conclude by examining the expectations of the modern customer with sophisticated, consumer-led demands from a leisure centre.

Products provided by a leisure centre

Since the leisure 'boom' of the 1960s and 1970s, which coincided with the building of many of our leisure centres, sales of goods and products have continued to grow all the time. Sports clothing and equipment retailing are now both major industries with many people employed as producers or sales persons. Leisure centre managers are keen to operate in this market as a means of

- Generating extra income for the centre
- Offering a wider range of service to customers
- Offering a complete service within one building from equipment hire or sales to high-quality playing venues.
- Widening the customer base and market share of the facility

Goods, equipment and accessories

In view of the range of sports and activities which can be undertaken in a typical leisure centre, then the corresponding range of equipment needed by customers is also very wide. Some typical examples include

- Rackets for badminton, squash or tennis
- Shuttles and balls for these sports
- Arm bands and floats for young learner swimmers
- Swimming goggles and trunks
- Footwear for all sports and activities
- Aerobics clothing

Many of the above are available for hire in the average leisure centre, while others are suitable for use only by one person and have to be purchased. Centre management has to decide on the range of products to be carried as sale stock, and the method of sale – whether to do this as an 'in-house' operation or to offer a franchise to an outside contractor.

Activity

List the advantages and disadvantages of both 'in-house' sales of products and of offering a contracted-out franchise.

Food and drink

We have already seen in this unit that there are many legal and licensing requirements for offering food and drink sales in a leisure centre. The management has the option of having in the centre

- A bar
- A cafeteria
- A functions suite
- Vending machines
- Poolside eating or drinking facilities

The decision as to which combination, if any, to offer will ultimately be determined by the size of the facility and its potential catchment area. It will be influenced by such factors as:

- The income-generating potential of these ancillary services
- The desire to offer a complete service to customers and be a true, multi-activity 'leisure' centre
- The space available or the capital funds available for any extensions required
- The specialist staff available within the organisation
- Whether to undertake catering and bar operations as an 'in-house' or contracted-out operation

Services provided by a leisure centre

The leisure centres built in the 1960s and 1970s were established to meet the growing demands for sporting activities and the need to refurbish older, existing facilities such as swimming pools which were many decades old and in a poor state of repair. These two demands came together in the concept of the leisure centre as a focus for community sport and recreational activities. In the latter context, this quickly extended to additional events and services such as craft fairs, antique fairs, animal shows, exhibitions and conference and meeting facilities. These served a twin purpose:

- Raising additional income for the centre
- Widening the activity base of the leisure centre to make it more attractive to a wider community of customers who might return to the centre to undertake another activity at a later time

Changing trends in the sport and leisure market have led to changes in the activities offered by centres. The health and fitness boom is a phenomenon of the 1980s and has resulted in a huge public demand for aerobics classes, both in water and on dry land.

This has led to a need for

- An ever-expanding range of classes at times suitable to customers
- The need for qualified instructors in these activities
- The need to provide ancillary services such as crèche and child-care facilities

The sport and leisure market of the late 1990s is a highly sophisticated and competitive environment in which centre managers have to try to constantly keep abreast of market trends and ahead of rival facilities and services.

Pricing policies in a leisure centre

As will have been found from the study of the mandatory units on this course, price is one of the 'four Ps' of the Marketing Mix comprising

- Product
- Price
- Place
- Promotion

All are linked together as a centre's management attempts to offer the best range of facilities and services at affordable prices in a highly competitive sport and leisure market. Some of the key factors influencing a leisure centre's pricing policy will include the following:

- *Costs* – Some activities are much more costly than others to put on. A swimming pool is the best example of this with high installation costs, high maintenance costs and high energy costs.

continued on page 82

Charnwood Leisure Centre: aerobics and aqua aerobics

Figures 10.11 and 10.12 give details of aerobics and aqua aerobics available at the centre

AEROBIC PROGRAMME
(Starting Monday 11th March 1996)

Day	Time	Class	Effort
Monday	9.30 - 12.30	FIT-N-FEMALE	(ALL)
	6.00 - 6.45	AEROBIC BLITZ	(B/I)
	7.00 - 8.00	POWER STEP	(I/A)
	8.00 - 9.00	BODY WISE	(B/I)
	8.00 - 9.00	ADVANCED AQUA AEROBICS	(A)
Tuesday	10.00 - 11.00	BEGINNERS STEP	(B)
	6.00 - 7.00	FAT BURNER	(I)
	7.15 - 8.15	ENERGY MAX	(I/A)
	8.00 - 9.00	AQUAFIT	(B)
	8.30 - 9.15	STEP ON IT	(B/I)
Wednesday	9.30 - 12.30	FIT-N-FEMALE	(ALL)
	12.15 - 1.00	FAT BURNER	(B/I)
	6.15 - 7.15	ENERGY MAX	(I/A)
	7.05 - 7.50	AQUA AEROBICS	(B/I)
	7.30 - 8.30	TUMS & BUMS	(B/I)
	8.30 - 9.15	STEP ON IT	(I)
Thursday	7.30 - 8.15am	WAKE UP WORK OUT !	(ALL)
	6.15 - 7.00	AERO FIT CONDITIONING	(B/I)
	7.15 - 8.15	HIGH ENERGY AEROBICS	(I)
	8.30 - 9.15	THE TRIPLE XPERIENCE	(ALL)
	8.30 - 9.30	SUPER CIRCUITS (GYM)	(A)
Friday	12.15 - 1.15	HAPPY HOUR	(B/I)
	4.00 - 5.00	AQUA AEROBICS	(B/I)
	6.30 - 7.30	POWER HOUR	(A)
Saturday	10.30 - 12.00	EXERCISE & GO	(I)
Sunday	10.15 - 11.15	FAT BURNER	(I)
	11.30 - 12.30	ENERGISER	(I)
	7.30 - 8.30	AQUA FIT	(B)

CLASSES MUST BE PAID FOR AT TIME OF BOOKING

KEY TO EFFORT
ALL - All Levels   A - Advanced   B - Beginner   I - Intermediate

VOUCHERS AVAILABLE - ASK AT IMAGES DESK
01509
SERCO 611080 Charnwood
Borough of
Browns Lane, Loughborough, Leics. LE11 3HE

Fig. 10.11 Aerobics programme for Charnwood Leisure Centre, Loughborough

Fig. 10.12 Aqua aerobics programme for Charnwood Leisure Centre, Loughborough

continued from page 79

- *Demand* – In the 1960s and 1970s there was an immense demand for squash facilities from the public. This has now levelled out or fallen slightly with resultant pricing implications. Any sport or leisure activity can become vulnerable to such fluctuations in demand.
- *Competition* – Many organisations are now competing for a share of the customer's 'leisure pound' and this has a major effect on pricing policy.
- *Local economic environment* – Leisure spending is influenced by basic economic factors and in times of, for example, high unemployment these may lead to alterations in pricing policy. This is discussed later in this section.
- *Organisational philosophy and objectives* – It has already been seen in this unit how important these are in formulating the programme of a centre. Pricing is clearly linked to programming. A private leisure centre and a publicly run one will have differing pricing policies owing to their differing objectives and place in the leisure environment.

Pricing in practice

If a leisure centre is suitably located, offering a good range of products and services and an attractive programme, then pricing will be the last piece of the operational jigsaw. Many of the multi-activity leisure centres were originally built by local councils to mirror the Sports Council's slogan of 'Sport for All'. This meant that they offered a service to all citizens in the council's catchment area at subsidised prices. That is to say, the centre, particularly if it had a swimming pool, could never match its operating costs unless it charged prices which would have conflicted with the providing authority's social objectives. The council would, therefore, provide a subsidy to offset the centre's operating deficit and thus keep prices low for all users. Moreover, certain categories of user would receive further concessions on activity prices; these included

- School children or other young persons
- Disabled people
- Senior citizens or early retired people
- Unemployed people
- Those in receipt of certain social security benefits

Indeed, some users in these categories would, in some local authorities, be granted completely free use of leisure centres. Some local councils have introduced special pricing concessions which are often referred to under the title of 'Passport to Leisure' schemes.

Passport to Leisure schemes

Many of these schemes were set up in the early 1980s at a time when unemployment, especially among young people began to climb dramatically as traditional industries such as steel-making went into decline. The schemes offered free use to certain users and they were also often linked to particular concessions on price for registered citizens living within a centre's immediate catchment area. These schemes became very popular and many authorities adopted them in a wider policy aim than simply dealing with problems posed by mass unemployment.

Leicester City Council has operated a Leisure Pass since 1985 (see Figure 10.13).

Fig. 10.13 Leisure Pass, Leicester City Council

Sheffield City Council calls its scheme the *Sheffield Leisure Card* and it operates on the following terms:

STANDARD LEISURE CARD

- A Standard Leisure Card entitles the holder to standard discount.
- This represents excellent value for money, card holders can recover the cost of a 1 year card in:
  12 *Visits to the Leisure Pool*
  4 *Games of Golf or Badminton at off-peak times.*
- Anybody is eligible to apply for a Standard Leisure Card.
- On applying for a Standard Card you may be asked for proof of your Residency.
- Standard Leisure Cards last for either 1 year or 3 years.

GOLD LEISURE CARD

- A Gold Leisure Card entitles the holder to maximum discount
  (often half the equivalent adult price).
- You are eligible for a Gold Leisure Card if:
  You are a registered student in full-time education
  You are aged between 5 and 17 years old
  You are in receipt of Income Support or Housing Benefit AND a Sheffield Resident.
- Gold Leisure Cards last for 1 year only with the exception of children aged 5 - 14 years old inclusive, who may apply for a 3 year card.
- On applying for a Gold Card **you may be asked** for
  proof of your Sheffield Residency **AND** proof of your age.
- 'Gold' refers to the extra discounts available. Your 'Gold' Leisure Card will look the same as 'Standard' Leisure Cards.
- Students will have to apply in person bringing their current N.U.S. card.

HOW MUCH WILL MY LEISURE CARD COST?

PRICES ARE NOW THE SAME FOR SHEFFIELD RESIDENTS AND NON-SHEFFIELD RESIDENTS.
Although non-residents are NOT entitled to a Gold Card unless they are full-time students.

	1 year	3 years
STANDARD CARD	£6.00	£14.00
GOLD CARD	£6.00	£14.00 — *5 to 14 year olds only*

LEISURE DESK OPENING TIMES

Leisure Desk, Ponds Forge International Sports Centre, Sheaf Street,
Sheffield S1 2BG. Telephone: (0114) 278 9199

The Leisure Desk is open at the following times for the sale of Leisure
Cards and Tickets for events either in person or for telephone enquiries.

Enquiries can also be made at any Leisure Centre or Swimming Pool and
our other outlets listed at the beginning of this form.

Monday	9.30 am	–	4.15 pm
Tuesday	9.30 am	–	4.15 pm
Wednesday	9.30 am	–	7.30 pm
Thursday	9.30 am	–	4.15 pm
Friday	9.30 am	–	4.15 pm
Saturday	9.30 am	–	3.00 pm

CONDITIONS OF SALE

1. Cheques/Postal Orders should be crossed and made payable to "Sheffield MDC" except at student unions/SYPTE.
2. The Leisure Card may only be used by the person whose photograph appears on the card.
3. The Leisure Card only entitles the holder to the benefits of the Council's Leisure Card scheme in accordance with the current terms and conditions.
4. The Leisure Card must be returned to the Leisure Desk if there are any changes affecting the Leisure Card holders entitlement.
5. Any abuse of the concession or misuse of the facilities will result in the Leisure Card being withdrawn.
6. The Council reserves the absolute right to withdraw a Leisure Card and the benefits of its use to any person who does not comply with any of the above conditions, or who does not abide by all the arrangements related to the scheme.

Printed by Sheffield Design & Print

R3003

Different price rates

A leisure centre will charge different price rates for different activities and at different periods of the day, with off peak charges being cheaper than the peak times when a known demand gives a greater guarantee of income. How this works in practice is illustrated in this price list for a leisure centre.

	£
Swimming	
Adult	1.50
Junior	0.75
Senior Citizen	0.75
Unemployed	0.75
Spectators	0.30
Student (off peak)	0.75
Swimming tuition	
Junior (1 hour)	2.50
Junior (45 min)	2.15

	£
Junior (30 min)	1.85
Junior (20 min)	1.40
Parent and Toddler	1.45
Adult (1 hour)	2.80
Adult (45 min)	2.25
Adult (30 min)	1.65
Private lessons (per 20 min)	2.00

Sports Hall

	£
Five-a-Side football Netball } off peak Basketball	15.00
Table Tennis (peak)	2.85
Table Tennis (off peak)	1.75
Squash (peak)	3.10
Squash (off peak)	2.60
Squash: Unemployed (off peak)	1.35
Squash: Junior (off peak)	1.35
Squash: Schools (off peak)	1.35
Student (off peak)	1.35

Skating

	£
Family	4.65
Individuals	1.90

Other activities

	£
Active Lifestyle	1.55
Fit and Female	2.65
Crèche:First hour	0.80
Subsequent hour	0.50
Racket hire (adult)	0.75
Racket hire (junior)	0.35
Aqua Fit (peak)	2.45
Aqua Fit (off peak)	1.85
Football coaching	1.80

Room hire (per 30 min)

	£
Freddies Suite	6.40
Brooklands Suite	12.90
Meeting Room	5.95
Dance Studio (peak)	20.25
Dance Studio (off peak)	14.95

Compulsory Competitive Tendering

The advent of Compulsory Competitive Tendering (CCT) since the late 1980s has (as already discussed in this unit) had a profound impact on leisure centre operations. The contract for offering a centre out to commercial tender may, at the discretion of the local authority (the client), lay down tight or slack guidelines as to the future pricing constraints on the operator (the contractor). However the contract is framed, the council will retain the ultimate right of approval on any pricing changes in the centre.

Membership schemes

Private sports centres, with a limited range of facilities and services, generally operate membership schemes. This gives them

- A guaranteed income and cash-flow situation
- The opportunity to use the pricing mechanism to select their client groups and thus offer a more 'exclusive' image and service

The growth of CCT has changed the activities and facilities on offer at many previously publicly run leisure centres. For example, a lot of investment has been put into health suites and many of these will operate membership schemes as a help in the process of recouping this outlay. If a membership scheme route is chosen, then the centre management will need to attract an optimum number of members to achieve a balance of value and economy. Tables 10.1 and 10.2 give figures for this balance in both public and private leisure complexes.

Table 10.1 Public leisure complex attendances

Active attendances per week	Active attendances per year	Optimum participation membership
2,000	100,000	1,000
4,000	200,000	2,000
6,000	300,000	3,000
8,000	400,000	4,000
10,000	500,000	5,000 plus limited social membership, say 10%

(*Note:* Based on usage levels of one visit per week on average by each member)

Table 10.2 Leisure club attendances (small swimming pool, squash, tennis, small fitness studio)

Active attendances per week	Active attendances per year	Membership
500	12,500	500
750	18,750	750
1,000	25,000	1,000
1,250	31,250	1,250
1,500	37,500	1,500 plus high social membership, up to 50%

(*Note:* Based on usage levels of one visit per two weeks on average. However, in the less exclusive clubs such as squash clubs and bowls clubs, the tendancy is for average participation rates to be much higher at around two visits per week, which means that some members will attend four or five times a week)

Activity

List the benefits and the drawbacks of a membership scheme being introduced in a council-owned leisure centre.

Expectations of customers of a leisure centre

All of Unit 10 has been concerned with this topic, as no leisure centre can exist without its customers and their spending power. The needs and demands of customers are constantly changing and we have already seen how centres can respond to these by setting out their customer service principles in the form of charters. The customer expects high-quality facilities, a good range of products and services and a well-motivated staff providing standards and attention to detail. In order to attempt to improve on all these vital aspects of service delivery, many leisure centre managers are using Performance Targets to measure staff and facility performance. In a similar manner, it is now common practice to undertake surveys and questionnaires to measure how customers feel about the facilities and services they have used.

CASE STUDY

Performance standards

Performance standards can include target figures to compare against the actual achievement. However, standards can be set for operational activities. Set out below are examples of standards which could be applicable to all staff, along with a set applicable exclusively to a catering area(s). Obviously, these can be expanded or reduced to suit individual requirements.

All staff

- Dealing with customers will have priority over everything else.
- Customers will receive undivided attention.
- Customers will not be discriminated against because of their age, sex, race, culture or colour.
- Customers will be greeted with an appropriate greeting, e.g. 'Hello. Can I help you?', and a smile.
- All queries and questions will be handled to the customer's satisfaction. This may mean referring them to someone else, where appropriate.
- Any customer who is looking anxious, lost, confused etc. will be approached and asked if there is anything that can be done to help.
- Any complaint will be treated as an opportunity to understand more completely the customer's expectations and as a way of improving the customer's satisfaction. If it is not possible to do this, the complaint will be referred to a member of management.
- If a customer is seen causing damage to the facility, they will be prevented from doing this if this can be done without risk to the member of staff. If this is not possible, a member of management will be informed immediately.
- If a customer is seen behaving in an antisocial way or heard using bad language, they will be asked to stop. If they refuse to stop, a member of the management will be informed.
- Staff will always behave in a way which conforms to the current health and safety policy.
- If there is an emergency incident, all staff will conform to the guidelines on emergency procedures.
- Any member of staff who is required to assist in the cafeteria will wash their hands thoroughly before doing so and wear an apron which will be provided.
- If a member of staff sees litter on the premises, they will pick it up immediately and deposit it in a litter bin.
- Full uniform, including name badges, will be worn by all staff whenever they are on duty.
- Staff will consume food only in the cafeteria or other place designated for the consumption of food.
- There will be no smoking by staff who are wearing a uniform.

Customer satisfaction assessment

Most facilities conduct some research and assessment of customer satisfaction now and questions will be geared to seek responses most useful to the organisation. Methods of soliciting information were included in an article in *Recreation 4* in July/August 1993 which discussed complaint and suggestions schemes, internal and other surveys and forum groups, among other things. A typical set of questions and style which can be adopted are as follows: Do you enjoy visiting this leisure facility? We would like to hear your views by completing this questionnaire. Please tick where appropriate

	Very happy	Happy	Unhappy	Very unhappy	Don't know
Equipment	☐	☐	☐	☐	☐
Maintenance of buildings	☐	☐	☐	☐	☐
Internal conditions e.g. ventilation, lighting and temperature	☐	☐	☐	☐	☐
Staff	☐	☐	☐	☐	☐
Activity programme	☐	☐	☐	☐	☐
Personal safety/ security	☐	☐	☐	☐	☐
Level of prices	☐	☐	☐	☐	☐
Cleanliness and hygiene	☐	☐	☐	☐	☐
Reliable service	☐	☐	☐	☐	☐

Which three of the nine services above are most important to you?
Starting with the most important: (i)   (ii)   (iii)

Have you noticed any improvements in services at this facility in the last twelve months?
- Greatly improved   ☐
- Improved services   ☐
- Haven't noticed any change ☐
- Worse service   ☐

Are you aware of our new improvement opportunity scheme which provides you with the opportunity to make comments, complaints or suggestions using printed cards available in the reception area?

Yes   ☐   No   ☐

If yes, have you used this system?   Yes   ☐   No   ☐

Which local paper do you read?

If you could change one thing in this facility, what would it be?

This facility will be holding a user forum called *Leisure Link* to encourage customers to air their views on the service provided. If you are interested or would like to be on a mailing list for activities and courses, could you please leave your name and address and indicate the appropriate activities.

1 Children's activities	☐	6 Swimming	☐	11 Football	☐
2 Women's activities	☐	7 Weights/Hi-tech	☐	12 Water sports	☐
3 Over-50 activities	☐	8 Badminton	☐	13 Snooker	☐
4 Coaching courses (adult)	☐	9 Squash	☐	14 Leisure Link	☐
5 Coaching courses (jr)	☐	10 Athletics	☐	15 Other	☐

Name   Address

Thank you for helping with this survey. Please return this card to reception.

Conclusion

Leisure centre operations are, as in any organisation, complex and interrelated. They are designed for a sole purpose, that of providing the customer with an attractive, safe and competitively priced environment in which to pursue sporting and leisure interests. With the competition now being so fierce to attract and retain customers, no leisure centre can afford to ignore any elements of the processes which this unit has sought to examine.

Assignment 10.3

Title: Leisure centre products and services
Performance criteria satisfied: 10.3.1, 10.3.2, 10.3.3, 10.3.4
Core skills satisfied at level 3: Communication 3.1, 3.2, 3.3, 3.4
                                   Information technology 3.1, 3.2, 3.3
                                   Application of number 3.1, 3.2, 3.3

Situation

Leisure centres provide a vast range of products and services to customers. This range is influenced by many factors. You have been asked to look into this in the context of your local leisure centre.

Tasks

1 Gather information on the products and services offered by your selected leisure centre.
2 Investigate the pricing policies which go along with this range of products and services.
3 Discuss how far the demands of customers influence products, services and pricing strategies.
4 Present your findings and conclusions, with suitable examples, in report form.

Unit 11
OUTDOOR ACTIVITIES

Element 11.1   Investigate the scope and provision of outdoor activities

Element 11.2   Examine the legal and regulatory requirements for outdoor activities

Element 11.3   Plan, carry out and evaluate a group outdoor activity

Element 11.1   Investigate the scope and provision of outdoor activities

Performance criteria

1   Describe locations where outdoor activities take place.
2   Describe with examples different types of outdoor activity.
3   Describe the different providers of outdoor activities and explain their roles.
4   Describe with examples the different users of outdoor activities.
5   Explain the reasons for participation in outdoor activities.
6   Explain trends in different types of outdoor activities.

Introduction

For the purpose of this unit we have interpreted outdoor activities as those normally described as outdoor pursuits, for example rambling, climbing, canoeing and gliding. There is a wide range of activities, so we are focusing primarily on selected activities from each of the operating environments of land, water and air.

The activities which we have concentrated on are

- Land based   Rambling/orienteering
- Water based   Canoeing
- Air based   Gliding

There is growing awareness of and participation in outdoor activities, reflected in the increasing number of activity centres which are providing an ever expanding range of courses for the novice through to the experienced participant.

This unit is intended to be a general introduction to the subject of outdoor activities and should therefore not be regarded as a definitive text. Anybody wishing to participate in outdoor activities should consult appropriate, expert sources of help and information before embarking on any programme of activities.

Activity

To help with the understanding of the reasons for participation it would be advisable for the tutor to organise either a small event or a residential trip.

Local activities may take the form of the following:

* A limited orienteering type activity either within the school grounds or the local park
* Abseiling or climbing under qualified supervision at a local crag or quarry

Suitable residentials could include:

* A residential organised through a recognised centre such as PGL Activity Holidays
* An expedition organised by a suitably qualified tutor possibly involving hill walking with an overnight camp

Students who take part in such events would be better able to evaluate the potential outcomes of participation in outdoor activities.

Locations where outdoor activities take place

Traditionally outdoor activities have taken place in some of the more remote and inaccessible areas of the country. However, due to the increasing levels of participation the access and opportunities to become involved are becoming greater. The increase in popularity has also generated a growth in activities taking place in an urban environment, such as indoor climbing walls.

There are various reasons for this. The most important factor is the improved transport networks and the rise of private car ownership. Mass car ownership has led to a greater accessibility of the more remote areas of the countryside. In one respect this has benefited many individual areas in terms of an increase in the number of visits or tourists but this in itself has created new problems such as traffic congestion. Many local councils have embarked upon schemes to reduce this problem by adopting initiatives such as the building of car parks, restricting access and park and ride schemes.

The improvement in the range and variety of maps available has aided access. Also there has been a willingness by the providers of activities to site venues nearer to the centres of demand, for example, the dry ski slope at Rossendale, Lancashire.

Advances in technology have also promoted all-year-round participation in some activities, for example, sledging at the Snow Zone in Speke, Merseyside and skiing at the Snow Dome in Tamworth, Staffordshire.

Traditional rural venues

Government legislation and in particular the Access to the Countryside Act 1949 led to the creation of the National Parks in England and Wales. Many outdoor activities take place within the National Parks, which can be regarded as traditional rural venues. In Scotland areas of outstanding natural beauty are designated as National Scenic Areas.

Within the Lake District National Park, for example, the following activities take place:

Land based	*Water based*	*Air based*
Walking	Water skiing	Hang gliding
Rambling	Canoeing	Parascending
Climbing	Power boating	Microlighting
Mountain biking	Sailing	Ballooning
Orienteering	Scuba diving	Gliding
Bird watching		
Pony trekking		

From the maps shown in Figures 11.1 and 11.2 it can be seen that the geographical regions which comprise the National Parks and National Scenic Areas all have similar landscape features, that is mountains, hills, rivers and lakes which provide suitable topographical conditions for outdoor activities to take place. Some examples of topographical features in National Parks and National Scenic Areas are given on page 97.

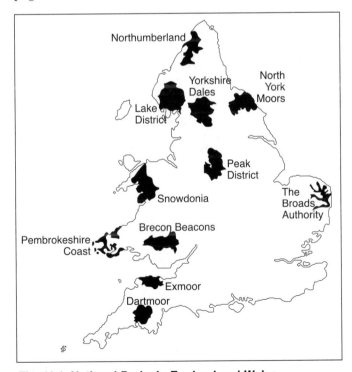

Fig. 11.1 National Parks in England and Wales

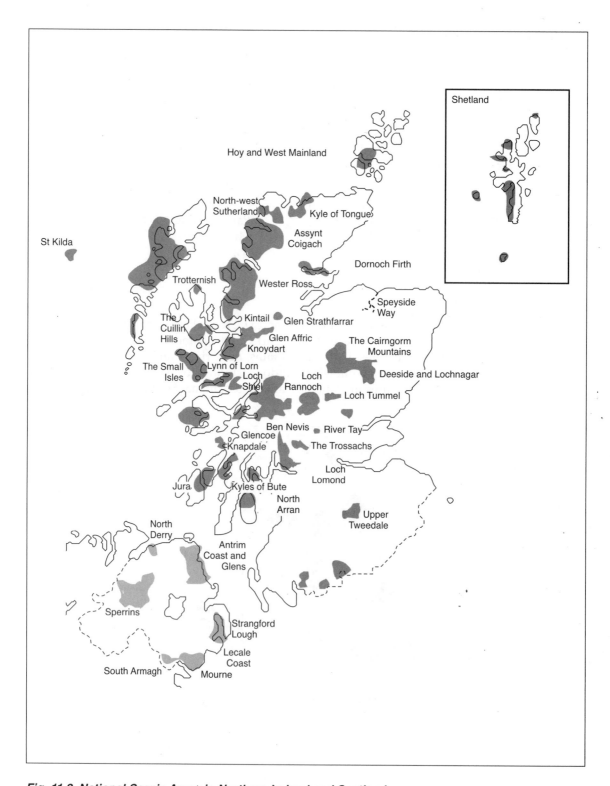

Fig. 11.2 National Scenic Areas in Northern Ireland and Scotland

Topographical feature	Region/area	Example
Mountains	Cairngorms	Cairngorm
	Lake District	Coniston Old Man
	Snowdonia	Cader Idris
Lakes/mere	Lake District	Bassenthwaite
	Snowdonia	Llyn Ogwen
	Scotland	Loch Lomond
Rivers	Norfolk Broads	River Cam
	Dartmoor	Rive Exe
	Scotland	River Dee
Caves	Peak District	Blue John Mines
	Yorkshire Dales	Gaping Ghyll
		Alun Pot
		Long Churn System
High moorland	North Yorks Moors	Fylingdale
	Northumberland	Cheviots
Gorges/ridges	Yorkshire Dales	Gordale Scar
	Lake District	Striding Edge
	Snowdonia	Crib Goch
	Isle of Skye	Cuillin Ridge

Activity

Using suitable Ordnance Survey maps showing any of the Scottish National Scenic Areas, try to identify some of the topographical features which are listed above.

Show the topographical features which you have identified on a rough sketch map of a National Scenic Area.

Urban venues

Increasingly there has been a demand to provide outdoor activities all year round. Technological advances have meant that purpose built facilities offering a range of activities normally associated with the outdoors are now feasible within the urban area, in most cases under cover.

The purists may argue that bringing such activities under cover is a contradiction in terms: by its very description an outdoor activity should take place in the open air. However, a growing interest in outdoor pursuits and the ability for participants to practise their skills in a more accessible location has led to increasing provision and participation within urban areas. Examples of outdoor activities in urban environments include climbing walls, outdoor dry ski slopes and indoor ski slopes with snow.

Climbing walls

Keswick Climbing Wall is located in a purpose built unit on a small business park close to the town centre (see Figure 11.3). The climbing wall allows climbers the opportunity to continue their activity when weather conditions may dictate that it is impossible to pursue outside. These indoor facilities also provide a more controlled environment for novices and junior participants where a number of easy graded routes can be provided in a close locality. There is also less likelihood of unforeseen events, for example rock falls or severe weather conditions. Should an accident occur then assistance will be more readily available than on a remote crag.

Fig. 11.3 Keswick Climbing Wall, Cumbria

The increased provision of climbing walls has seen the development of a number of trends within the sport of climbing, including

- The traditional outdoor climber who uses the indoor facilities for winter training
- The indoor climber who wishes to develop skills which will possibly lead to participation in indoor competition
- Novices who are introduced to the sport through climbing walls

Outdoor dry ski slopes

Rossendale ski slope is situated in the town of Rawtenstall in central Lancashire. This outdoor dry ski slope tries to recreate the facilities and atmosphere of a traditional alpine skiing resort. Included within the facilities are a main slope of 200 metres, an intermediate slope of 70 metres and a nursery slope of 35 metres. There are five ski tows to enable the skiers to reach the top of the slope. To promote evening skiing the centre is also floodlit.

The facility operates many different courses for all grades of skiers and snowboarders, for example

- Beginner lesson one   – Essential first steps
- Beginner lesson two   – Controlling your speed
- Beginner lesson three   – Beginning to turn
- Beginner lesson four   – Mastering snow plough turn

These will lead to advanced beginner courses and intermediate courses, followed by advanced courses which include slalom skiing, moguls and snowboarding. In addition, instructor courses are held. All courses are run under the supervision of qualified instructors.

Equipment for skiers can be either hired or purchased at the centre as there is a specialist ski shop. Refreshments are available in the licensed cafeteria.

The siting of these types of venues is very important as it requires a large catchment area to be profitable. This site in central Lancashire is well connected to the local motorway network providing easy access from north Manchester, Lancashire and West Yorkshire, as illustrated in Figure 11.4 on the following page.

Indoor ski slopes with snow

Technological developments and the influence of economic motives have made it possible to reproduce indoor ski slopes with artificially produced snow. A successful example of this is the Tamworth Snow Dome, Staffordshire, which opened in April 1994. Here the environment of alpine skiing is reproduced both in the sports available and the social facilities. The Snow Dome incorporates a 150 metre run which is equivalent to a graded blue run and has a consistent snow depth of 16 cm. An escalator system enables skiers to ascend the slope and once the evening's activities have finished there is a choice of a ski bar or the café bar to relax in. As with many skiing resorts there is also an equipment shop and expert advice on hand. A selection of the facilities available at the Snow Dome is shown in Figure 11.5

To enable the maximum usage of the ski slope there are various nominated sessions available, such as school classes, women's morning ski, ski fit sessions and tiny tots on skis.

HOW TO GET TO *Ski Rossendale*

BY CAR: With excellent motorway links, Ski Rossendale is only a short drive away from all over the North West, situated at the end of the M66, North Manchester.

BY BUS: Only 45 minutes from the centre of Manchester! Please ring Rossendale Transport for details on 01-706-212337 or 213677.

THE NORTH WEST PREMIER SKI CENTRE

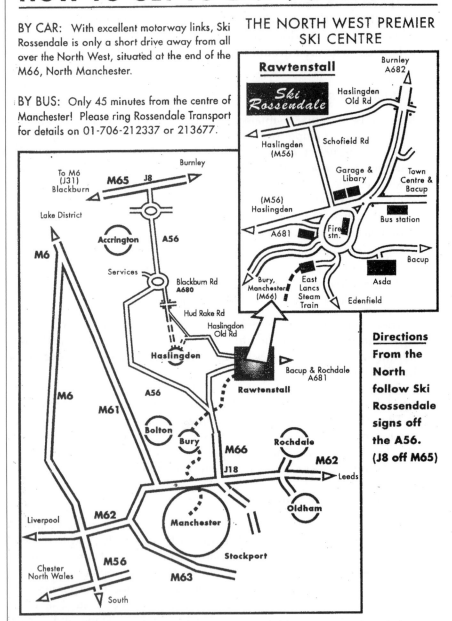

Directions From the North follow Ski Rossendale signs off the A56. (J8 off M65)

BY STEAM TRAIN: A great day out on the East Lancashire Railway through the picturesque Irwell Valley from Bury to Rawtenstall to visit Ski Rossendale. (Weekends & Bank Holidays only) Ring ELR on 0161-764-7790.

Fig. 11.4 Ski Rossendale, Lancashire

Fig. 11.5 *Snow Dome, Tamworth, Staffordshire*

Different types and providers of outdoor activities

All outdoor activities take place in one or a combination of three environments:

- On the land
- On the water
- In the air

These environments determine the nature of the activity. Here are some examples of the types of activities which take place in each of the three environments.

Land based	Water based	Air based
Rambling	Waterskiing	Hang gliding
Orienteering	Sailboarding	Microlighting
Mountain biking	Ice skating	Kite flying
Rock climbing	Scuba diving	Parachuting
Caving	Kayaking	Model aircraft
Pony trekking	Canoeing	Light aircraft
Skiing	Dingy sailing	Ballooning
Snowboarding	(inland and sea)	Parascending
Abseiling	Fly fishing	Paragliding
Bird watching	Narrow boating	
Cave diving		
Cycling		

Participation in outdoor activities can take various forms and the nature of the activity will depend upon the organising body or provider. The following five case studies illustrate a variety of types and providers of outdoor activities.

Geography field visit

An A Level geography field visit may involve studying glacial features in valleys such as Great Langdale in the Lake District. As part of the field study the pupils might view the geomorphological features from a variety of locations in order to fully appreciate the extent of the glacial impact. This may involve examining features such as corries, hanging valleys, arêtes and drumlins. In order to observe such features the pupils may need to ascend the fell side, for example at Rossett Gill towards Angle Tarn. Therefore pupils engaged in a group educational activity would in effect be taking part in the outdoor pursuits of fell walking and navigation. Other field visits could be to coastal areas, for example Robin Hood's Bay, North Yorkshire (see Figure 11.6).

*Fig. 11.6
An A-level geography field visit, Robin Hood's Bay, North Yorkshire*

Provider/organiser: School/college (public sector)
Reason/role: Educational, cultural, social
Types of activities: Hill walking, navigation

Leadership training courses

A group of individuals who are experienced hill walkers enrol upon a course to develop their walking and navigation skills. The course organisers may operate in the public, private or voluntary sector.
Typical course providers:

- Plas y Brenin (public sector – Sports Council National Centre for Mountain Activities)
- YMCA Lakeside (voluntary sector – outdoor centre)
- Paul Hughes & Associates, Howlbarrow Farm (private sector – outdoor centre)

All of these centres organise mountain leadership training courses. Although the sectors have differing commercial aims and objectives, all providers must attempt at a minimum to cover the costs of providing such courses. The costs will include overheads, such as instruction fees, accommodation, and possibly equipment costs and its maintenance.

Provider/organiser: Outdoor pursuits centre from one of the three economic
                        sectors
Reason/role: Educational, skill development, vocational, personal
                        development
Types of activities: Group leadership in an outdoor environment

Canoeing courses

A local canoe club wishes to provide canoeing courses for its novice members during the summer months, and so holds regular weekly meets on a local lake or reservoir. For example Bolton Canoe Club holds regular training evenings on Crompton Lodges. The club provides qualified instructors and in some cases the canoes. Although subscriptions are paid to the club by members, the organisation of the club and the training sessions are run on an entirely voluntary basis by the club coaches and its committee members.

Provider: Bolton Canoe Club (voluntary sector)
Reason/role: Skill development, social
Type of activity: Canoeing instruction

Glider flight tuition

North Wales Gliding Club is located near St Asaph in Clwyd (see Figure 11.7). The club is run on a voluntary basis which is supported by membership subscriptions, glider hire and the use of volunteers. In the summer the club organises training weeks whereby private individuals who are non-members may embark on a course of glider flight tuition. Any profits which are made from the training weeks are reinvested into the club and provide extra funds for new equipment and equipment maintenance. There is also much social activity which is aimed at raising funds for the club. The summer course members may find themselves a part of this social activity; indeed for many of them this is their annual holiday.

Provider: North Wales Gliding Club (voluntary sector)
Reason/role: Skill development, personal development, social and cultural
Types of activities: Gliding, navigation, ground based launch and landing, maintenance work

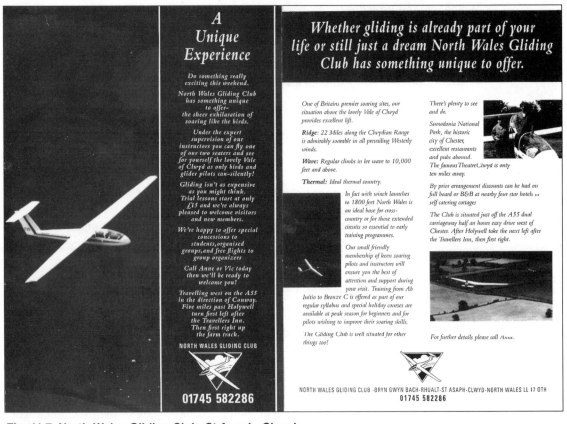

Fig. 11.7 *North Wales Gliding Club, St Asaph, Clwyd*

CASE STUDY

Outdoor pursuits centre

Longsleddale Outdoor Pursuits Centre is located in the eastern Lake District (see Figure 11.8). It is a voluntary charitable organisation that aims to encourage young people and adults to enjoy outdoor activities in safety. In order to fulfil these aims the Centre offers a wide variety of courses including:

- Fell craft
- Mountain safety

- Orienteering
- Climbing
- General outdoor activities
- Adventure weekends
- Duke of Edinburgh's Award Training and Assessment
- Field courses

Longsleddale Outdoor Pursuits Centre

The centre is based in two seventeenth-century barns by Stockdale Beck near the head of Longsleddale Valley

At the eastern edge of the Lake District National Park this is possibly one of the quietest and most unspoilt of the valleys in the Lake District

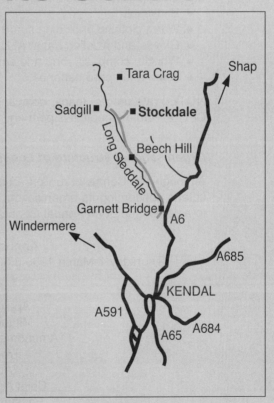

Fig. 11.8 Longsleddale Outdoor Pursuits Centre

These courses generally last for a weekend due to the voluntary nature of the Centre Staff, although longer courses can be arranged if specifically requested.

The Centre is aimed primarily at organisers of youth groups, including schools, youth clubs, scouts and guides. The idea is to give young people experience of outdoor activities at a reasonable cost. Participants are advised to bring the following personal equipment.

1 Food for the stay, including
   2 breakfasts
   2 packed lunches
   Main meal for Saturday
   Tea, coffee, milk and sugar
   Extra snacks

2 Thermos flask for a hot drink whilst out on the hills

3 Warm sleeping bag and toiletries

4 Tea towel

5 A change of clothes for use in the Centre

6 Equipment for walking
   • Boots with Vibram type soles
   • Waterproofs (cagoule and overtrousers)
   • Rucksack
   • Warm clothing, including spare jumper, socks and windproof jacket
   • Gloves and woollen hat at ALL times of the year
   • Whistle, compass, map and survival bag
   • Torch and spare batteries

NOTE Waterproofs, maps, compasses, and survival bags may be borrowed at the Centre. Radio reception is poor and radios and cassette players are not encouraged.

Organisational structure of Longsleadale Outdoor Pursuits Centre

Although the Centre is run on a voluntary basis it still has to comply with various criteria concerning its organisation. Suitably qualified club members are elected on to a committee at an Annual General Meeting (AGM). Here is a typical agenda:

Annual general meeting
Thursday 7 March 1996 8.00 p.m. The Royal Oak, Bradshaw, Bolton

Agenda
Apologies for absence
Minutes of last meeting
Amendments to the Constitution
Treasurer's Report
Auditor's Report
Chief Administrator's Report
Equipment Officer's Report
Building Committee Report
Chairman of Instructors' Report

Election of Officers

President	Membership Secretary
Vice President	Finance Chairman
Chairman of Executive	Finance Secretary
Treasurer	Chairman of Instructors
Booking Secretary	Instructors' Secretary
Chief Administrator	Building Chairman
Executive Secretary	Auditors
Training Officer	Ordinary Members
Equipment Officer	

Any other business

The committee manages all aspects of the Centre, for example, finance, purchase of equipment, election of a president, memberships and safety aspects. All meetings follow a written constitution which determines the way in which the Centre must operate and manage its affairs. An example of this from the constitution is point 7:

Membership of the centre shall be open to:
Individuals who are interested in furthering the work of the centre and who have paid the annual subscription as laid down from time to time by the committee.

At the meetings of the committee various items are discussed, for example the equipment officer's report. Here is an example of an equipment audit and report.

Equipment officer's report
AGM 1996
Equipment audit

12	Rope Trail Helmets	3	Climbing Ropes
16	Climbing Helmets	1	Abseil Rope
24	Rucksacks	4	KISUs
24	Cagoules and overtrousers	3	Safety line/Walking Ropes
8	Tops	1	Stretcher Rope
7	Waist Belts	3	Complete Tents
3	Stoppers	3	Incomplete Tents (spare parts)
2	Jumars	8	Compasses
8	Slings	9	Maps
4	Betta-brakes	50	Pairs of Boots
2	'8 Descendeurs'	6	First Aid Kits
13	Karabiners		
1	Large Sit Harness		
3	Medium Sit Harness	}	all with 1 Karabiner attached
7	Small Sit Harness		

The six tents are getting beyond repair and we need to look at re-ordering soon. The lost sleeping bag was found.

Typical activities available at the Centre include rock climbing, hiking, gorge walking, orienteering and problem solving activities. These activities are all under the supervision of both a qualified senior instructor and an instructor, who will be assisted by at least one trainee.

All of these people voluntarily donate their time and services at weekends in order for these activities to take place.

Provider: Longsleddale Outdoor Pursuit Centre (voluntary sector)
Reason/role: Skill development, personal and social development
Types of activities: Hiking, climbing, walking, orienteering

Activity

Look in the classified section of a range of outdoor activity journals (e.g. *High, Climber and Hillwalker, Compassport, Canoest, Descent, Surfer, Sport in the Sky*) for examples of providers of courses in a variety of activities. Find out which economic sector the centres operate in and list the courses provided.

Users of outdoor activities and reasons for participation

Outdoor activities are engaged in by a wide variety of participants from enthusiastic amateurs, who may be complete novices, to highly experienced professionals. One of the reasons for participating in outdoor activities is the challenge which the different types of activities present. However, not all of the challenges are equally attractive to all participants. The reasons for participation therefore may be explained by a combination of:

- *Personal factors* – individual interests, personal skills and abilities
- *Social factors* – the enjoyment of working as a team member being involved in group activities or conversely the enjoyment of solitary pursuits
- *Environmental factors* – opportunities which an individual is exposed to, for example it may be easier for a rural dweller to participate in hill walking than someone living in a town or city

When we consider the different types of users, there is no one definitive participant: active involvement in outdoor activities is open to almost everyone. Figure 11.9 shows how a participant will belong to a combination of different categories. An example might be a novice on a business trip, who may initially have been recruited as an individual but engages in team building exercises. Another example is a group of scouts or cubs who may go away on a camp for recreational purposes. All will be members of a patrol, which will most probably be composed of males between the ages of 10 and 15, and will probably be either novices or of limited experience.

When considering reasons for involvement we must take into account the anticipated or perceived outcome for the participant. Reasons could vary among individual participants and may include the development of personal skills which could be team building, for enjoyment or for professional or educational motives. The involvement could be viewed as a system which has inputs and outputs. In our example we consider various categories of participant and a variety of expected outcomes.

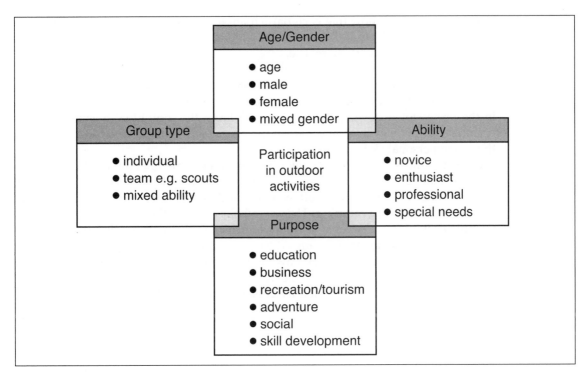

Fig. 11.9 Characteristics of user types

User type	Activity	Outcomes
Special needs: group/individual Users requiring close supervision and monitoring May have limited physical or mental ability or possibly behavioural problems	Canoeing	Widening personal experience Confidence building Possible physical/ mental development Social skills Self-discipline Self-esteem
Tourist (recreational) A group of ramblers on a walking holiday	Walking the Pennine Way	Develop physical ability Social development Environmental awareness Confidence building Team building
Individual professional	Sailing instructor	Job satisfaction Income Build communication skills Develop physical skills Help others to learn Develop leadership skills

The three examples show that each participant has a different set of outcomes. Some of these may be skills that the individual expects to develop from taking part in the activity but may not actually realise.

In the example of an outdoor activity centre which provides courses for business people, we can consider the outcomes from two perspectives. When a company sends a group of its executives to an outdoor centre it will view this as an investment in the professional development of its staff. From the individual businessperson's point of view, however, taking part in the course will enhance the development of their own personal skills.

Consider the scenario of a major motor vehicle manufacturer who sends its regional managers to an outdoor centre where they will participate in a series of events which might include hill walking and navigation, raft building, assault courses and overnight camping. The overall objective for the company is to improve the efficiency of its sales force. It hopes to achieve this by improving the skills and efficiency of its management team. At the same time each individual taking part in the activities will develop a self-awareness of their capabilities, limitation and potential. As part of the exercise the executives will be required to self-evaluate their performance and from this to identify personal growth and development points (see Figure 11.10).

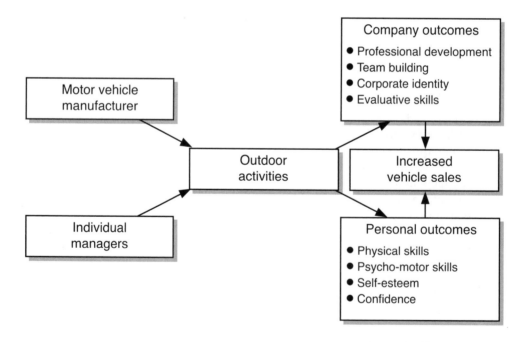

Fig. 11.10 *Company and personal outcomes of outdoor activities for business people*

For the company the overall goal is to increase its profitability by increasing the sales of its vehicles. A more highly motivated workforce which works as a team should help the company to achieve this objective. The motor vehicle manufacturer should therefore consider the course as a worthwhile financial investment.

As a contrast, let us consider a junior school party who visit an activity centre on an adventure holiday (see Figure 11.11).

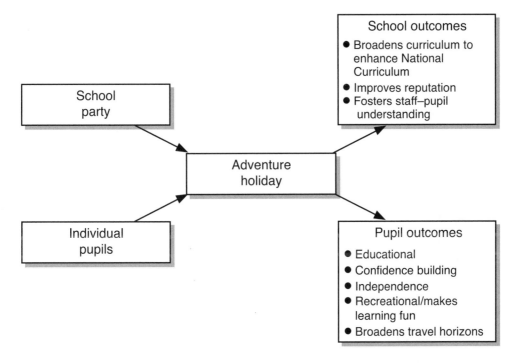

Fig. 11.11 *School and pupil outcomes of adventure holiday for school children*

Activity

Describe an outdoor activity with which you have been involved or would like to become involved. List the benefits and outcomes which might arise from participation in your chosen activity.

Trends in different types of outdoor activities

In line with the general growth of the leisure industry since the 1950s, participation in outdoor activities has increased enormously.

Factors influencing trends

Some of the factors which have influenced this trend of increased participation are as follows.

Leisure

There has been a general increase in the amount of personal leisure time and a reduction in hours of the average working week.

Income

The rise in disposable income means that the majority of the British population now has more spare money available to spend on leisure activities. For example, average weekly disposable income per household was £150 in 1970; this had risen to £215 by 1992.

Education

Education has encouraged increasing awareness by the general public of the countryside as a recreational resource.

Legislation

The National Parks and Access to the Countryside Act 1949 was the forerunner of the designation of the National Parks of England and Wales.

Health

People are more knowledgeable about the benefits of a healthy lifestyle and the importance of keeping fit.

Transport

The rise in private car ownership enables people to travel widely.

Technology

Technological advances in equipment and facility design have led to innovations such as indoor artificial ski slopes like the Snow Dome illustrated in Figure 11.5

Media

The role of the media, especially television, has been important in widening the public's horizons and helping to create role models. Programmes such as the Channel 4 series *Board Stupid* highlighting the development of snowboarding help to inform the public of new developments.

Government

An example of government involvement is the creation of the Central Council for Physical Recreation (CCPR), which helped to develop specialist centres in outdoor activities, for example Glenmore Lodge and Plas y Brenin.

Past developments

An examination of the recent history and significant events/people of some of the more popular outdoor activities, for example walking, cycling and mountaineering, helps to highlight the growth of interest in outdoor activities from the traditional outdoor types such as caving and walking through the growth boom of the 1990s of 'action sports' such as hang gliding, sailboarding and mountain biking.

Significant dates	Activity	Role models/events
1946	Various	Outward Bound Trust established
1950	Various	Establishment of Eskdale Outward Bound Mountain School
1953	Mountaineering	Sir Edmund Hilary and Sherpa Tensing made ascent of Everest
1956	Duke of Edinburgh (DOE) Award Scheme	John Hunt became director of DOE scheme
1956	Mountaineering	Sports Council set up Plas y Brenin as national centre of excellence
1959	Mountaineering	Scottish CCPR set up Glenmore Lodge in the Cairngorms
1950s and early 1960s	Fell walking	Alfred Wainwright wrote a series of guides to to the Lakeland fells
1960	Water sports	Ocean Youth Club encouraged participation in water sports
1965	Cycling	Tommy Simpson became world road race champion
1965	Climbing/ mountaineering	Televised climbs by Chris Bonnington, Joe Brown and Don Williams created general interest
1971	Sailing	Chay Blyth achieved solo passage east to west
1978	Sailing	Naomi James was first woman solo round the world
1981	Mountain biking	Introduced into UK

As can be seen from the chronology, there have been many significant sporting events and personalities associated with them which have influenced participation. This is not a definitive list: there are many interrelated factors which have contributed to the development of outdoor activities.

Numbers of participants in outdoor activities

While it is difficult to define exactly which sports are considered to be 'outdoor activities' it is equally difficult to ascertain the number of people participating in outdoor activities. For example, is an outdoor activity the same as a countryside activity? Furthermore it is difficult to distinguish between regular and one-off participants.

Statistics on participation in outdoor activities are hard to obtain as there have been very few surveys conducted on recreational participation. There have been spasmodic surveys by a variety of organisations such as the *National Countryside Recreation Survey* of 1984 which was carried out by the Countryside Commission. The *General Household Survey* contains basic data on the most popular sports but does not give specific details on outdoor activities. Some governing bodies, but not all, collect data on the number of participants in their particular sport. National Parks collect data on the activities undertaken by their visitors. Figure 11.12 shows the number of visitors to the Yorkshire Dales. Below is a breakdown of the types of activities undertaken by visitors in 1991-92. From this information it can be seen that walking is by far the most popular activity in the Yorkshire Dales.

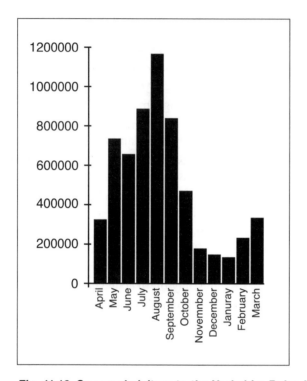

Fig. 11.12 Seasonal visitors to the Yorkshire Dales National Park

Breakdown of activities undertaken by visitors to the Yorkshire Dales

Active pursuits	%	Passive pursuits	%
Long walk (over 5 miles)	27	Sightseeing in the countryside	43
Walk (2.5 to 5 miles)	23	Picnicing	40
Cycling	2	Exploring the village	34
Climbing	1	Stroll (up to 2 miles)	28
Caving	1	Relaxing/sunbathing	22
Fishing	1	General touring	21
Canoeing	1	Visiting a tourist attraction	15
Riding	*	Bird watching/nature study	7
Hang gliding	*		

* less than 0.5%

Leisure pursuits	%
Visiting a pub	30
Visiting a restaurant/pub	26
Shopping for gifts	15
Other shopping	9
Visiting friends and relatives	4

N.B. Some visitors will participate in more than one activity.

Source: Yorkshire Dales National Park, Education Factsheet

Another factor which makes the collection of such data difficult is the fact that many of the areas where outdoor activities take place, such as the National Parks and Areas of Outstanding Natural Beauty, are also major centres of tourism: a simple census of visitor numbers will mask the true extent of people participating in outdoor activities. Although it would be possible to conduct a survey of the number of registered participants with national governing bodies, many people may not necessarily register prior to participation.

Future developments

Since the 1970s, the introduction of a number of new sports has been possible because of improved technology. Examples of these include the introduction of mountain biking from the USA in 1981, hang gliding, microlighting, parascending and jetskiing. The increased number of activities available has not been reflected in an increased number of participants in every activity.

Gliding

The example of gliding illustrates this point. In the period 1983 to 1994 the number of clubs has increased by only seven and the number of members, initially on the increase from 9,500 in 1983, reached a peak of 10,586 in 1990 but has since shown a decline to 9,522 in 1994 (see Table 11.1 on following page for full statistics).

The reason for the decline in the number of people participating in gliding could possibly be explained by the increasing popularity of other forms of air activity, such as hang gliding and microlighting.

Mountain biking

Mountain biking activities are now equal in popularity to a quarter of all walking activities and is still showing an increase in participant numbers. One reason for this is that mountain bikes are now cheaper to buy, and secondly, bikers are transporting their bikes to the countryside by car in order to explore new areas. One result of the increase in participation has been incidents of bikers riding on land without the landowner's permission. The Sports Council in conjunction with the Countryside Commission produced a Mountain Bike Code of Conduct which gave new participants guidelines on where to cycle.

Table 11.1 Participation in gliding activities

	1983	1984	1985	1986	1987	1988	1989	1990	1991	1992	1993	1994
Clubs	95	96	99	99	99	96	99	101	101	102	102	102
Flying members	9,550	9,669	9,999	9,845	10,121	9,892	10,296	10,586	10,125	9,623	9,409	9,522
Club two-seaters	239	229	264	267	274	275	278	280	280	285	281	285
Club single-seaters	205	206	223	211	249	228	242	242	256	256	247	251
Privately owned gliders	1,189	1,180	1,277	1,300	1,303	1,375	1,434	1,508	1,488	1,614	1,730	1,577
Launches (in thousands)	402	457	407	433	449	420	487	452	452	434	443	411
Hours flown (in thousands)	123	146	153	145	151	144	192	170	149	153	156	150
Gliding certificates issued	1,898	1,859	1,625	1,522	1,706	1,373	1,719	1,368	1,326	1,013	909	819
Bronze badges issued	430	446	419	384	433	423	519	471	464	479	441	414
Silver badges issued	223	296	261	240	222	204	418	282	278	225	284	318
Gold badges issued	58	76	75	54	59	53	82	116	81	80	48	73

THE MOUNTAIN BIKE CODE OF CONDUCT
for cross-country and cross-city cycling

RIGHTS OF WAY
- Bridleways – open to cyclists, but you must give way to walkers and horseriders.
- Byways – usually unsurfaced tracks open to cyclists. As well as walkers and horseriders, you may meet occasional vehicles which also have right of access.
- Public footpaths – no right to cycle exists. Look out for finger posts from the highway or waymarking arrows (blue for bridleways, red for byways, yellow for footpaths).

Please note – these rights of way do not apply in Scotland.

OTHER ACCESS
- Open land – on most upland, moorland and farmland cyclists normally have no right of access without express permission from the landowner.
- Towpaths – a British Waterways cycling permit is required for cyclists wishing to use their canal towpaths.
- Pavements – cycling is not permitted on pavements.
- Designated cycle paths - look out for designated cycle paths or bicycle routes which may be found in urban areas, on Forestry Commission land, on disused railway lines and other open spaces.

GENERAL INFORMATION
- Cyclists must adhere to the Highway Code. A detailed map is recommended for more adventurous trips.

FOLLOW THE COUNTRY CODE
- Enjoy the countryside and respect its life and work.
- Guard against all risk of fire.
- Fasten all gates
- Keep your dogs under close control.
- Keep to rights of way across farmland.
- Use gates and stiles to cross fences, hedges and walls.
- Leave livestock, crops and machinery alone.
- Take your litter home.
- Help to keep all water clean.
- Protect wildlife, plants and trees.
- Take special care on country roads.
- Make no unnecessary noise.

SAFETY
- Ensure that your bike is safe to ride and be prepared for all emergencies.
- You are required by law to display working lights after dark.
- Always carry some form of identification.
- Always tell someone where you are going.
- Learn to apply the basic principles of first aid.
- Reflective materials on your clothes or bike can save your life.
- For safety on mountains refer to the British Mountaineering Council publication "Safety on Mountains".
- Ride under control downhill since this is when serious accidents often occur.
- If you intent to ride fast off-road, it is advisable to wear a helmet.
- Particular care should be taken on unstable or wet surfaces.

COMPETITIONS
- Events are organised by a number of clubs and national bodies. They can only take place with the permission of the landowner and/or highway authorities as appropriate.

AND FINALLY
- Enjoy yourself.

The growth in the popularity of mountain biking is also reflected in the increasing number of competitive events which are available to cyclists. The newspaper report on page 118 is of a typical mountain bike event, the Bolton Mountain Bikes' downhill mania event which was held at Rivington Pike in March 1996.

Hill walking and climbing

The number of people participating in hill walking and climbing has shown a substantial increase since the mid-1980s. The British Mountaineering Council (BMC) estimated that in 1993 there were approximately 4 million hill walkers and 700,000 outdoor climbers of whom 150,000 were active. However, the fastest growing aspect of climbing is in the use of indoor climbing walls where it is estimated that during 1993-94 there were in excess of 1 million user visits. The use of indoor climbing walls is expected to increase and since 1994 many more walls have opened either as purpose built facilities or within sports centres. The overall number of clubs affiliated to the BMC has increased from 302 in 1989 to 320 in 1996 reflecting the overall increasing popularity in the sport. However, it must be remembered that many people actively participate in climbing without joining an official club.

Mountain bike mania

A Bolton club will be going rapidly downhill this weekend – and it should be a thrill a minute.

Bolton Mountain Bikes will be hosting a big Downhill Mania event at Rivington, with top stars competing for a total prize purse of £3,500.

The highlight will be on Sunday, after practice sessions on the Saturday, when about 150 of the best British riders will be taking a daredevil route 1,250 feet down a stony track from near the summit of Rivington Pike to the Pike car park in the shortest possible time.

Action

The action will take place between 10 a.m. and 4 p.m.

While Sunday is reserved for the cut throat competition, Saturday will be given over to family mountain biking with the West Pennines ranger service joining forces with local mountain bike clubs to stage a taster day.

There will be experts on hand in the area of the top barn to give free advice on maintenance, advice on the use of the West Pennine Moors' network of bridleways and tracks that cyclists are allowed to use. The rangers say the aim is to encourage proper use of the area for cycling and to avoid conflict that occurs when cycles are ridden on public footpaths.

Also there will be British downhill champion Will Longden and trade stands. The Saturday event runs from 10.30 a.m. to 5 p.m.

Throughout both days of the event Bolton Vauxhall dealers Kirkby Central will have a range of off-road vehicles for people to test drive.

(*Bolton Evening News* 14 March 1996)

Examine the legal and regulatory requirements for outdoor activities

Performance criteria

1 Explain the main legal and regulatory requirements affecting an outdoor activity.
2 Explain the potential safety hazards of different types of outdoor activity.
3 Describe the measures to be taken to overcome safety hazards for individuals and groups.
4 Explain the resources that are necessary to run a group outdoor activity safely.

Legal and regulatory requirements affecting an outdoor activity

In March 1993 there was the tragic incident where four young students died while taking part in a canoeing expedition at Lyme Bay, Dorset. Prior to this accident there was little specific legislation in place, with the exception of the Health and Safety at Work Act 1974, relating to both outdoor activities and outdoor activity centres.

The Lyme Bay tragedy was the catalyst which focused the government's attention on the necessity of legislation to protect the safety of participants. Legislation has now been introduced for both providers and participants at outdoor activity centres.

Government action

The government plan of action, introduced on 11 November 1993, refers to commercial centres which provide activities for participants under the age of 18 years.

The original four point plan comprised

- An immediate survey of outdoor activity centres followed by a programme of inspection visits by the Health and Safety Executive (HSE) over two years.
- Making publicly available factual information about the inspections and any enforcement actions arising from them.
- New comprehensive and detailed guidance by the Department for Education and Employment (DFEE) with the assistance of the HSE to provide information to schools and local authorities on the lessons which they should draw from the Lyme Bay tragedy.
- Changes in documents on coaching in schools to make explicit the legal duty of care concerning health and safety

(*Source:* Department for Education and Employment, *Safety in Outdoor Activity Centres: Guidance*, September 1994)

Code of practice

A code of practice was published in May 1994 by the ACAC (Activity Centre Advisory Committee). The ACAC is an advisory committee which was set up in 1993 by the English Tourist Board. The membership is drawn from the public and private sectors of both the leisure and educational areas. The following organisations were involved in the setting up of ACAC:

- English Tourist Board
- Health and Safety Executive (HSE)
- Sports Council
- Association of Head Teachers
- Central Council for Physical Recreation (CCPR)
- Mountain Leaders Training Board (MLTB)
- Council for Outdoor Education Training and Recreation

This code of practice covers such important areas as guidance on planning and managing visits, insurance, assurances sought from outdoor activity centres, emergency procedures and legal responsibilities.

Guidelines on planning and managing visits

Preliminary considerations

These will include

- The aim of the visit
- Skills of the provider
- Skills and competencies of the accompanying school-based staff

Curriculum

It has long been recognised that well-structured outdoor activities and residentials can greatly enhance the school curriculum. This will manifest itself in a series of activities which is based on progressive skills, learning and understanding. The activities involved must also be relevant to the work of the curriculum thus allowing opportunities to participate and opportunities for participants to record their achievements.

Reconnaissance

Wherever possible organisers should gain as much prior information concerning the management of their chosen centre. This information will relate to centre safety, centre safety standards, centre personnel and qualifications of personnel. This information can be used to assess the potential risk.

Risk assessment

There is always an element of risk involved in outdoor activities. The intention is to reduce this risk as far as is practicably possible. To achieve this organisers (teachers) and providers (centres) must carefully consider certain factors including

- Type of activity
- Location
- Competence and experience of participants
- Ratio of participants to qualified staff
- Quality and suitability of equipment
- Weather, season and timing

Selecting participants

Care must be taken when planning events and organising staff must use several criteria when considering the suitability of participants. Criteria will include

- Purpose of the visit
- Educational objectives
- Size of group to participate
- Individual needs of the participants

Staffing the visit

There are certain considerations to be borne in mind when planning an activity:

- Party leader
- Suitably qualified in the proposed activity
- At least one member of the supervising staff should hold a nationally recognised first aid certificate

Figure 11.13 is an example of a form used by organisers of educational visits and residential courses.

EV2

MID-CHESHIRE COLLEGE

APPROVAL OF EDUCATIONAL VISIT LASTING MORE THAN ONE DAY/RESIDENTIALS

1	Party Leader to complete this form and submit to Head of Faculty
2	Head of Faculty to sign and submit to Principal: - six weeks prior to departure for visits in Britain - twelve weeks prior to departure for visits overseas
3	Copies to . . .

Faculty of:

Course/Groups Involved:

Destination (If overseas name of countries to be visited):

Purpose of proposed visit and educational objectives:

Does the programme include any other "hazardous activities"?
Please include details if you are not sure - see Educational Visits: Code of Practice booklet)

Fig. 11.13 Form used by organisers of educational visits (continued on following page)

Please attach itinerary

Dates and Times:

    Depart MCC   date   time

    Return MCC   date   time

Total number of days, including departure & return date:

Name of Member of Staff in Charge of Visit (Party Leader):

Names of Accompanying Members of Staff:

Number of students on visit (Male and Female):

Full Postal Addresses and Telephone Numbers of all Accommodation to be used: (if home stay accommodation attach separate list).

Full Name, Address and Telephone Number of Package Tour Agent (if applicable):

Bonding arrangements (eg ABTA or Trust) please state:

Transport Arrangements (give details of operator if appropriate and include flight numbers etc.

Accommodation Arrangements

Form EV5 to be attached giving financial details.

I have read 'Educational Visits: Policies & Code of Practice" and confirm that the above arrangements comply with the guidance given.

I confirm that I will complete the following documentation when approval is received:

Form EV1 : Details of Staff and Students   [ ]

Form EV4 : Parental Consent/Health Declaration   [ ]

Form EV5 : Estimate of Expenditure and Income   [ ]

Form EV3 : Overseas Visit Checklist (if applicable)   [ ]

Code of Conduct Letter (if applicable)   [ ]

Party Leader: Name:

Signature: ....   Date: ....

Head of Faculty: Name:

Signature: ....   Date: ....

APPROVAL OF EDUCATIONAL VISIT

I approve the arrangements outlined in your application, subject to the above documentation being completed:

Signed: ....   Principal   Date: ....

Signed: ....   Chair of Governor Date: ....

Copies: Head of Faculty, Party Leader, Assistant Accountant

Fig. 11.13 Form used by organisers of educational visits (continued from previous page)

Staffing ratios

These will depend upon the activity, age and location, examples:

- One adult to fifteen pupils where the activity might include trips to sites of historic interest, fieldwork and local walks
- One adult to ten pupils for overseas residentials
- One adult to six pupils may be appropriate for children under the age of 8 or students with special needs. Ratios of one to one may be appropriate in certain circumstances, depending on the student's ability
- Higher ratios may be appropriate for higher risk activities

Parental consent

These forms must be completed in advance for every pupil taking part in the visit. The form must state any special requirements which the pupil may have, including

- Details of any medication which the child requires, plus dosage
- Telephone number in case of emergency
- Swimming ability if appropriate
- Special dietary requirements

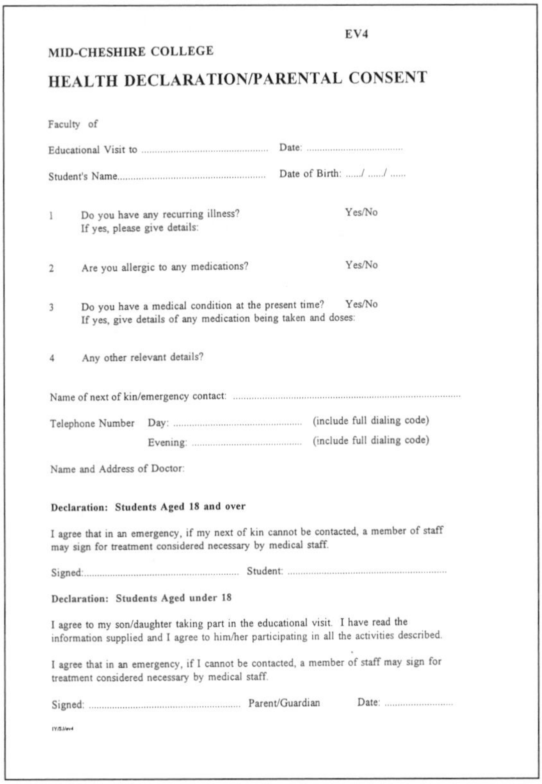

Fig. 11.14 Example of parental consent form

Activity Centres (Young Persons' Safety) Act 1995

The guidelines listed above formed the basis of the Activity Centres (Young Persons' Safety) Act 1995. Further details of the Act are given in the briefing document issued by the National Youth Agency:

Early in 1995 a Private Member's Bill - The Activity Centres (Young Persons' Safety) Bill was introduced by David Jamieson, Labour MP for Plymouth, Devonport, following the Lyme Bay canoeing tragedy in which four young people from his constituency died. The Bill received Royal Assent on 28 June 1995.

The main provisions of the Act are

- to set up a system of compulsory registration
- to set up an independent inspectorate to carry out initial safety checks at all centres, carry out random spot checks and follow up complaints
- inspection teams, subject to consultation, would be employed by a central licensing body operating in similar ways to OFSTED inspectors by having a code or framework of good practice to guide their investigations
- inspectors will be able to serve a notice of improvement or remove a company's accreditation and shut it down if safety measures are not up to standard

- prison sentences of up to two years would apply if operators continued to provide activities without a licence
- the system will be self-financing with the centres themselves paying for the inspection teams and for compiling the register.

Guidance and implementation – consultation

The Health and Safety Commission has been charged with drawing up proposals for regulations and guidance to implement the safety provisions of the Act. A consultative document has been issued which sets out its proposals for a statutory scheme for the licensing of adventure activities for young people under 18.

The document explains its approach to licensing and why its proposals should be focused on the activities presenting the highest risk to groups and why it should be restricted to activities provided commercially. Its key features and the Commission's role are also covered.

Alongside this statutory licensing scheme it suggests that a parallel voluntary approval scheme run by the same body and open to providers of activities not in the scope of the statutory scheme should be set up. The document sets out how a wider voluntary approval system might be run, the differences between the schemes and the relationship between them.

Statutory licensing – the criteria

There is widespread recognition that some degree of risk is unavoidable if adventure activities are to accomplish their essential purpose allowing young people to develop by meeting challenges they do not necessarily face every day and to experience a sense of achievement in overcoming them. But not all activities are equally hazardous, and the nature of the hazards varies - some put only individuals at risk, others have the potential to cause harm to numbers of young people.

In the light of the above, the Commission considers that the following criteria should provide the basis for deciding which adventure activities should be subject to statutory licensing:

- there is a significant risk of death
- the competence of the instructors/leaders is crucial
- the activity is vulnerable to changes in weather or the natural environment
- there is a significant risk to the safety of the group, if things go wrong.

Regulation of voluntary organisations

The Commission does not wish to cut across the freedom of voluntary and national youth organisations to offer the opportunity to members to participate in adventure activities, on a non-commercial basis. It therefore proposed that voluntary associations should not be subject to statutory licensing except when they choose to act in a commercial manner.

Key features

The Commission proposes statutory licensing of the following activities: caving, climbing, mountain walking, paddlesports, sailing and skiing.

The Act requires persons to be licensed, not places. The 'person' granted a licence could be an individual or it could be a body running an activity centre. It could also be a non-profit-making club or a voluntary youth organisation but only if it chooses to behave in a commercial manner. Education authorities, school governors, proprietors and teachers already have legal obligations of care.

Providers seeking a licence to offer adventure activities within the scope of the scheme will have to satisfy the licensing authority that a suitable and sufficient risk assessment has been done and suitable safety arrangements have been developed and implemented. Providers will also need to give documentary evidence to the licensing authority that they have proper systems for the management of the safety risks of the activities in place.

A licence will not be given until there has been an inspection by licensed authority inspectors. For a large centre offering a range of activities, an inspection could involve a team of inspectors and take two or more days.

At the other end of the scale, inspection of a highly trained and competent individual, seeking a licence to offer instruction and leadership in a single activity, should just involve: confirmation of qualifications, that safety issues are understood and a check of the necessary equipment. The timetable for future inspections varies but licence-holders will be subject to spot check inspections or investigations of complaints at any time.

Comments are also sought on the fees and appointment of the licensing authority amongst others.

The voluntary scheme

It is clear that there is a demand from schools and from parents for some assurance that all providers are managing safety effectively. Many commercial providers of activities which do not meet the Commission's criteria for inclusion in the statutory scheme wish to participate in a scheme which would confer a level of approval on the safety of their business.

Voluntary associations also want to be able to demonstrate that they are applying the same standards in respect of the safety of their members as would be required for activities offered on a commercial basis. The Commission recommends that the industry (providers, consumers and experts) should develop a parallel voluntary approval scheme and that the licensing authority should run it. If this approach finds favour, the Commission proposes to nominate as licensing authority, a body capable of setting up and running a voluntary scheme based on safety criteria consistent with the statutory scheme.

Unlike the statutory licensing scheme, a voluntary scheme would not be subject to regulatory restrictions. The framework could therefore be developed in ways that better fit the diversity of its scope. For example, the licensing authority could give approval to the codes of National Governing Bodies which approve providers. It could also approve the codes of trade or voluntary associations which vet their own member providers. The licensing authority itself could also approve providers directly. These would result in the award of a 'kite-mark', not a licence, but in these ways the licensing authority would be able to offer approval to any provider who met the standards it set.

To assure public confidence, certain key elements would need to be common to the statutory and voluntary schemes. In particular the licensing authority would need to publish guidance to providers on the conditions and standards they would have to meet to gain its approval. Like the regulations and guidance for the statutory licensing scheme, this would need to cover:

- risk assessment

- information to instructors and participants on safety measures and arrangements

- the competence of instructors in the activities which they supervise

- appropriate equipment properly maintained

- emergency and first aid arrangements.

The licensing authority would need to develop and publish the competence standards expected for other activities, as the Commission is doing for those in the statutory scheme. The Commission would expect the licensing authority to work constructively with the national governing bodies and HSE in the development of appropriate standards.

Regular inspection would be a vital element in the public assurance offered by an approval scheme. The licensing authority will need to develop appropriate arrangements for inspecting providers who seek approvals under the voluntary scheme. In line with the statutory licensing scheme, inspection should focus on safety management systems. In planning inspections, the licensing authority would have to take account of the ad hoc nature of adventure activity provision in the non-commercial sector.

The Commission recognises that there will be scope for confusion between the statutory and voluntary schemes. The licensing authority should distinguish between the statutory and voluntary schemes in its publications and its approval markings. However, if both schemes are run by the same body to equivalent safety standards, a seamless service should be available to both providers and consumers. The resulting single point of enquiry for schools and parents will result in a powerful commercial pressure for providers to opt into the voluntary scheme where there is no statutory obligation on them to hold a licence.

Voluntary codes of practice

We have looked specifically at legislation concerning outdoor activity centres and courses which have been organised through educational establishments such as schools and colleges and voluntary establishments such as youth groups.

In order to ascertain safety requirements specific to individual activities, it is necessary to research the codes of practice established by the national governing bodies (NGBs), for example, the British Canoe Union (BCU). Governing bodies produce voluntary codes of practice for instructors and participants which will suggest how the activities might be carried out in a safe and proper manner.

Guidelines for voluntary participation in outdoor activities

The voluntary codes of practice form the guidelines of national governing bodies' programmes of qualifications. Individuals wishing to become qualified within outdoor activities must achieve their award through the relevant governing body. They must also be extremely competent and possess a thorough understanding of their specific sport.

Although it is not a statutory requirement that anyone instructing in outdoor activities holds the relevant NGB qualifications, it is a preferred practice by the Health and Safety Commission that all instructors are suitably qualified to the criteria laid down in the national governing body voluntary codes of practice.

For example, in the sport of climbing, all novices under qualified instruction will be made familiar with safety procedures. These may not necessarily be adequately explained and taught by an experienced yet unqualified climber. An example of a safety procedure is the attachment of an individual to a rope in a safe and proper manner which will require the tying of knots. All qualified instructors will have had to demonstrate their competence in such techniques during an assessment.

Potential safety hazards of different types of outdoor activities

There is a wide diversity of potential hazards associated with the range of outdoor activities available; we shall focus on three pursuits:

- Land based   Orienteering

- Water based   Canoeing

- Air based   Gliding

Each activity will be covered as a separate case study and will include a description of suggested measures and precautions which can be taken to minimise safety hazards. The case studies will also include details of the resources necessary to provide outdoor activities in a safe environment.

It must be remembered that with any outdoor activity, which by its nature is challenging, there is always the chance of unforeseen circumstances. However well equipped the participants might be or despite the experience of the instructors, groups or individuals will always be exposed to conditions which are hazardous to their safety.

Orienteering (land based)

Governing body

British Orienteering Federation (BOF)
Riversdale, Dale Road North, Darley Dale, Matlock, Derbys DE4 2HX

Venues

Typical venues include forests, moorland, heathland and mountainous regions.

Equipment and facilities

- Compass (e.g. Silva)
- Ordnance Survey or specialist orienteering map in 1:10,000 or 1:15,000 scale or 1:40,000 Harvey map
- Polythene map bag
- Sturdy shoes/trainers
- Full body clothing (e.g. Helly Hansen T-shirts, tracksters or overpants)
- Whistle
- Control flags
- Control card descriptions
- Control punches

If the participant is a club member then special club colours may be worn.

Factors to consider when organising an event include the following:

- *Organisers' considerations* – first aid kit, first aider, provision of shelter (e.g. tent), list of competitors (including abilities), refreshments
- *Weather conditions* – these must be assessed in order to decide whether or not to alter courses and to advise participants as to what to take.
- *Venue* – type of terrain will determine the distance and speed of competitors over the course e.g. forest trails are quicker than rocky, mountainous areas
- *Type of participant* – novice, special needs, experienced, representative standard, or children
- *Participants' skills* – courses must be designed to suit all abilities, taking into account length, time allowed, siting of control, map reading skills
- *Event standards* – colour coded, badge event, world championships, string course

Hazards

As orienteering is primarily an individual sport in wild, unfamiliar country, any injuries or problems are accentuated for the following reasons:

- Lack of knowledge of precise location of casualty who may have stumbled or fallen – difficulty in finding casualty
- Time delay between accident and treatment – casualty's condition may deteriorate
- Competitors are subject to adverse weather conditions and, even with full water and windproof body cover, may still be at risk of hypothermia if competing over long periods of time in severe weather

- For novice competitors attempting more challenging courses, there is the risk of over-extending their competition time while carrying inappropriate equipment

Ideally novices and juniors when first introduced to the sport should practise on permanent orienteering courses.

As with many outdoor activities the safety of the event is governed by the organisation, knowledge and experience of the organisers and by the understanding which the participants have of the event.

Other factors to consider may include the group or party size, the expectations of the party, the ratio of instructors to party members and the experience of organisers and party members.

It always has to be borne in mind, however, that with any challenging outdoor activity, there is always the chance of unforeseen circumstances.

Environmental and physical conditions

As the largest number of participants in outdoor activities take part in land-based activities, certain additional features which are not discussed in the case studies on water-based and air-based activities need to be considered here.

Anybody who participates in outdoor activities needs to have a basic understanding of the relationship between weather systems and physical landscape features. One of the fundamental principles of safety at altitude is an understanding of the progressive lowering of air temperature in relation to height climbed.

The rate at which air cools as it rises is approximately 1 degree centigrade for every 100 metres climbed. Figure 11.15 shows how the temperature may vary between sea level and the summit of 700 metres, which is a common height found in the UK. Climbers must therefore be prepared for a substantial fall in temperature as they ascend.

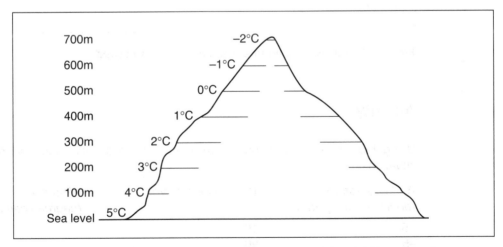

Fig. 11.15 How temperatures may vary between sea level and 700 metres above

The actual temperature felt by climbers is accentuated by the wind chill factor. This is of particular concern as land surfaces become more exposed with increasing height and receive varying amounts of sunlight. For example, a north-easterly facing slope is likely to be considerably colder than a south-westerly facing slope at the same altitude.

Figure 11.16 shows how air temperatures are affected by wind speed. For example, where the air temperature is 0 degrees centigrade in a wind of 20km per hour, this would equate to a wind chill effect of minus 10 degrees centigrade.

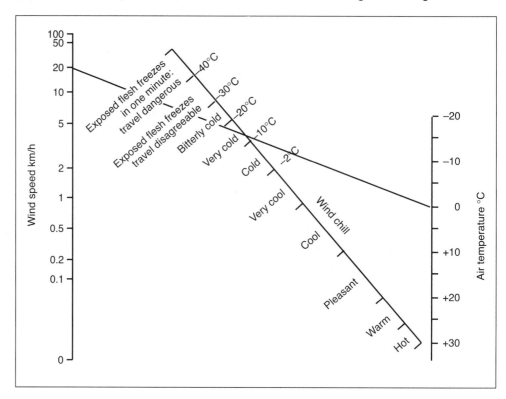

Fig. 11.16 How air temperature is affected by wind speed

Activity

Using Figure 11.16 as a guide, calculate the wind chill effect for the following situations:

Air temperature (degrees centigrade)	Wind speed (km/h)	Wind chill (degrees centigrade)
+5	10	
−5	20	
0	50	

The reverse situation may occur on the hills during the summer months: although the temperature will still decline at the same rate there is the possibility of over-exposure to the sun and its heat. In these circumstances the effect of a breeze may deceive the climbers as to the actual exposure to ultra-violet radiation and heat. This may therefore result in sun burn or sun stroke.

In both circumstances the answer would be the use of adequate and suitable clothing. In cold temperatures waterproof and windproof clothing is essential. If possible several layers should be worn with an outer waterproof and windproof garment. This type of clothing can be purchased in many specialist outdoor shops where an inner fleece jacket can be purchased with an outer shell jacket. Examples of well-known makes include Berghaus and Karrimor.

In warm weather, loose-fitting natural fibres are preferred with a hat to provide cover for the head.

Human resources

The coaching structure of the BOF is as follows:

- Level 1   Instructor's award
- Level 2   Club coach
- Level 3   Regional coach
- Level 4   Senior coach

Further details of the training required to achieve each level are listed in the BOF guidelines, available from the above address.

Canoeing (water based)

In this case study we concentrate on kayaking. A kayak is a craft for one or two people who sit facing forwards; movement is by the use of a double-bladed paddle. (In a Canadian canoe the participator kneels down and uses a single-bladed paddle.)

There are many types and shapes of kayaks, representing their different uses; however, all should have a cockpit area with a seat in the deck, foot rests, buoyancy aids and end grabs.

Governing bodies

British Canoe Union (BCU)
Mapperley Hall, Lucklow Avenue, Nottingham NG3 5FA

Scottish Canoe Association
SCA Office, Caledonia House, South Gyle, Edinburgh EH12 9DQ

Venues

The BCU categories for inland venues are as follows:

- Grade I   Flat water, lakes
- Grade II   Moving water, no obstacles
- Grade III   Obstacles, fast flowing water
- Grade IV   Obstacles, boulders
- Grade V   Turbulent
- Grade VI   Turbulent

For categories III, IV and V it is essential to be trained in white water skills. Grade V water is generally accepted to be international competition standard, conditions depending upon the event, for example slalom or white water racing.

Equipment and facilities

Before purchasing canoe equipment a novice should contact a specialist dealer for advice. Inappropriate equipment in the hands of a novice is a hazard in itself.

The choice of canoe will depend upon the individual's ability and requirements, for example whether the canoe is for use in slalom competition white water or general purpose touring.

Certain equipment is a prerequisite for safety:

- *Paddles* – these must be of the correct length for the user
- *Helmets* – any helmets used in canoeing must cover the temples and the forehead so as to avoid serious head or facial injuries in the event of capsizing
- *Buoyancy aids* – the wearing of a buoyancy aid which conforms to BS4983 is compulsory. Buoyancy aids include not only life jackets but also the buoyancy aid fitted inside the canoe
- *Clothing* – although it is not essential to wear specialist clothing it is advisable if participants are likely to spend a long time on the water and most certainly get wet. Specialist clothing can include wet or dry suits, thermal vests, gloves and canoe boots.
- *Spray deck* – this is generally made of neoprene or nylon and is used to form a watertight seal between the canoeist and the canoe cockpit. Until a certain degree of competency has been achieved the use of a spray deck is not recommended.

Due to the high risk of potential accidents it is advisable for individuals who wish to participate in canoeing to join a recognised club where they can learn all of the relevant skills, such as capsize routines under controlled conditions. Details of affiliated clubs can be obtained from the BCU at the address shown above.

The benefit to the individual of belonging to a club which is affiliated to the BCU is that the club can offer guidance on insurance matters and access agreements to stretches of water.

Hazards

The potential hazards were demonstrated when a novice canoeist capsized while on the River Tryweryn in North Wales. As a member of a recognised club she was attending an open day and failed to read the river conditions accurately. This resulted in her passing her exit point and entering a more turbulent part of the river. Her canoe capsized and became wedged against a metal grid designed to stop debris, such as trees, floating downstream. She was eventually freed from this dangerous situation by other members of the canoeing club.

Human resources

The structure for qualifications is split into various awards:

- BCU one star   Encouragement award for novices
- BCU two star   Evidence of competence at basic skill level and orally

- BCU three star   Competence on rivers
                              Ability to right craft
- BCU four star   Training instructor
- BCU five star   White water skills
- TI   Training instructor (minimum age 16 years)
- I   Instructor (minimum age 18 years)
- SI   Senior instructor
- E1 and E2   Advanced stages of the SI qualification which indicate that the post holder is competent to assess the preceding qualifications

Gliding (air based)

Governing body

British Gliding Association (BGA)
Kimberley House, Vaughan Way, Leicester LE1 4SE

The BGA produces many factsheets on gliding. Here is an extract from one of them.

If you haven't tried it before, here is

SOMETHING ABOUT GLIDING

to give you an idea of what it is about

You will soon be up in the air, but first of all you should know how to handle a glider on the ground, and how its controls work. In the air the instructor will demonstrate how the glider is manoeuvred; it has dual controls so you will be able to handle it and feel what it is like to fly yourself. If you have some aptitude or have done a little previous flying, the instructor may let you have a shot at doing the landing after only a few flights.

Gliding is a strange sport. It is exciting and beautiful, frustrating and cold, challenging and unexpected, and heavy on time unless you come to love it very much. When you try it you can decide for yourself, and if you study these notes in advance, you will have more time to look around and enjoy your flying.

First flights

The two seater in which you will fly will have a wing span of 50/60ft; it may have side-by-side or tandem seating, and it may have an open cockpit or perspex canopy. You will be launched into the air by a winch or a tow car, or towed up by a light aeroplane. The winch or car will give you about 1,000ft of height and a flight of 4/5 minutes, and the aeroplane will take you to, usually, 2,000ft and give you a flight of 15/20 minutes.

On a winch or car launch the instructor has to climb the glider steeply to gain height, so do not be surprised at the angle at which you go up. After the instructor has released the cable, he will fly the glider at its normal speed – some 40/45 knots, and you will be able to feel the controls for yourself. You will quickly find that no strength is needed to control the glider; it is quite stable in flight, and you only need a light and gentle touch to guide it. You will be delighted at the wonderful view, and the quietness. A glider is not, of course, silent, but the airflow sound is much more pleasant than the monotonous drone of an engine.

After a while you will find that it is not that difficult to fly more or less at the right speed, and to make gentle turns. Do not worry if it all seems a bit strange; the instructor can correct with his dual controls any mistakes you may make.

If upcurrents can be found the instructor may do a few circles in them to show you how a glider soars. On days of wind or strong thermals the air may be rough. If the instructor thinks that it will be too turbulent for you to enjoy flying, he will not take you up.

If you think you like gliding, do not hesitate to ask the instructor all the questions about learning to fly that you can think of. Most clubs have booklets or leaflets that you can take away to read at your leisure.

How a glider flies

A glider flies, just as does an aeroplane or a bird, when the speed of the air flow over the wings is enough to cause lift. In an aeroplane this speed is provided by the engine pulling through the air. The glider obtains its speed by gliding downhill, using gravity as motive power. Unless the pilot can find upcurrents of air, he can only glide steadily downwards until the ground is reached and he has to land.

If, however, he can fly in an upcurrent which is going up faster than he is gliding down, the glider will gain height, and the flight will be prolonged. This is soaring.

Whether the pilot is gliding down or soaring, he must always fly the glider at a speed which will enable the wings to provide enough lift to support it. If the glider is flown, at any time, slower than the minimum speed necessary it will stall. The stalling speed of most gliders is around 35/40 knots.

A pilot soars across country by circling round and gaining heat in warm air currents, called thermals. Having used a thermal in this way, he then flies straight, and often quite fast, in the direction he wants to go. During this straight flight he will be gliding downwards, losing height, and looking for another thermal to take him up again.

Gliders are designed to have flat gliding angles, that is, they will travel a long way for little loss of height. Training gliders have a gliding angle of about 1:25, and competition gliders about 1:40. This means that theoretically such a glider will travel 40 miles from 1 mile, or, 5,280ft high. In real life the actual distance varies because the pilot uses up some height when selecting his landing field. The distance flown is also affected by whether the pilot is helped along by a following wind, and covering the ground fast, or whether he is struggling against a head wind, and only making slow progress over the ground while gliding down.

When the air is moist, the rising thermal upcurrent will produce a cumulus cloud at its top. The pilot uses these cumulus cloud markers dotted about the sky on a fine summer day to show him where the thermals are. If the air is very dry, cumulus clouds will not develop at the top of the thermals, and they are said to be "blue". Thermals rise generally to about 3,000ft to 5,000ft in the summer in Britain. In winter any thermals that develop are usually so weak that only birds can use them.

Gliders can also soar in the upcurrents over the hill produced by the wind being forced up over the rising ground. These upcurrents are known as slope or hill lift. In the lee of mountainous regions atmospheric wave systems sometimes develop.

These are like gigantic versions of waves or ripples in water. Gliders can be soared in the upgoing part of waves which may sometimes go very high indeed - even 10 miles, or roughly 50,000ft high.

Most cross-country flights in gliders are intended to end on airfields, or at other gliding clubs - the pilot having declared his goal before take off. If, however, the thermals die away, or the pilot fails to find them, he will have to land in a field. Having selected a suitable field, of grass or stubble, from the air, the pilot will use his airbrakes, which steepen the glide path, to land in it accurately.

The glider will be retrieved by the pilot's partner or friends, who will bring the trailer to collect it.

(*Source*: British Gliding Association)

Gliding started to become popular in the UK during the late 1920s with some of the earliest clubs being located at Dunstable and the Midland Gliding Club at Long Mynd in Shropshire. Some of the pioneers of the sport include Derek Piggott and Fred Slingsby, with more recent notable pilots including the naturalist Sir Peter Scott and the actor David Jason.

Gliding was included in the 1936 Olympics in Berlin. However, since the Second World War it has not appeared but there is a move towards its reintroduction.

Venues

Gliding clubs are usually located in rural or semi-rural locations where there is sufficient flat land for the runway. Careful consideration must be given when siting an airfield. Two main factors to be considered are access and topography.

Access from the national road network is important as gliders sometimes need to be towed on trailers for competition purposes; also gliders which have landed off site need to be returned by road. The North Wales Gliding Club near St. Asaph is situated on farmland adjacent to the A55 dual carriageway which is the main route from the north-west of England to North Wales (see Figure 11.7).

Topography will depend upon the method of launch of the gliders. In the case of an aero tow launch a reasonably flat site/runway of approximately 600 metres is required. In the case of a winch launch approximately 1,000 metres is required. The topography will also determine the gliding lift-off conditions, for example a combination of wind direction in relation to the location of the hills can produce hill lift and thermals. The North Wales Gliding Club operates on winch launch using hill lift.

A full list of affiliated clubs is available from the British Gliding Association.

Equipment and facilities

As with any outdoor activity specialist advice should be sought before becoming involved. Specialist knowledge will be available at any of the member clubs recognised by the BGA. Because of the high capital cost of purchasing a glider an individual novice will be relying upon the craft provided by the club. For example, at the North Wales Gliding Club there is a variety of gliders to cover the range of individual skill levels from twin-seated aircraft for the novice under instruction to single-seated craft for the experienced pilot.

The range of gliders available at the North Wales Gliding Club includes

2 K8 single seaters
1 single seater Sky Lark
1 Bergfalk 4
1 Super Blanik

There is also a selection of privately owned gliders which are stored at the airfield by their owners.

The club-owned gliders are housed in a hangar. The club also owns three winches and four tractors to help with movements on the ground and with the launching of craft.

Ground hazards

Gliding involves a small degree of risk, which can be minimised by the use of correct and appropriate training procedures which are organised by the Chief Flying Instructor (CFI) and the Club Safety Officer. For example, the towing cable on a winch launch system presents a hazard. People must walk behind the glider on take off and not across it. There is also the risk of cable/rope breaks. Therefore all personnel on the ground must be aware of safe walking areas.

Air hazards

The North Wales Gliding Club operates a very comprehensive training programme for prospective pilots. This extends from the complete novice (ab initio) having a trial lesson to an easy solo flight to Bronze C standard with cross-country endorsements.

The individual's training is rigorously monitored by the club's instructors, who can assess a pilot's capability by referring to the training sheet, which lists a series of manoeuvres and courses of action in which the trainee must show competence. The training sheet is kept by the pilot in a personal log book. The instructor fills in the sheet, marking D for demonstrated, A for attempted, I for improving or S for satisfactory.

- Ground handling
- Cockpit checks
- Control effects
- Straight flight
- Use of trimmer
- Gentle turns
- Further control effects
- Medium turns
- Continuous turns
- Turn reversals and speed control
- Speed control
- Winch launch
- Cross-wind take off
- Cross-wind landing
- Round out and landing
- Airbrakes and aiming point

- Circuit planning
- Slow flying
- Stall and recovery
- Neg - G - demo
- Stall reinforcements
- Cable break: high
- Cable break: medium
- Cable break: low
- Wing drop and recovery
- Steep turns
- Full spin and recovery
- Solo Super Blanik
- Solo K8

The trainee must also keep a record of launches, both assisted and solo, and the amount of time spent in the air.

It is essential that all gliders carry a certificate of air worthiness which will be granted by the BGA registered inspector.

All participants should be able to navigate using air maps. They must also be aware of the prevailing weather conditions as the use of air currents, wave clouds and thermals is fundamental to the sport.

Human resources

As with all outdoor activities the qualification structure is based on an individual's ability, experience and skill level. Within gliding the qualifications range from novice, bronze/silver/gold award through to instructor. The content of these awards is based on

- Number of launches and landings undertaken
- Ability to carry out safety checks within the aircraft
- Ability to carry out general aircraft inspections
- Number of flying hours accumulated
- Learning of new flying skills

Plan, carry out and evaluate a group outdoor activity

Performance criteria

1 Identify objectives for a group outdoor activity.
2 Produce a plan for a group outdoor activity incorporating essential factors.
3 Carry out a planned group outdoor activity.
4 Describe the evaluation criteria for a group outdoor activity.
5 Collect evaluation feedback from relevant sources.
6 Evaluate the success of the outdoor activity for the group.

We shall treat this element as one practical task which demonstrates the procedure for setting up an outdoor activity. The task will include the setting of objectives, planning, implementation and the discussion of criteria which can be used to evaluate such an activity. We shall use the example of a group of four 16-year-olds who are to undertake a practical expedition, such as for a Duke of Edinburgh's Award. The exercise will consist of planning a two-day back-packing expedition with one night under canvas. The group will need to set themselves objectives and to ensure that these objectives are as far as possible achieved.

The four young people will work together as a team. They will, however, have an adult supervisor in attendance whose role will be to observe and evaluate the performance of both the group and the individuals and to ensure their safety.

Outdoor activity

Duke of Edinburgh Award: practice hike in Lake District, undertaken in summer by four young people, 16 years of age, who are all of good health and experienced back-packers.
Map title: Ordnance Survey Outdoor Leisure Series No. 4 English Lakes North Western Area and No. 6 South Western Area.

Objectives

To successfully navigate between Seathwaite car park and Coniston Information Centre using the following grid references and allowing for an overnight camp.

Day 1

Seathwaite Car Park 235123 to
Coniston Village Information Centre 302977 by way of
Styhead 220095

Esk Hause 233081
Overnight camp north side Throstle How crag 228047

Day 2

Cockley Beck 247017
Great Carrs 271009
Eastern end of Levers Hause 271995
Levers Water Weir 282993
Coniston Information Centre

Team building

In order to successfully complete this hike the group will need to develop team-building skills such as communication, responsibility, decision-making, empathy, group organisation and patience.

These skills could be demonstrated through the following decision-making processes:

- What equipment should be taken?
- Who will carry the equipment?
- Who will cook?
- Who will be responsible for navigating?

It is important that all the members are actively involved in any decisions made and that they are supportive of individual and group decisions.

Skills acquisition

Each member will independently navigate sections on both day 1 and day 2 thus providing evidence of their ability to competently use a map and compass and to be able to make decisions as situations occur on the ground. In the event of a navigational error it is essential that the individual is able to recognise the fact that an error has been made at an early stage. All members must be able to relocate both themselves and the group.

Health and safety

It is essential that the group is aware of the importance of health and safety in such an activity. This can be ensured by choosing a safe and easily definable route avoiding any potentially dangerous areas. The young people must also be aware of their own ability and also the ability of the group. If any group member should show signs of discomfort, corrective action must be taken immediately. In the event of an accident the group must be able to assess the situation and provide treatment as appropriate.

The group must also keep health and safety in mind when planning their equipment. A first aid kit, survival blanket or, better still, a large polythene bag which an individual could crawl inside for warmth is essential.

Customer satisfaction

Not only is the hike a test of skill and endurance but also all involved must derive personal satisfaction in the achievement of their objectives. There must also be an element of group satisfaction in the successful completion of the exercise and for the individual in having played an important role in the group's achievement.

Preparation

To help plan the activity and to ensure that all the essential factors have been covered, the group will need to prepare detailed route cards and comprehensive equipment lists.

Route cards

Detailed route cards are illustrated in Figure 11.17.

Suggested clothing to be worn on expedition

Suitable footware (not smooth soled) and woollen socks
Thermal layer for next to skin
Shirt
Jacket – fleece, pile or woollen pullover
Windproof trousers/tracksters (not denim jeans)
A complete change of clothes should be taken.

Equipment list

Large comfortable rucksack containing

- Sleeping bag
- Spare clothes and socks
- Stove and fuel*
- Water container*
- Torch, spare batteries and bulb
- Tent, poles and pegs*
- Sleeping mat
- First aid kit*
- Food*
- Spare matches
- Waterproof outer garments with leggings
- Hat and gloves
- Kisu – large group survival tent

(*group items)

GROUP DETAILS: S. PEARSON, 2 ASSISTANTS, 12 x 14-14 OLD PUPILS

PLACE	GR	HGT (m)	GRID BRG	DIST (km)	CLIMB (m)	TIME (min)	TIME (time) hr min	NOTES
LOCATION: CONISTON OLD MAN							**MAP:** O.L. S.W.	
DATE: 24 OCT '95			**START TIME:** 9.45				**FINISH TIME:**	
1 WALNA SCAR	289970	225	335	1·2	85	25	25	
2 CROWBERRY HAWS	284981	310	272	1·0	160	30	55	
3 LOW WATER	276982	550	118	0·9	250	40	1·35	Attempted by site decision
4 OLD MAN	272978	880	016	0·9	–	20	1·55	Retreat by same path
5 LOW WATER	276982	580	100 / 008	0·4 / 1·0	– / –	25	2·20	Through boulder valley
6 LEVERS WATER	280990	480	140 / 53	0·4 / 0·3	– / –	12	2·32	
7 RUW	286991	330	132	1·2	–	18	2·50	Follow path rising/descending
8 PATH BEND	293984	210	018	1·6	200	40	3·30	
9 PATH BEND N.W.	289999	330	000	1·5	–	20	3·50	
10 CAR PARK (T.I.B.)	306009	140	**TOTAL** 10·4				3·50	# 56 DOUBLE PACES PER 100M # # 4 KMS/HR PLUS 1 MIN PER 10M ASCENT #

GRID TO MAG ADD #   # MAG TO GRID GET RID

EMERGENCY ROUTES – DESCEND TO CONISTON VIA APPROPRIATE PATH
EMERGENCY PHONE NO.

GROUP DETAILS:

PLACE	GR	HGT (m)	GRID BRG	DIST (km)	CLIMB (m)	TIME (min)	TIME (time) hr min	NOTES
LOCATION:							**MAP:**	
DATE:			**START TIME:**				**FINISH TIME:**	
1								
2								
3								
4								
5								
6								
7								
8								
9								
10			**TOTAL**					# 56 DOUBLE PACES PER 100M # # 4 KMS/HR PLUS 1 MIN PER 10M ASCENT #

GRID TO MAG ADD #   # MAG TO GRID GET RID

Fig. 11.17 Detailed route cards

Venue

A suitable weekend should be identified. A venue will be chosen in consultation with the tutor, who will ensure that it provides sufficient scope for the event and that the planned activity is realistic. The leader should take into account the time of year and consideration should also be given to route planning in case of extreme bad weather. A range of safety routes must therefore be considered.

Fig. 11.18 Students involved in outdoor activities in the Lake District

Evaluation criteria

The evaluation will be in two parts, first via the accompanying supervisor who will gather information through observation of the group's abilities and record them onto a matrix (see Figure 11.19). The matrix has two components

- The individual's performance
- The group's performance

The second part will be gathered after the event through the members writing an evaluation of the activity and a verbal discussion both with the individual and the group (see Figure 11.20 on page 144).

Feedback

Feedback will take place during the individual evaluation discussion using the forms shown in Figures 11.19 and 11.20 as the basis for any opinions. Group feedback will be given by the supervisor following the group evaluation session on the same basis.

ASSESSOR'S EVALUATION									DATE	
	CONTRIBUTION TO TEAM	SELF MOTIVATION	ENVIRONMENTAL AWARENESS	NAVIGATION SKILLS	PHYSICAL ABILITY	EQUIPMENT RESPONSIBILITY	PERSONAL EQUIPMENT	HEALTH/ SAFETY	AWARENESS OF OBJECTIVES	
NAME										
NAME										
NAME										
NAME										
Group	ROLES & RESPONSIBILITY	GROUP INTERACTION	SAFETY	PLAN FOLLOWED	EMERGENCY RESPONSE	GROUP SUPPORT	OVERNIGHT CAMP	SUCCESS OF OBJECTIVES		
PLAN										

ASSESSOR'S COMMENTS

Fig. 11.19 Assessor's evaluation matrix

NAME Adam Dandy	DATE 25.4.96
TASK to complete Planned walk	LOCATION Blencathra.

What did I set out to achieve? to meet time and destination Plans.

I had to Climb up a ridge on the way to **Blencathra** to the top back down and on to Keswick

Did I meet these objectives?   Yes ✓   No

What did I find difficult? Climbing up the ridge against the force of the wind

How satisfied am I with my performance?   Very pleased   ✓Pleased   Not so pleased

What criteria have I used to measure my success? Time, condition.

What could I have done to improve my performance? taken a hat and gloves.

How well did I operate as a team member?

Quite well, I think, I waited for anybody lagging behind and had a go at map reading

What new skills have I learned?

To take compass bearings from maps.

What were the advantages and disadvantages of our plan?

We had a hard climb to begin with which got the hardest part out of the way

What improvements would I make to the plan with the benefit of hindsight?

Taken allbody waterProofs.

Assessor Comment a) You have evaluated both team + personal considerations

b) There is no comment on team decision to alter the proposed route, because of the weather conditions

Fig. 11.20 Student's self-evaluation form

Unit 12
HEALTH RELATED FITNESS

Element 12.1 Investigate the effects of exercise on the human body

Element 12.2 Develop a fitness programme

Element 12.3 Examine injury prevention and recovery procedures

Element 12.1   Investigate the effects of exercise on the human body

Performance criteria

1   Describe different body types.
2   Describe main types of exercise for fitness training.
3   Explain the effects of exercise on the human body of different age groups.
4   Explain how eating and drinking affects the ability to exercise.

Introduction

This unit is related to several others covered in GNVQ Leisure and Tourism; there are aspects which are covered in Unit 13 Planning for Sports Coaching and Unit 15 Human Physiology. This unit enables you to apply some of the background information gathered from Units 13 and 15 and allows you to enjoy getting involved in the practical aspects of fitness.

Health is a general term relating to the overall well-being of the individual; this includes physical, mental and social well-being. Fitness relates specifically to the physical condition of the individual.

Some people are naturally more able than others at sport; this is all connected to their physical and psychological make-up. What makes a winner and how do you ensure you maximise each individual's potential?

In order to devise a suitable fitness programme the coach must understand the requirements of each individual and must understand the effects of exercise on the human body. The coach must then be able to relate these characteristics to the individual sport or activity. Health related fitness is a specific business; one programme does not suit all.

Different body types

Endomorph, mesomorph and ectomorph

The most common method of categorising body types was introduced by an American researcher called Sheldon. He described three extreme body types, although most of us possess a combination of the characteristics of all three (see Figure 12.1). They are

- *Endomorph* – oval shaped body with the majority of body fat centred around the hip, waist, thighs and bottom. The shoulders and wrists are much thinner and the body is widest from front to back as opposed to side to side. Muscles tend to be poorly toned and limbs are flabby.
- *Mesomorph* – a heavily muscled stocky body where weight is concentrated in the upper body; the bones are large and heavy. Mesomorphs who are inactive in later life will tend to accumulate unwanted fat.
- *Ectomorph* – an extremely thin individual with sharp features. The skeletal system appears fragile and the neck protrudes, forehead is high, the arms and legs spindly. The muscle formation is minimal as is the amount of body fat.

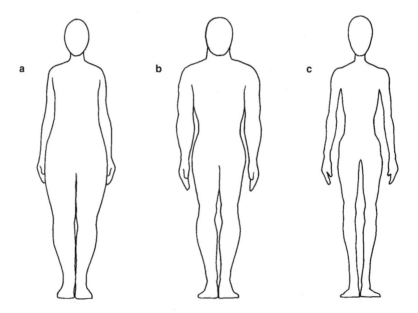

Fig. 12.1 Body types: endomorph, mesomorph and ectomorph

As most of us are part endomorphs, mesomorphs and ectomorphs there is a scoring system to categorise our body type in prominence. A scale of 1 to 7 is used; the higher the rating the more dominant the body type. For instance a scoring of 2, 6, 2 refers to an individual who has a low endomorph score, a high mesomorph score and a low ectomorph score.

When related to athletes, Tanner in the 1960 Olympics found the competitors were predominantly mesomorphs and ectomorphs with none scoring above 4 for endomorphs. This is to be expected as athletes tend to carry less than average body fat. Some sports demand certain body types. A gymnast would tend to be low endomorph as would a high jumper; a high jumper would be high ectomorph; a rugby player who demands great muscle power would tend to be high mesomorph and a swimmer or rower would tend to lean in this direction too. If you were to study a group of successful athletes in a similar sport you could almost feel you were looking at one 'species' of human being.

Body typing

Body typing (or somatotyping) has been used to select potential champions at particular sports; it has been widely reported that the Eastern bloc countries used this sort of method at an early age so as to train and produce sporting world beaters. However, it is not foolproof: there are always exceptions to the general rules. Also a 'winner' is not made out of pure physiology; aspects such as tactics, skill and mental preparation are significant too.

 Activity

In small groups discuss what you think your body type is and which sport you are most suited to. Complete this on your own and about both yourself and your friends and then compare your responses.

Main types of exercise for fitness training

The demands of a sport will be reflected in the fitness programme; some sports rely heavily on aerobic efficiency such as marathon running, swimming, cycling and triathlons, whereas others are purely anaerobic, such as 100 metre sprint and javelin throwing.

We need to produce energy in order to produce muscular contraction; this is illustrated in Figure 12.2 on the following page.

Anaerobic exercise

If adenosine triphospate (ATP) is produced without sufficient oxygen, the body is said to be obtaining energy and so muscular contraction anaerobically. There are two anaerobic energy systems, the creatine phosphate system and the lactic acid system.

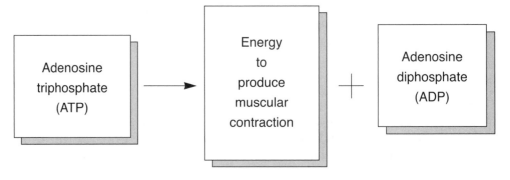

Fig. 12.2 Energy production

Creatine phosphate system

ADP + CP → ATP + creatine

Creatine phosphate (CP) is a substance stored in the muscles to produce energy; muscular contractions can take place without the presence of oxygen for a limited time. Stores of CP are used up within 30–60 seconds, so if exercise is to be maintained another source of energy must be found. Activities that may use this energy system are sprinting and throwing events.

Lactic acid system

ADP + glycogen → ATP + pyruvic acid*

*Lactic acid is produced when there is insufficient oxygen

This energy system also produces ATP without oxygen, but this time ATP is formed by the breakdown of glucose. Glucose is stored as glycogen in the muscles and liver. The glucose and then glycogen is obtained from the diet through the consumption of carbohydrate. When ATP is produced, a substance called pyruvic acid is also produced; if there is insufficient oxygen then the pyruvic acid is further converted into a substance called lactic acid. Lactic acid can be debilitating in the extreme, causing muscles to completely seize up. More often there is a burning sensation and a heavy feeling in the muscle. Exercise cannot be sustained without oxygen and eventually lactic acid will be converted back into pyruvic acid which will be converted into ATP, with bi-products of carbon dioxide and water.

The oxygen debt

When you exercise anaerobically you are breathless; you are in need of oxygen; this deficiency is known as the oxygen debt and this debt must be repaid as soon as possible. The heart rate and respiratory rate remain elevated for some time after exercise has finished in order to repay this debt. The oxygen debt can be said to be the extra oxygen required if the task were to be completed anaerobically.

Fitness levels will effect the body's ability to exercise anaerobically and the speed at which lactic acid is produced or CP stores are diminished.

Aerobic exercise

ADP + glycogen → ATP + pyruvic acid*

*With oxygen produces carbon dioxide and water

During aerobic exercise, sufficient oxygen is available for the production of ATP and so exercise can be maintained indefinitely. This type of exercise is the least intense and there is no oxygen debt to be repaid. The body maintains a steady state. During the oxidation process that produces ATP, pyruvic acid is produced; this is converted to carbon dioxide and water and is removed through the lungs.

What is fitness?

Both the aerobic and anaerobic energy systems need to be tested in a fitness programme in order to produce the best performance possible.

Fitness is an individual concept; it has a different meaning to each individual. The natural follow on question to 'Are you fit?' is 'Am I fit for what?'. The physical demands placed on the body differ depending on the activity; you may be fit enough to run for the bus but not to run a marathon, or you may be fit enough to sustain an active lifestyle without extreme tiredness but not be able to play a game of football for 90 minutes.

There are four components of physical fitness:

- Endurance
- Strength
- Flexibility
- Speed

Endurance

Endurance is the efficiency of the cardiovascular system, that is how effective are our heart and lungs in using the oxygen we breathe in and producing energy for muscular contraction. In order to improve endurance, the training programme will concentrate on aerobic exercise; the body will be developed to maintain aerobic exercise longer.

There are six main benefits of endurance training:

- There will be an increased ability to breathe in and out; a trained athlete can breathe in and out over 200 litres a minute for 20 minutes; an untrained person will operate at between 60 and 80 per cent of this capacity and only for a very short period
- Trained athletes are able to operate closer to their maximum, known as VO2max
- A trained athlete consumes more fat and less carbohydrate during energy production and therefore has reduced body fat and so is leaner, increasing the power ratio of the body
- A trained athlete can cope with hard work effectively and can recover more quickly; the resting pulse rate is lower; stroke volume can be double that of an untrained person; the heart is larger with stronger muscles and thicker walls; blood pressure is reduced; there are lower levels of fat in the blood and there is a

higher level of haemoglobin in the blood therefore the blood of a trained athlete carries more oxygen compared to an untrained person

- Muscles that are trained use fat as opposed to glycogen as a fuel and so less lactic acid is produced
- The muscles hold greater amounts of oxygen and so exercise can be maintained for longer periods of time

Strength

Strength can be defined as the ability of the muscle to apply force measured by the maximal singular contraction. There are three types of strength: static, explosive and dynamic strength.

- *Static strength* – the limbs remain constant as does the muscle length; the force is applied against an immovable objective, for example a rugby scrum or wrestling
- *Explosive strength* – the maximal force is applied in one explosive act such as a shot putt, javelin throwing and high jump
- *Dynamic strength* – the muscles here contract to support the body over a period of time and this is connected directly to the endurance training of the athlete; the muscles can contract maximally only for a short period of time up to approximately 3 minutes as they then start to produce lactic acid and will eventually give way; an example of dynamic strength is rowing

The benefit of developing the strength of the athlete is clear; the trained athlete will be able to apply a greater force for longer and this can be the difference between winning and losing.

Flexibility

Flexibility is the range of movement around a joint or series of joints; this is often an aspect of fitness that is forgotten; most sports do involve an element of flexibility even if it is just the ability to reach further for the ball in a game of tennis. The benefits are more obvious in some sports where reaching and stretching are integral parts of the activities, gymnastics and dance for example. Flexibility should be part of every training programme for the following reasons:

- Flexibility exercises should form part of a warm up and ease down programme; flexibility gradually extends the muscles and so helps minimise the risk of muscle strain.
- The more flexible the body, the less likely the chance of overstretching injuries.
- Flexible athletes have a greater range of movement and so can perfect their technique accordingly; for instance a swimmer will be able to reach further and so increase stroke length, while for an athlete, a longer stride can be significant in a hurdles event.
- One muscle pulling against another in pairs gives controlled movement (slow moves, steady moves, holding position).
- Regular and well-chosen exercises encourage the connective tissue of the joints to remain supple. Connective tissue hardens with age (from the mid-20s) and so

athletes become less flexible and the brittle tissue is more likely to be torn (as in cartilage injuries).

Flexibility can be categorised in the following way:

- Static stretching – the limb is extended beyond its normal range normally for a period of 10 seconds.
- Ballistic stretching – the limb is extended beyond its normal range repeatedly for a period of up to 30 seconds; although this type of flexibility exercise increases the range of movement there is an element of risk by the 'bouncing' action as the muscle is not able to repeatedly extend and contract without a chance of strain. Ballistic stretching has been used by untrained aerobics instructors which is dangerous as the participants at aerobics session are often the more 'sedentary' exercisers.
- *Passive stretching* – the limb is extended beyond its normal range by a second party, which can be a partner or an object. The stretch is held for up to 10 seconds. The stretching must be gradual and if working in partnership each person must know when the maximum stretch has been reached.

Speed

Muscles are made up of fast twitch and slow twitch fibres; if individuals possess more fast twitch fibres they are at a physiological advantage; speed training is connected to reaction times; external factors such as illness, fatigue and drugs can affect speed. Speed training relies on practice of rapid movements.

Benefits of exercise

The benefits of exercise have been physiologically described but there are other benefits such as a general sense of well-being, increased awareness and a reduction in stress levels.

A fit person often has a healthy glow; the toned physique is often supplemented by clear skin and an adventurous nature! A fit person has an awareness of his or her body and its limitations and so is often more confident and has a powerful sense of self-esteem. The ability to exercise also helps relax the individual and the frequent exerciser benefits from the release of endorphins, a hormone which creates a 'high'. There is also the social benefit of fitness programmes; the competition can be fun and many lifelong friends are made through this activity. Stress levels can be reduced in frequent exercisers as they learn to control the levels they apply to themselves.

Activity

Are you involved in training programmes? Which aspect of fitness do you concentrate on most? Which do you neglect? What training methods does your programme consist of? Is it suitable?

The effects of exercise on the human body of different age groups

(This topic is further discussed in Element 13.3: Determine the additional requirements for coaching children.)

The effects of exercise apply to all age groups but certain groups do have particular considerations. While the body is developing, excessive strength training can hinder the normal physiological development of the body (puberty); weight training programmes should be developed to improve endurance, not muscle bulk.

Once the body starts to physically slow down, exercise should be appropriate for the limitations of the individual; so for example a marathon runner may want to reduce mileage.

Disabled athletes can usually participate in any sport: improvisations are widely accepted and disabled competitions are integrated with able-bodied events such as the Commonwealth Games in Victoria 1994.

Training programmes are individual and this principle is particularly important where age is concerned.

How eating and drinking affects the ability to exercise

The ability to exercise successfully necessitates a holistic approach to a fitness programme; it is of little value devising a specific plan for an event including a taper, aerobic endurance and suitable body type for example and then the night before the event eating a 'stodgy' meal and consuming too many pints of beer! Performance will be negatively affected. A balanced diet aids recovery. The value of the training programme is lost if an unsuitable diet is followed.

Unit 15 on Human Physiology includes a discussion of nutritional requirements. When explaining how eating and drinking affects the ability to exercise, we need to consider

- Type of food
- Calorie intake
- Timing of eating
- Alcohol intake
- Water intake

Type of food

An athlete needs a balanced diet that consists of sufficient quantities of the main food groups, concentrating particularly on complex carbohydrates (60 per cent of the total intake) for effective energy release. We all need the vital nutrients; we all need to monitor our fat intake as too much fat is linked to heart disease; we all need to monitor our sugar intake because excess carbohydrate is stored as fat; we all need to reduce our sodium intake as this is linked to heart disease through hypertension. Athletes are no different; however, an athlete expects the body to perform maximally and without this balance the body simply will not do this. For example, a car will drive best on the specific petrol suited to that car; it will drive on other types of petrol but not with the same performance. Athletes should study their diet closely, analysing consumption of the food groups; this is an integral part of a training programme.

Calorie intake

We all need to consider our calorie intake if we are to remain at the correct body mass; quite simply the energy equation states that if we consume too many calories for our lifestyle we will store these extra calories as fat; if we do not consume sufficient calories we will have inadequate fat stores around the body to the point of energy being produced through muscle tissue wastage (atrophy).

Timing of eating

We should not consume a large meal directly before a training session because all our energy will be concentrated on the digestive process and not on our ability to perform. Muscle glycogen supplies are replenished most effectively if carbohydrates are consumed in the first hour after training; exercise is an appetite depressant and so this is sometimes difficult; however, it is advantageous to eat in this first hour.

Endurance athletes sometimes carbohydrate load immediately prior to a competition; in the week before the competition the level of carbohydrate in the diet is altered. A low carbohydrate intake is maintained for two or three days followed by a diet that is very high in carbohydrate. The diet is based on the principle that the initial lack of glycogen available to the body is overcompensated by producing far greater quantities during the period of high carbohydrate intake. This enables the athlete to use glycogen as an energy source for longer. This principle is contested and some coaches feel that as long as intense training schedules are reduced prior to competition to allow the muscle glycogen levels to recover to their maximum levels, there is no need to alter the diet.

Alcohol intake

Alcohol is a social drug and has been consumed for pleasure for centuries. It has a strong affect on the mind and body, particularly when consumed in large quantities. Many athletes consume alcohol; in fact part of the sporting celebrations will involve a traditional toast and a few pints of beer; this is after the event and as long as the alcohol is not consumed in excess has little effect on performance. However, regular heavy drinking and success in sport are not associated. Alcohol causes the following side-effects:

- An inability to concentrate
- Reduced reaction time
- Increased recovery time
- Reduction in the ability to maintain an aerobic level of exercise
- Dehydration
- Reduction in body temperature

All of these effects are significant to maximal performance but have different degrees of significance for each sport; for example the ability to concentrate is likely to have a huge effect on precision sports such as archery or snooker; marathon runners will be greatly affected by a reduction in their aerobic endurance; skiers are likely to be affected by a reduction in body temperature.

Excess alcohol consumption should be avoided.

Water intake

As adults our bodies are composed of 65 per cent water; dehydration can seriously affect performance even if the loss of fluid amounts to only 2–3 per cent. An athlete training intensively needs up to 20 pints of fluid a day; if this is not consumed, the role that water plays in the body is hindered. Water is the major constituent of body tissues; it aids the digestion and absorption processes and aids temperature regulation through sweating. The more active a sport, the more we tend to sweat and therefore more fluid needs to be consumed to keep the body in a balanced state; during a marathon there are feeding stations every 3 miles for this purpose.

We tend to drink when we are thirsty. Thirst is actually a defence mechanism of the body to remind us to drink; performance is likely to be hindered if we allow the body to get to this state so a better idea is to constantly top up the fluid intake by regular drinks.

Activity

In small groups discuss the following questions. Have you ever tried to compete after drinking alcohol? How did you feel? Were you successful?
The effects of dehydration are far reaching. Have you ever ran or jogged for more than 15 minutes without drinking? Find someone who has and ask them the effects.

In conclusion, the human body is a finely tuned mechanism which will produce sustained, skilful and rapid movement. The ability to perform will depend on how we train our bodies. A fitness programme involves the various aspects of fitness, diet and relating these to the specific demands of the sport.

Assignment 12.1

You are a highly trained coach. You are appointed by the governing body of your chosen sport to select and develop a squad of potential world beaters. In the form of a presentation illustrate what would make a 'winner'.
Include

- The importance of body typing
- The types of exercise
- The concept of 'fitness'
- The effects of exercise on the body
- The role of diet in the training programme

Develop a fitness programme

We have discussed the fundamentals of exercise related to the human body, types of exercise and other effects on the body. Now we concentrate on the practical aspects such as the activities to use, safety considerations and developing a specific plan for an individual.

Fitness programmes

Type of exercise

Every sport has different characteristics; participants will need to concentrate on the different types of exercise in varying degrees; the specific programme must reflect those needs. For example, a 100 metre sprinter will follow a different programme from a marathon runner, although they are both runners. Sprinters need to develop their anaerobic capacity particularly as their muscle contractions are fuelled by the creatine phosphate energy system. Due to the nature of the anaerobic systems, training methods cannot just work these as they can be developed only over very short periods. As a consequence aerobic exercise is an integral feature, along with technical development of the sprinter's programme. Marathon runners use aerobic energy systems throughout their event; training will include long and time-consuming sessions to develop aerobic capacity and the anaerobic threshold. The marathon runner may need to call on the anaerobic energy system during a sprint for the line or a sudden change in pace, so this should also be trained, but not to the same degree.

The person interested in keeping fit and maintaining a suitable body weight should concentrate on the fat burning aerobic system. The ability to sprint is not often required in everyday life but having superior levels of stamina helps to create a general well-being.

Frequency of exercise

The sprinter is concentrating on shorter bursts of maximal work and so must allow adequate recovery time for the muscles to eradicate any lactic acid; this can be achieved through active rest, that is through aerobic sets and also through a rest day in the training programme. The marathon runner also needs rest days to allow the muscle glycogen levels to reach their maximum; this can take up to a week for an athlete covering frequent large distances. This recovery period needs close consideration prior to competition. Many athletes feel they need to train every day and train hard every day and a great many suffer injuries and illness through over training; there is a fine line between optimal and over training and this is why a coach who is both experienced and qualified must develop a fitness programme. The everyday exerciser will naturally allow rest days, generally exercising three or four times per week. Recovery time is an essential part of the programme, not only physiologically but also to maintain motivation and interest; any fitness programme should have at least one rest day per week.

Intensity of exercise

'Variety is the spice of life': the same principle applies to the frequency of exercise. The types of exercise need prioritising and need to be trained in different ways, to ensure that training remains enjoyable. Physiologically the energy systems need to recover and so you cannot constantly train hard all the time.

Duration of exercise

A marathon runner is likely to train for 20–30 hours per week in sessions of up to 3 hours; the sprinter does not need this amount of time and would probably train for about 20 hours per week with sessions of up to 2 hours in duration. The everyday exerciser need devote only 3–4 hours per week in periods of up to 1 hour to maintain a well-toned and trained body.

Individual demands

It is essential that the fitness programme is related to individual demands: one programme does not suit all.

The main types of equipment used in a fitness programme

Specific fitness programmes for a particular sport obviously require the equipment related to that sport; a swimming programme will require a swimming pool, costume, goggles, kick board and so on. However, a general fitness programme tends to centre around more traditional fitness sessions and there are three main types of equipment.

Free weights

Free weights are weights of varying sizes that are fixed to bars and used to increase local muscular endurance, strength and muscle bulk; they can be used to train the majority of body parts and are available through many public and private leisure centres.

Multi-gym

This type of equipment is similar to free weights but the weights are fixed, generally to a series of stations in a fitness room. The stations include leg press, pectoral press and biceps curl. These are readily available in public and private leisure centres and small multi-gyms are suitable for the home.

Circuit equipment

Equipment used for circuit training is usually multi-purpose, for example a skipping rope, a bench or a mat. The facility providing this service requires considerable resources to purchase this equipment in large numbers and for safe storage. Circuit training is usually performed to music and concentrates on general stamina and local muscular endurance. There are many types of circuits that can be regularly changed to add progression and maintain interest. A general session may need twelve mats, six benches, two skipping ropes and two cones; a circuit session designed for 'aerobics' enthusiasts may include a mat, a slide, a step, a pole and a set of hand weights for each participant.

Other items needed for a fitness session may include a stopwatch or pace clock and a whistle. All fitness sessions require one common piece of equipment that is often forgotten – the availability of water to replace lost fluids.

Fitness testing procedures

When we start compiling a fitness programme we need to identify the starting point for the individual; we do this generally by some simple tests; they range from simple tests performed through exercise to physiological tests that a doctor or nurse may perform. Table 12.1 on the following page simplifies these tests.

Suitable activities for a fitness programme

Training programmes are based on the principles of overload and progression. It is important to assess the individual with certain practical measures such as those just discussed, to ensure that the programmes are based on these principles and are not just guesswork!

Principle of overload

In order to train our body effectively we have to work it harder than we normally would. We can do this in three ways:

- Increase the intensity of exercise
- Increase the frequency of exercise
- Increase the duration of exercise

By achieving this our bodies will be able to respond to stress more effectively and so when we place an extra demand in the latter part of a race our bodies will respond.

Table 12.1 Tests to be performed before a fitness programme is compiled

Aspects to be tested	Name of test	Characteristics of test	Comments to be noted
Cardiovascular efficiency	Eurofit Endurance test	Shuttle runs: subject runs at a predetermined pace between two objects spaced 20 metres apart. The pace becomes progressively faster and the point at which the subject drops out is the indicator of cardiovascular endurance	- Equipment and space needed can be limiting - Can be used as a competition therefore popular with young atheletes - Difficult for untrained person
	Step test	- Resting pulse rate is measured prior to test - Subject steps up on to a bench or step for 3 minutes while the pulse rate is measured - Recovery rate is then measured and timed to establish cardivascular efficiency	- Can be easily performed in limited space - Can be used with the highly trained athlete and untrained person alike
Blood pressure		Pressure is calculated by by measuring the pressure needed to stop the flow of blood through the artery. Two readings are taken: - Systolic – maximum reading as the heart contracts - Diastolic – minimum reading as the heart is relaxed	- Performed only by a doctor or a nurse - Difficult to make generalisations as BP can change rapidly - Conclusions should be made *only* from a series of tests

Continued on following page

Aspects to be tested	Name of test	Characteristics of test	Comments to be noted
Flexibility	Sit and reach	Subjects sits with feet flat against a box and reaches as far forward as possible. The extent of flexibility is measured by a plate. The test is repeated using the best score.	• Measures upper body flexibility only • Results can depend on the extent of a warm up • Easy to administer
Anthropometric	Height	Subject is mesured barefoot and up against a flat surface. The point of measurement is the vertex of the head.	
	Weight	The scales are placed on a level surface and subject is weighed wearing normal clothing	
Body fat percentage	Skinfold tests	Skinfolds are measured using callipers at four sites • Tricep • Bicep • Sub scapular • Anterior supraliac The measurements are totalled and then referred to standard body fat tables	• Difficult to standardise • Use as a guide only

Principle of progression

In order for our performance to improve we must gradually keep stressing our bodies further. Our bodies will adapt to this increased stress and eventually they will reach their optimal fitness levels. This overload must be progressive as we cannot expect our bodies just to perform at much greater levels without a gradual improvement; we are also likely to suffer from overtraining and injury if we do not progress gradually. The greatest improvement seen in performance is during the beginning of our sporting careers; we then tend to plateau and eventually have to train maximally just to maintain performance. The principle of progression also is a motivational factor; a lack of pressure and achievement in training would tend to lead to boredom.

Principle of reversibility

The sad part about training and fitness programmes is that all the hard work and effort can easily be lost through the principle of reversibility. The body reacts to a lack of stress as well as stress overload; many of the benefits of hard training can be lost within about three or four weeks. The most rapid deterioration is in aerobic capacity and flexibility; speed and strength deteriorate more slowly.

Role of instructors

Instructors of a fitness programme must be able to identify the timing of progression and overload; this is a fine art and demands an experiential and theoretical background in training.

Activities in fitness programmes will take into account the three principles of overload, progression and reversibility; whatever the sport or activity the principles remain the same and an instructor will consider these closely.

Devising a fitness programme for a participant

Once we have identified the fitness level of the individual and all their specific needs we can go on to develop a fitness programme that if completed should help that individual achieve many of their aims and objectives. To illustrate this here are two different examples.

Participant 1 – Sarah, aged 26 with a 9-month-old baby. She is about 10 lb overweight according to government guidelines and would like to improve muscle tone particularly around the hips, stomach and thighs. Her body type is 5, 3, 2 (see Element 12.1.1). She enjoys good health and has no present medical conditions preventing her from exercising. She would like to meet people; she enjoys music and she needs a reliable crèche when exercising.

The fitness programme will concentrate on mainly aerobic exercise as this will help burn fat; it will also include local muscular endurance exercise to promote muscle tone. It will consist mainly of group work and will be provided by Sarah's local authority leisure centre as there is a registered crèche provided at minimal cost adjacent to the fitness room.

A weekly programme will consist of

- 1 hour aerobics
- 1 hour body conditioning
- 1 hour step
- One swimming session of 30 minutes
- Three rest days between exercise sessions

These have been chosen because

- 75 per cent of exercise concentrates on improving aerobic fitness
- The three land-based exercises also contain an element of local muscular endurance which in turn concentrates on the problem areas identified by Sarah

- The swimming will provide a change and a relaxing break which will also help Sarah's body to recover effectively
- There are three rest days to ensure fatigue is prevented
- The exercise is not continuous and involves group work so Sarah will be able to socialise and maintain her motivation
- There are likely to be others in the groups trying to achieve the same aims and objectives and so Sarah again will be encouraged to persevere
- The programme can be easily altered to be sensitive to Sarah's needs
- Sarah could also join a sliming class run at the leisure centre to supplement her fitness programme.

Participant 2 – Ben, an 18-year-old international competitive swimmer who has competed in the Olympic Games. Ben trains for up to 25 hours per week and is aiming to increase his strength and his flexibility while maintaining his endurance. Ben is a middle-distance freestyle swimmer and trains as part of an elite squad. He does not work or study at college.

A standard weekly programme during off peak training will consist of

- Nine 2 hour swimming sessions which concentrate on aerobic, anaerobic, anaerobic threshold exercise and stroke technique; the specific sets in training will depend on the session
- Three 1 hour dry sessions to include weight training using free weights and a multi-gym to build strength, plus 10 minutes flexibility at the beginning and end of each session
- Two 1 hour circuit training sessions to add another dimension to endurance training that can include a more social aspect to maintain motivation
- One 1 hour lab testing to measure body fat, including a weigh in, to monitor Ben's diet and how Ben is coping with intensive training; also to ensure Ben does not over-train.

Total = 24 hours

Training includes two rest days and rest of at least 3 hours between dry and swimming training and 8 hours between swimming sessions.

These two fitness programmes are very different, both require different equipment, varying lengths of time devoted to the programme and different levels of coaching. However, they both must be monitored and regularly evaluated and adapted depending on the specific need at the time.

Procedures for ensuring safe practice during a fitness programme

(See also Element 13.1)

A fitness programme needs to be well organised by an experienced coach or instructor; this helps minimise the risk of accidents and promotes a safe environment for the individual to progress. What may seem perfectly acceptable to the unqualified eye is likely to alarm those with experience in organising and implementing fitness programmes.

Appropriate facilities and equipment

The instructor must ensure the facility is suitable with the correct fixtures and fittings. For instance a fitness room for aerobics should be heated to approximately 18–21 °C. This temperature is comfortable to exercise in and warm enough to allow muscles to warm up gradually. Muscles do have a greater tendency to pull when used in cold temperatures. The floor covering should be suitable, for example a sprung floor for high impact aerobics is preferable as this minimises the strain placed on muscles. A non-slip floor is essential for badminton and squash where the athlete will have to reach and stretch.

Equipment used should be passed up to British safety standards and should display a kite mark. It is foolish to use a cheap alternative; these tend to need more maintenance and replacing more often and do not tend to provide the service that customers would expect. The equipment should also be designed specifically for the purpose it is to be used for; for example, cross country skis are not appropriate for a downhill skier.

Suitable programme

The instructor should plan a suitable programme that includes a comprehensive warm up and cool down and exercise that is applicable to the fitness levels of the individual. A warm up and cool down should consist of slow stretches to all major body parts concentrating on the muscle groups that are to be used the most; the pulse rate should be increased gradually. A runner would not just run a 10 kilometre race without performing some flexibility exercises and some gradual jogging; the runner would not just finish the 10 kilometres and stop; a period of jogging and then some flexibility exercises would follow. This minimises strain placed both on the muscles and the cardiovascular system.

Assignment 12.2

In groups of two or three prepare a training programme for a sport or activity of your choice; it may be to improve your physical appearance or it may be for your whole GNVQ group to complete a half marathon or you may be an elite athlete working towards the national championships.
Include

- A description of the programme
- Equipment used
- Fitness testing procedures used
- Suitable safety considerations
- Reasons for all your choices

During the programme keep a diary of your training and use it to comment on your progress and record your likes, dislikes, ideas and suggestions for the future.

Element 12.3 Examine injury prevention and recovery procedures

Performance criteria

1 Describe factors contributing to injury.
2 Describe factors contributing to injury prevention.
3 Explain basic procedures for treating injuries.
4 Explain the components of a recovery programme.

Factors contributing to injury and injury prevention

People involved in sport or physical activity are likely to experience injury. Most injuries are fairly minor and require a little extra rest and the participant is ready to resume the training programme; however, a more serious injury requires immediate attention and action in order to minimise the damage. Your ability to both treat and prevent an injury is vital to the safe organisation of a fitness session. Planning of the actual activity and foresight as to the possible dangers are integral to this.

Initial assessment

As with all activities there a number of factors that demand consideration prior to an individual actually participating in an activity. The coach must be aware of the characteristics of each individual, in other words be aware of the advantages and disadvantages involved in the participation by the individual. These factors can be assessed in a number of ways:

- Experience of working with the individual on a previous occasion
- A questionnaire prior to activity
- A formal or informal interview prior to activity
- By keeping a watchful eye over participants and being aware of the danger signs that may suggest either further damage to an existing injury or increased possibility of injury occurring in the first place.

In order to prevent injury the coach must take a holistic view of the participant, considering physiological, psychological, social and environmental factors.

The coach must ask a series of questions prior to the activity in order to comply with the Health and Safety at Work Act 1974, which states that you must not place any colleague in any personal danger. This is also a moral obligation as the coach is in a position of responsibility.

A simple checklist would include the following aspects:

- Physical fitness
- Physique
- Demographics
- Alcohol and other drugs
- Technique
- Safety

Physical fitness

Assess the physical characteristics of the individual – can the participant realistically be expected to complete the activity successfully? An overweight and untrained person who has not exercised before and would now like to begin a fitness programme should not be expected to complete a 'Do or Die' circuit training session as the body is unlikely to react favourably to the shock of intense exercise and so will be placed under excessive stress (see Figure 12.3).

Fig. 12.3 Fit to run a marathon?

Physique

Is the individual suitable for the activity? Given a comprehensive training programme, can the individual be expected to complete the activity without the risk of excess stress being placed on the body? It would be unwise for an extreme endomorph to participate in the high jump, for example, as the risk of injury will be increased due to the individual's inability to cope with sudden jerky movements.

Demographics

Are the demographic details of the individual suitable for the activity? Age, gender and psychological factors will be included here. An intense session of rugby which included mainly mesomorphic young men would be inappropriate for an unwilling and untrained woman, or an untrained middle-aged man. The risk of injury is increased by including a broad cross-section of participants in body types, ability and demographics. These aspects should be viewed with caution and not used to categorise a session. However, beware of discounting a participant purely on age or gender; these are only part of the complete profile.

Alcohol and other drugs

A number of factors will increase the risk of injury and these usually demand immediate attention. Alcohol (see Element 12.1) affects the individual physically and psychologically. Under the influence of alcohol individuals will generally not be as perceptive, will be unable to make an accurate decision and will be physically putting their bodies under extreme stress. This must be avoided and any individual showing signs of consuming alcohol prior to a session should be prevented from participating and counselled as to the reason for the consumption initially. Participants taking drugs for medical reasons should discuss the implications of the drug with the coach and refer to a doctor if further clarification is necessary. Social drugs, of which alcohol is one, should be treated similarly but with greater emphasis on the reason for consumption and then education. Drugs of this kind and sport do not mix.

Technique

The coach must recognise the important role of accurate technical guidance within a session. The risk of injury can also be increased through poor technical ability in an activity. For example, aerobics includes a great deal of emphasis on stretching; if the body movements are not precise and stretch a muscle inappropriately, the muscle is placed under stress and this is likely to cause injury, particularly if the bad habit is constantly repeated. The role of the coach is to spot the bad habit and alter the technique accordingly.

Safety

The coach also has a responsibility to plan the session with safety in mind. The facilities and equipment used must be appropriate for the activity and the participants; the session must include a comprehensive provision for warm up and cool down and the fitness testing procedures must be completed prior to the activity (see also Unit 13).

Activity

In small groups discuss any limitations you may need to consider if you were planning a session for yourselves. How would you incorporate this into your planning process?

Basic procedures for treating injuries

Once an injury occurs, the coach must be clear what to do; this is a time where quick and accurate thinking is demanded in order to minimise the injury. The following guidelines are useful in assessing the situation and treating specific injuries.

Assessing the situation

- How serious does the injury appear?
- Ascertain what happened
- Ask the casualty for details of the accident and injury
- How many casualties are involved?
- Has the injured participant suffered this injury before?
- Contact the registered first aider

In each establishment there will be a registered first aider; this person is suitably qualified to provide first aid and if necessary help decide if further professional help is required. The role of the first aider is to minimise further damage and provide reassurance to the casualty until this help arrives, not to treat a serious injury. As a coach you will know who your registered first aider is and you will know how to contact them. It is often sensible for a coach to be a registered first aider as sporting activities possess a high risk of injury at some time.

Treating specific injuries

There are particular procedures for specific injuries; these can be categorised into three areas: head, spinal and soft tissue injuries.

Head injuries

Apply the principle of ABC – airways, breathing, circulation (Figure 12.4).

- *Airways* – Check the airways are clear
- *Breathing* – Give mouth-to-mouth resuscitation if breathing cannot be detected
- *Circulation* – If the casualty has no pulse, external cardiac compression must be applied

Once the presence of breathing has been confirmed, place the casualty in the recovery position.

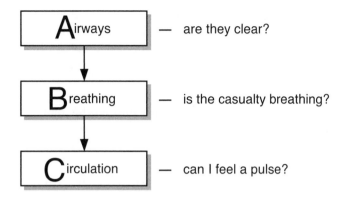

Fig. 12.4 How to assess the severity of a head injury

Spinal injuries

- Never move the casualty: this can cause further damage
- Call for an ambulance immediately
- Talk to and constantly reassure the casualty, who is likely to be frightened

Soft tissue injuries

These are the most common injuries and as a coach you will almost certainly come up against these. The aim is to decrease circulation which will in turn decrease internal bleeding and swelling.

Apply the principle of RICE – rest, ice, compression, elevation (Figure 12.5).

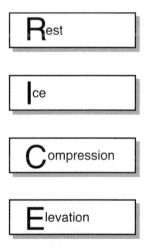

Fig. 12.5 How to treat soft tissue injuries

- *Rest* – Stop using the injured part of the body immediately as further use is likely to increase damage and risk causing permanent damage.

- *Ice* – Ice should be applied to the injured part; this will allow the blood vessels and surrounding tissues to contract and will reduce blood flow to the injured area. Swelling is likely to be reduced. Do not apply the ice direct but through a cotton towel or similar. Remove the ice every ten minutes and repeat at three-hourly intervals if necessary.
- *Compression* – In order to keep swelling to a minimum apply direct pressure by wrapping a bandage tightly around the injured body part.
- *Elevation* – Again to decrease circulation raise the injured body part above the heart. The force of gravity will help reduce blood flow and drain excess fluids from the injured area.

It is important to remember that only trained medical personnel can treat a serious injury to the best effect and you as a coach must assess the situation quickly yet accurately so as to reduce the severity of the injury.

Components of a recovery programme

Once an injury has occurred you can affect the rate of recovery by your actions. Apply the following principles:

- Never move a casualty with a spinal injury
- Place a casualty in the recovery position if unconscious

If an injury is caused by overuse, the injured part should be rested; the period of rest is determined by the severity of the overuse; the only person able to quantify this is a sports injury specialist, usually a physiotherapist. Uninjured parts of the body can still be trained.

Once the injury has been adequately rested, training can be resumed; this must be progressive and not to a stage where overtraining injuries recur; the training programme therefore needs constant monitoring and, where necessary, adaptation.

Isometric exercises increase the strength of the muscle by static contraction; the muscle length remains constant and the amount of tension applied can be progressively developed. A recovery programme should incorporate these type of exercises.

If an injury does not heal following these principles it is likely to need further treatment, possible surgery or retirement from that particular activity. Again a qualified medic specialising in sport is the best person to answer this. To train with an injury and not listen to the body is folly; the injury will only get worse over time and can have eventual debilitating effects.

Assignment 12.3

Have you ever been injured? What treatment did you receive? Could it have been better? What recovery programme did you follow?

Think of prominent sports stars who have suffered an injury. What was their injury? How long did it take them to return to competitive action? Do you know anyone who has been forced to stop participating in sport because of an injury?

Unit 13
PLANNING FOR SPORTS COACHING

Element 13.1 Explore the coaching process and the roles of the coach

Element 13.2 Plan a coaching session for a selected sport

Element 13.3 Determine the additional requirements for coaching children

Element 13.4 Prepare guidelines for safe practice in sports coaching

Element 13.1 Explore the coaching process and the roles of the coach

Performance criteria

1 Explain the coaching process.
2 Explain the roles of the coach.
3 Describe the skills required for coaching.
4 Describe areas of knowledge required for coaching.
5 Identify and give examples of areas of knowledge required for coaching selected sports.

Introduction

Planning a sports coaching session may seem a simple task on first thought: however, planning a successful sports coaching session is a comprehensive and challenging task and makes the difference between future repeat customers and a one-off session. The process is stage by stage, covered by the elements in this unit. Each element is further broken down into performance criteria; there are further sub-stages in the complete planning process.

If you are to plan a successful session, you must include all aspects of the performance criteria for each element in your planning process; this way there should be no gaping holes in your session and you should enjoy satisfaction among your customers.

This unit is subsectioned with direct reference to the performance criteria; there will be ample opportunities for you to provide evidence for your portfolios. Remember to cross-refer where possible between elements and between units.

The coaching process

If you are in charge of organising and coaching a session there are a number of vital aspects to consider prior to the session running. The coaching process has to be considered from first to last and then repeated and reconsidered at regular time intervals (see Figure 13.1).

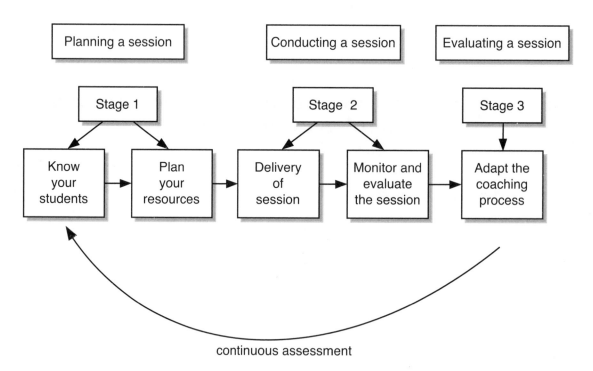

Fig. 13.1 *The three-stage coaching process*

Planning a session

Information must be collected and organisation completed prior to your session. The information needs to be adapted for the specific needs of your session. A checklist is an appropriate way to ensure that you gather as much relevant information as possible; if you have a list to refer to it will minimise the chances of forgetting something important.

Student checklist

- Who are my students?
- What are their demographic details?
  - what sex are they?
  - what age are they?
  - what are their socio-economic details?
  - what are their aims and objectives?
- Are my students able-bodied or disabled in any way?
- Is my session adaptable for participants with disabilities?
- What level of ability or experience do my students have?

Resources checklist

- What facilities are available?
- Are they suitable in terms of
  - size
  - access
  - attractiveness
  - adaptability
  - locality
- Is there sufficient car parking?
- Are there any catering facilities?
- Is the facility suitably insured?
- Is sufficient equipment available on site?
- Is the equipment of a satisfactory standard?
- Is the equipment safe, durable and appropriate for the task in hand?
- What are the domestic arrangements of the facility?
- Where are the toilets, fire exists and first aid facilities?
- What are the security arrangements?
- How do I book the facility?
- How many supervisors do I need for the session?
- What are the costs of the session for staffing, hire of facility and hire of equipment?
- Is a deposit required in advance?

Once you have matched the demands of the student to the supply of the resources, the next part of the process is the actual delivery of the session.

Conducting a session

Following a similar process to planning a session, the use of a checklist is generally the most suitable approach.

- What are the aims and objectives of the session? (Remember these should be measurable and realistic.)
- What will my students be able to achieve by the end of the session?
- How will I structure the session?
  - time available
  - breakdown of time

- demonstrations
- practice
- games
- awards
- presentations
- refreshments
- breaks (how often and how long)
- warm ups and cool downs
- How will I maximise my students' learning?
- Will I coach individually or as a group or a combination of the two?
- How will I praise and encourage my students?
- When will I introduce the students to the domestic arrangements of the session?
- What behavioural code will I adopt?
- How will I ensure safety of all participants at all times?
- Will I include a general or sport specific warm up and ease down?
- How will I end my session?

The majority of these questions have no simple answer that applies to all coaching sessions. The specific conducting of the session needs to be directly referred to the Stage 1 planning process (see Figure 13.1). For instance, a warm up for experienced competitive swimmers will be very different from a warm up for children playing hockey for the first time; the behavioural code and the tone of delivery you adopt for your session will also vary accordingly.

Evaluating a session

It is essential to evaluate your coaching process for the following reasons:

- To review your coaching process
- To improve future sessions
- To hear fresh ideas from your students

Your students should feel that they are being heard and that their opinions are valued. You and your students should finish the session as a partnership which will naturally progress to the next session and encourage repeat custom.

Methods of evaluation

- Informed feedback throughout and at the conclusion of a session, often in the form of simple questions
- A questionnaire at the end of a course; this formal written evaluation should allow anonymity if necessary
- A quick off-the-cuff SWOT analysis studying the following:

  Strengths
  Weaknesses
  Opportunities
  Threats

The method used will depend on the student group and the sport being coached.

Three-stage planning

Every coach needs to progress through the three-stage planing process for each coaching session. Without a checklist the session would quickly deteriorate and, as in any industry, the customer will seek a more professional approach elsewhere.

An experienced coach, taking a session at the same venue week after week, will obviously have a shorter checklist prior to the session. However, even an experienced coach needs to adapt each session depending on the stage in the season of the sport, the progress of the students and so on.

Every coach needs to evaluate the coaching process. The most successful coaches take time and effort and plan carefully and comprehensively every time.

Activity

You are preparing a seminar for prospective coaches at a conference to be held at the National Water Sports Centre, Home Pierrpont, Nottingham. There will be coaches from many different sports, such as swimming, canoeing and karate. All the coaches are looking for a background in how to plan, conduct and evaluate a session.

Prepare a handout which will consider these options and apply to all of the coaches on the seminar. Ensure the handout is not only relevant and precise but also eye-catching.

Interview and observe an experienced coach before, during and after a session. Prepare a checklist that covers the planning, conducting and evaluation of the session. Discuss with the coach the process followed and why. Add your own comments.

The roles of the coach

A coach will assume many differing roles when delivering a session or programme. To be successful the coach needs to develop a high level of skill in a range of areas. As with all people who take part in sport, a coach will only improve these skills during time, with practice and commitment.

The coach as organiser

Organising does not stop once the group or individual are in front of the coach, with the correct kit, equipment and enthusiasm. In fact it is only just beginning. Preparation is the key to delivering a good session. Once a session is underway the coach needs to be able to

- Give clear explanations of key points (demonstrations are usually easier to understand)
- Decide the best position from which to deliver demonstrations
- Stop the group, at a relevant time, in an effective manner
- Bring the group round quickly for explanation or demonstrations
- Instil discipline into the session

The coach as problem solver

Problems may occur during a session or programme. Coaches need to be aware of the types of problems that can occur, and be confident in their ability to deal with them.

Here are some examples of potential problems:

- Students are not making progress
- Students are misbehaving during sessions
- Students are losing interest and enthusiasm
- Parents of students (where applicable) are becoming over-involved

Coaches will approach situations differently but the problem should be resolved eventually. When dealing with a problem, a coach needs a range of attributes, including the ability to be firm but fair, confidence, to be fully aware of the facts and most of all, to be in control.

Activity

Suggest ways in which you would deal with the following problems if they occurred during one of your coaching sessions:

- The group has trouble in maintaining concentration
- A child's parent constantly shouts advice to the child as you are trying to coach
- One of your more able students suddenly becomes disruptive

The coach as a communicator

All coaches need to be able to express themselves clearly, not only by the spoken word but also non-verbally. It is important that the tone of voice, body language and facial expressions all match the message you are trying to relay.

The coach needs to be able to maintain attention and interest during a session as well as injecting enthusiasm throughout. The best way to achieve this is by

- Speaking clearly
- Being brief but informative
- Ensuring communication is relevant and two-way
- Being positive and helpful at all times
- Practising voice projection, tone and volume

Skills required for coaching

The coach has a varied and challenging role which covers many areas. The coach requires several different skills:

- Organising
- Problem solving
- Communicating

- Adapting
- Analysing and evaluating
- Encouraging trainee self-motivation
- Encouraging trainee self-evaluation

Organising

Coaches have to organise

- Themselves
- The students/participants
- The resources needed
- Time
- Aims and objectives
- Change and improvement

Problem solving

A coach has to be able to study performance in both training and competition. A short and long-term coaching plan will need constant analysis and evaluation which will lead to adaptation and problem solving through flexibility. For instance you may start a coaching plan with twenty sessions; however, the plan could easily be disrupted by unavoidable factors such as illness or poor weather conditions and so on. You must be able to understand these factors and plan an element of flexibility so your overall aims and objectives can still be achieved.

Communicating

The ability to communicate is an essential skill of coaching. You may possess all the technical, experiential and physiological knowledge but without the ability to express this expertise to the learners, its benefit is void. The type of communication used will depend on the learners involved; each individual will demand a different emphasis and a skilful coach will be able to choose the correct style accurately.

Consider these factors when communicating:

- *Tone* – express the meaning of the words through emphasis, to introduce mood
- *Volume* – your learners must be able to hear and understand you clearly
- *Language* – the choice of words should be appropriate for the level of student and skill
- *Non-verbal communication* – impression is created before a word is spoken; gestures, appearance and eye contact should encourage two-way communication.

Adapting

Adapting sessions for different age groups or different ability groups is an essential skill required by a coach.

When coaching children it is important to make sessions safe. This often involves changing the rules while maintaining the essential features of the game.

The coach can also

- Group children of similar size, age or ability together
- Reduce the size or weight of equipment to suit the group
- Shorten the length of games

Analysing and evaluating

Coaches need to be able to analyse two things. The first is the performance of the pupil, where the coach must have the expertise to identify faults and correct them accordingly. The second is the ability to analyse themselves and evaluate their own performance as a coach.

In order to identify and rectify faults, coaches require an in-depth knowledge of the sport they are coaching. They need to be able to observe performance and break down actions into smaller components. Coaches should also have a good knowledge of their pupils and know what makes them 'tick'.

When analysing and evaluating their own performance, coaches need to take a detached look at themselves and answer some simple but important questions. One easy way to do this is to prepare a self-evaluation checklist, to be completed after each session.

Here is an example:

- Date
- Time
- Activity
- What went well with the session?
- What did not go well with the session?
- What was achieved during the session?
- How could future sessions be improved?
- Any other comments?

You can add other questions to your list, but remember to ensure it is completed after each session.

Activity

Prepare your own checklist and complete it after your next session. See if it helps you analyse and evaluate your performance.

Trainee self-motivation

Coaches need to be aware that all people are different, and therefore respond to differing approaches. People participate in sport for a variety of reasons, for example

- To have fun
- To get fit
- To compete and win

Understanding these reasons will help the coach discover the motivation of the performer and will ultimately assist in developing 'trainee self-motivation'.

The coach needs to take the time to get to know individual performers and help them to motivate themselves. Communicate on a regular basis with all your students and find out what they are looking for. Treated correctly, students will become self-motivated and perform to their potential.

Trainee self-evaluation

As with the coach, performers need to be able to evaluate their own performance and as they become more confident and experienced rectify (or suggest ways to rectify) problems.

It is unrealistic to expect novice performers to have these skills, but they should be encouraged to improve their ability to self-evaluate as well as improving their physical performance.

The best way to achieve this is to talk to your students and help them along the way, suggesting how they can self-evaluate. Support them at all times and do not allow them to become too critical of their performance, unless it acts as a stimulus to improvement.

Activity

Take time to discuss with your students their motivation for participating in the sport you are coaching and ask them how they motivate themselves. Note their responses and see if they have changed in three months' time.

A coach requires many skills to be successful. Some of these skills you may have already, others may need to be developed over the years. A coach, like students, will improve with hard work and dedication. Above all, coaching needs to be enjoyable if both coach and student are to perform to their maximum.

Activity

The skill of communication can be assessed constantly; to understand the level of importance associated with this consider the following situations:

- A successful lecturer and an unsuccessful lecturer
- A sports commentator you enjoy listening to and one you do not
- A newsreader

What are the different characteristics of communication and how do they differ from situation to situation and between success and failure?

Areas of knowledge required for coaching, with examples from selected sports

Another aspect of coaching to consider, once the planning and general roles are finalised, is the specific area of knowledge required for a chosen activity or sport.

A coach will generally be expected to have a coaching qualification verified by the governing body of that particular sport, for example a swimming coach should have a Club Coaches Certificate awarded by the Amateur Swimming Association. The qualification will ensure that theoretical aspects and some practical aspects are understood by the coach. However, as with all professionals, added experience gathered over the years along with theoretical certificates will ensure that all areas of knowledge will be covered in detail.

Areas of knowledge include

- Techniques and tactics of the sport
- Psychology
- Fitness, nutrition and physiology
- Safety
- Knowledge of individual abilities

Techniques and tactics of the sport

It is essential to keep abreast of the latest developments within a sport and to be able to readily identify technical improvements within an activity. For example, in tennis a coach must be able to identify the correct grip on the racket, as this can influence a competitor's ability to reach and return a shot. Tactics can include rule changes within a sport, which can influence the outcome of a competition, for instance the back pass rule in football introduced in the 1992–93 season.

Psychology

The difference between a winner and a loser can often be the mental ability of the competitor. The ability to handle stress and pressure will ensure technical and tactical skills are not just forgotten during competition. Many competitors, having reached a final and with everyone watching, have 'lost their nerve'. The coach needs to be able to identify methods of relaxation in order to counteract this stress; this can include massage, competition rehearsal or the use of music; the method will depend on individuals and their stress adaptation.

The coach must identify the level of stress which is beneficial to performance (see Figure 13.2).

Fitness, nutrition and physiology

Each sport has different physiological demands depending on its physical intensity, for example a marathon runner will need to maximise aerobic fitness whereas a snooker player will need to concentrate on flexibility in order to maximise reach.

Each individual coach must identify the physiological aspects important to the specific sport and then must relate this to the individual competitor. A teenager during puberty will need a different fitness, nutrition and physiological programme to a 30-year-old experienced competitor. The physiological composition of these two examples will perform maximally only with very different programmes.

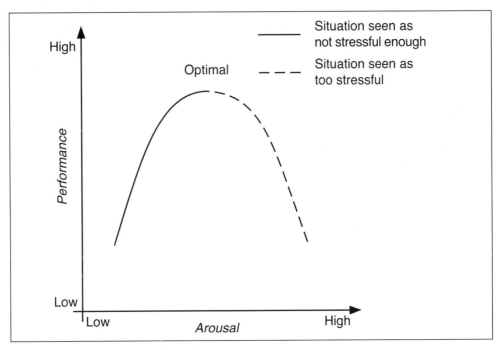

Fig. 13.2 Levels of stress in performance

Safety

Coaches are now compelled to abide by the Health and Safety at Work Act 1974 and the Children Act 1989 along with other legislation such as Control of Substances Hazardous to Health (COSHH) 1988.

The two main areas for concern are resources and learners.

- *Resources* – all equipment and facilities used must be checked for suitability. Equipment should not be damaged in such a way as to put anyone at any risk.
- *Learners* – the provider of the sessions must ensure that learners are coached by reliable and knowledgeable staff. A great deal of damage can occur from inappropriate training which is often caused by the ignorance of the coaches.

Coaches must also be checked for their suitability to coach. The high-profile aspects of drug taking, a problem which has had such a high profile at an elite level must obviously be avoided; coaching session and coaches should be regularly supervised by independent parties. Much publicity has been given to the case of Paul Hickson (1995), coach to the British national swimming team at the Seoul and Los Angeles Olympics, who is currently imprisoned for a series of sexual offences against swimmers who were placed within his trust. A complaints procedure and an open management policy should be applied to minimise any such risks, as now adopted by the Amateur Swimming Association.

Knowledge of individual abilities

Every individual will need a different long-term coaching plan; the different demands may include physiology, nutrition, tactics, techniques, aims and objectives. The coach has to balance in most cases the demands of a group and the individuals within the group. This can lead to conflict, particularly if there are two rival competitors within the same group. The successful coach will be able to strike the balance and ensure that all learners receive equal attention and that their worth is recognised.

Assignment 13.1

Within your class organise a small coaching session. Discuss the skills required to conduct your session, the differing demands of your classmates and the most important qualities you will need to coach the session. What are the characteristics of your ideal coach?

Element 13.2 **Plan a coaching session for a selected sport**

Performance criteria

1 Identify resources required for a coaching session for a selected sport.
2 Respond to factors influencing the planning of a coaching session.
3 Prepare a plan for a coaching session for a selected sport.
4 Explain the requirements for conducting a coaching session.
5 Explain the contribution a coaching session makes to a long-term development plan.

This element allows you to put into practice the issues discussed when studying the coaching process. The performance criteria are applicable to all coaching sessions and ensure that a session incorporating this comprehensive amount of planning will be successfully executed.

Our selected sport is competitive swimming and the following example includes evidence of all the performance criteria identified in this element.

Resources required for a coaching session in competitive swimming

Background

This is a programme devised for a leading national side who are at the start of the off season training period. There are approximately 25 swimmers in the session who are all national qualifiers and are all considered senior swimmers (over 15 years). All swimmers are experienced and have trained as a team for at least one complete season. The swimmers specialise at different events.

Facilities

A swimming pool with six lanes and competition facilities, suitable changing for the number specified and for both sexes. If possible dry side training should be available, for instance a weights room with swim benches and an area for warming up by flexibility exercises.

Time

The facility is needed for at least two hours per evening after 5 p.m. (these are senior swimmers with both employment and educational commitments and some travel up to 25 miles to training). Some swimmers will need extra training up to two hours per morning, finishing before 8 a.m.

Equipment

Equipment needed over and above permanent fixtures is minimal; 20 kick boards, pull buoys and pairs of flippers would be useful, but most swimmers own these themselves. The coach will need a stopwatch, pace clock, a wipe board and markers and a noticeboard.

Assistance from other staff

The coach will need to be a qualified lifeguard in order to comply with health and safety regulations and will at times need an assistant for backup during certain sessions.

Factors influencing the planning of a coaching session

Session goals

- To improve basic aerobic capacity
- To concentrate on technical aspects of each individual's chosen stroke
- To allow some socialising (swimming is time consuming and intensive so a session must include a fun element)
- To allow the coach to gather feedback after a competition the previous weekend

These are all relevant because of the timing of the session in the long term plan. Remember this is at the beginning of off peak training.
The coach will also need to consider safety regulations and participants' needs.

Planning a coaching session in competitive swimming

Starting the session

- Time 5–7 p.m. 20 September
- Coaching staff available
- Six lane 25 metre swimming pool with dry training area
- Pace clock, kick boards, pull buoys, backstroke flags, flippers and all other equipment provided
- All swimmers changed and on dry training area
- Ten minutes of flexibility concentrating on upper body
- Assistant coach ensures all equipment is set out

Content of session

Swimmers in the pool (approximately five per lane grouped by ability and swimming clockwise/anti-clockwise by lane)

- Warm up
- Swim 400 metres front crawl
- Pull 400 metres back crawl
- Kick 400 metres medley
- Swim 400 metres front crawl
- All at moderate pace

Main set 1

- Swim 10 x 100 metres front crawl on 90 secs holding pulse rate at 140
- Swim 10 x 100 metres front crawl on 85 secs holding pulse rate at 150
- Swim 10 x 100 metres front crawl on 80 secs holding pulse rate at 150
- Extra 2 minutes' rest between sets
- Swim easy 200 metres back stroke

Technical emphasis

Drill 12×25 metres choice stroke on 40 seconds reducing stroke count each 4 and each set – concentrating on reach and push phase of each stroke.

Main set 2

- Swim 3×400 individual medleys on 7 minutes, swimming progressively faster each repetition but keeping pulse below 160
- Ease down 4×50 metres choice stroke 1–4 regressive

Finishing the session

Assistant coach puts equipment away
After changing: team meeting to discuss the training session and the long-term objectives

Requirements for conducting a coaching session

As this group is an advanced and elite squad they possess a deal of self-discipline and experience. However, a behavioural code is necessary. It may include

- No toilet stops unless authorised by the coach
- No general fooling around: a swimming pool can be a fatal environment
- Any questions or suggestions must be addressed to the chief coach immediately

The coach must be able to empathise with the swimmers and respect their opinions while also maintaining authority. It is essential that a coach can be heard, particularly in sporting environments which are often noisy. Interpersonal skills are vital so development can be based on trust and respect.

The contribution a coaching session makes to a long-term development plan

This session is at the beginning of a yearly plan which in the sport of swimming is a medium or long-term plan. Many sports follow this basic plan:

Off peak training

September to January
Minimal competition and maximum training

Aims

- To improve aerobic endurance
- To improve technical aspects of the sport
- To discuss individual and team aims for the following season
- To learn from the previous season's performance

Mid-season

January to April
Some competitions, but not major national or international championships

Aims

- To build anaerobic endurance
- To maintain aerobic endurance
- To sharpen competition techniques
- To prepare for major competitions
- To evaluate and adapt progress this far.

Peak season

April to July
Major competitions

Aims

- To maintain aerobic endurance
- To maximise anaerobic capabilities
- To produce optimal performances

Rest period

August

Achieving success

All the qualities of the coaching process are part of an integral plan to achieve success, whether it be at an elite level or as a beginner. By studying this example it is clear that the coaching cannot be successful without a great deal of effort and thought; the principles applied are general.

Assignment 13.2

Consider a sporting activity you enjoy. Devise a coaching plan which is short, medium and long term to illustrate your intended development. Consider what you want to achieve, what you need to achieve it and how you will achieve it. Choose one aspect and keep a log of your development highlighting the points raised within this element.

You are the coach of a rising star. This athlete has a choice of coaches but you want this challenge. The athlete has the chance to reach the Olympic Games the following year and you have to put forward a proposal to achieve this. You must impress! Remember to include

- Specific resources necessary
- Factors influencing your coaching process
- Your method of coaching, including safety aspects
- A long-term plan

Performance criteria

1 Explain the implications of the Children Act 1989 for coaching children.
2 Describe developmental factors relating to children which affect coaching.
3 Describe the benefits that sport can have for children.
4 Propose ways of adapting selected sports for children.

Introduction

All of the planning details discussed in Element 13.2 require consideration when children are the subject; children, however, are a special group who need special attention. We are required by law to ensure the safety of children for whom we are responsible; we also have a moral responsibility to do so as children are left with their coaches or carers in good faith. Children will often follow a coach's instructions explicitly and consequently we must make sure as coaches that our instructions are clear and correct.

A child includes anyone under 16 years of age; for the purpose of this element it is recommended that we take a more open view and consider the ability of the group to be coached; the principles to be discussed are worth considering if the group comprises 17-year olds. Be flexible in your approach.

The implications of the Children Act 1989 for coaching children

The Children Act was initially enforced in November 1989 and has implemented some basic and far-reaching changes in child welfare. The implications of the Act now encompass areas that had not previously been considered on such a scale. Leisure facilities and coaching of children are two such areas. The law is complex and a great deal of information has been produced and publicised regarding paternity cases and those involving children's homes; the registration and relevant documentation regarding the coaching of children is not so well publicised.

The area we are concerned with is covered under the general heading 'day care for children'. In the past a local authority had the power to impose requirements with regard to the care of children; the Children Act states that a local authority has the duty now to impose reasonable requirements where the care of children is concerned.

Registration of coaches

All staff involved with the care of children under the age of 8 are registered with their local authority; to evade registration is an offence; staff are assessed for their suitability to be in the proximity of children as opposed to their fitness to look after children as with childminders and day nurseries.

The coaches will be asked to complete documents that question their qualifications and suitability to work with children. A police check is also carried out to study any previous convictions and to check an individual's criminal history.

Not only are the coaches questioned but also the premises where children are likely to be cared for are inspected to ensure that they are suitable for children and the activity chosen. A local authority will need to document the number of children cared for, the equipment to be used, the staff/child ratio and any records that are maintained. The local authority does have some discretion and the requirements are tailored to the individual situation. The local authority will from time to time inspect and review the registration and any changes to staff or facility must be reported immediately.

Facilities that are likely to require registration include crèche facilities, playschemes and children's clubs.

Developmental factors relating to children which affect coaching

Just as with adults, the group you will be coaching is likely to be of mixed ability and your planning must satisfy as many of your students' needs as possible. This role is greatly emphasised when your students are children. The range of ability is likely to be vast, because there are so many factors involved, including the physical and psychological profile of the individual child. We can all remember the physical education class at school with the tall, well-developed and popular girl outclassing the small, thin and underconfident boy, but how did it feel at the time? Our planning and coaching should ensure we can empathise with all children and include them into the session so they may enjoy the benefits.

Children are not mini-adults; they require special attention.

Physical development

Muscles

In an adult male the muscles comprise 40 per cent of the total body mass; in women it is about 24 per cent; the muscle composition of a child is quite different. A baby will possess all the muscle fibres at birth but they are small and watery; by adolescence they have become much thicker. The gain in strength is dramatic between the ages of 11 and 17 and boys will at this time become stronger than girls; this may be as a result of not only a more energetic lifestyle but also the male hormone testosterone, which increases in production at this time. This growth spurt that occurs during puberty is often quite alarming for the child; the route to adulthood has never been an easy one.

Also at this time girls have to contend with the starting of their periods (menstruation). The physical effects during the earlier years particularly can be quite debilitating, with stomach cramps, headaches and general lethargy.

Bones

At birth, bones are softer and have a greater water content than those of adults; from infancy to puberty, bones harden (ossification) and also increase in number. This physical development results in more skilful movement but a loss in flexibility; for instance babies cannot support their head at birth and their legs and hips can be manipulated in a way that an adult's cannot.

Fat

At the age of 6 or 7, the levels of fat that are stored around muscles and bones start to increase until puberty. The body fat levels differ between the sexes, with boys generally storing less fat than girls. Social and environmental considerations can affect this: an athletic girl will often possess similar body fat levels to an average boy. Body fat levels vary throughout our life.

Psychological development

The psychological development and experiences of a child prepare the child for adulthood; the memories of childhood are with us for life and will shape our personality.

Self-image

As children develop so does the way they see themselves. As a small child we often see ourselves purely as a description. For example, I am a girl; I am six years old; I weigh 5 stone and so on. As a child gets older these descriptions start to incorporate feelings, emotions and beliefs. They also become progressively more comparative. For example, I am tall for my age; I like to listen to music; I am a very good swimmer; I am the best runner in my class.

By the time that children reach puberty the self-image becomes almost totally related to their beliefs and is far removed from the physical characteristics. The self-image becomes an ideology. The self-image also becomes closely related to how children feel that they are perceived by their peer group.

Confidence

The confidence of a child can vary from time to time; we rarely feel confident about everything but we usually feel confident and relaxed about some aspect of our life. The confidence of a child is an individual characteristic; some children appear shy and withdrawn; some want to lead the class continually. The levels of confidence are related to self-image; more positive children tend to see themselves as above average in comparison with their peers; some children are confident whatever their ability. The closer that children get to puberty, the more their confidence seems to be related to how their friends see them.

Social and emotional development

The ability to socially interact is developed greatly through team games; you have to communicate to take part. Some children are naturally outgoing and very lively and enjoy the banter and competitiveness of sport; however, some children do not react positively to this environment and almost dread the session, some to the point of feigning illness in order to miss the session. Both the positive and negative experiences remain with the child in memory for life; the horror of physical education lessons is well documented. The coach must be able to balance the session and must invest extra time and effort in building the confidence of the reluctant participant.

Skills

This is an integral part of the physical considerations; some children are physically more able than others; some are able to handle pressure and failure well, others either openly or secretly dread this. The rates at which children develop vary vastly and some children will never have the physical or psychological attributes necessary for some activities. As a coach you can only nurture the best from each child. I can use an example from my own childhood to illustrate this; as a keen and successful athlete I would always dread the sessions that included ball games: my ability to catch and anticipate the ball was nothing short of lousy! It was not until I was speaking to a colleague at university that I realised that my lack of success was due to a limitation of my eyesight; it was really irrelevant how hard I practised as this would not improve my hand/eye co-ordination. A coach should be aware of these potential problems: with children they are common.

These aspects need to be considered during the planning process; the coach must empathise with each individual and must be able to do this quickly in order to maximise the benefits of the session.

Activity

How do you see yourself? Discuss with a partner how you would describe yourself. How can your self-image be related to your ability to learn? Consider any sporting childhood experiences that are distinctive to you and how these affected your participation in sport. If you do not participate, why not? Can this be associated with your self-image or a childhood experience?

The benefits that sport can have for children

There are five main benefits for children when they participate in sport:

- Appreciation of fair play
- Regard for rules
- Competition and co-operation
- Enjoyment
- Personal development

Sport prepares a child for life; all the characteristics listed above are qualities that many of us would say are essential for success in adulthood. The ability to survive in the 'rat race' revolves around the ability to handle competition and co-operation. Generally a child involved in sport will learn to handle failure and learn to be objective in this instance. The child will learn the art of self-discipline through appreciation of fair play and rules.

Other benefits to a child are individual. Sport may help a child develop a motor skill; there may be a medical benefit; it may simply help improve a child's self-esteem. The superior coach will be able to recognise potential benefits to a child and concentrate on achieving these.

Activity

Visit a school or talk to some children. Find out who enjoys sport and why. What do they enjoy most and least about coaching sessions?

Ways of adapting selected sports for children

It would be both impractical and unrealistic to expect a child to enjoy an adult sporting environment; most sports need modification for children to some extent. This is to ensure that a child can develop and enjoy the sport and not be overawed by a full-size football pitch, for example. This improvisation is essential as first impressions are lasting and can put a child off a sport or activity for life.

Adapting time

This aspect is probably the most flexible in terms of improvisation. The time spent on an activity must reflect the concentration span of the participants. Children have shorter concentration spans than adults, particularly if they are not kept active. This concentration span is the time one can spend productively listening; it is usually between 10 and 15 minutes. This does not mean that a sports session should only last this long, but that activities should be varied at 10–15 minute intervals.

A warm up could take the first 10 minutes of a session, followed by an introduction to the activity, followed by some drills, perhaps with some relays. Each time you are giving the participants a new stimulus and so creating new interest.

The length of competition is also flexible; the rule book states that a game of football lasts 90 minutes; this would be wholly inappropriate for a group of 6–9 year olds where a game played in two lots of 10 minutes would be far more beneficial. Change activities when you, the coach, decide it is necessary: you are in charge!

Adapting resources and equipment

Children are likely to need a scaled down playing area and smaller equipment than adult participants. In some sports this can be easily achieved as the equipment or facilities are especially provided. For example, small skis are easily bought and ski resorts provide nursery slopes. A swimming complex usually includes a small learner facility with shallow water and easy access for children.

Some sports are not so obviously adapted. A game of hockey for 6–9 year olds would be dangerous with the hard hockey ball; you can easily improvise by using tennis balls instead or by introducing the game of unihoc which uses plastic sticks and a plastic puck. The full-size hockey pitch is too large for small legs! Play the game using cones for goals and with simple markings, perhaps width-ways across the pitch to begin with.

Adapting group size

As with adults, where possible ensure that the group size is the optimum for learning. Ideally this may mean smaller groups for children; in practice this may be quite different as school children are often taught in groups of up to 40. Remember to bear in mind safety levels of supervision.

Changing rules

All sports can be adapted to a certain degree to be made suitable for children; some may need no adaptation. As a coach your insight will allow you to plan suitably for children, maintaining their interest and showing them the positive qualities of participating in sport. You can change the rules as you like in order to do this.

Activity

Choose two sports, perhaps your two favourite sports: how can these be improvised for a group of 6–9 year olds?

Assignment 13.3

You are head of physical education at a junior school and you have recently recruited a new member of staff to run your competitive sporting teams. This person is used to teaching adult beginners but has not coached children a great deal. You have spent a great deal of effort to ensure that the coaching sessions are suitable for children but your new member of staff requests some guidance notices covering the main considerations as a backup.

Compile these notes with examples including

- The implications of the Children Act 1989
- The developmental factors which must be considered when coaching children
- The benefits of sport for children
- Suggest adaptations for two of the sports for children aged 6–9 years and of mixed ability
- Try to present these notes in a distinctive way so your new member of staff remembers the points you raise easily.

Element 13.4 Prepare guidelines for safe practice in sports coaching

> Performance criteria
>
> 1 Explain the safety checks made at a venue by the coach.
> 2 Explain the requirements for coaching safely.
> 3 Describe factors affecting participants' safety.
> 4 Prepare written guidelines for safe practice when conducting a coaching session for a selected sport.

Safety checks made at a venue by the coach

Safety should always be in the mind of any sports coach before, during and after any session, not only out of moral obligation but also as a consequence of legal requirements such as the Health and Safety at Work, etc. Act 1974, the Children Act 1989 and Control of Substances Hazardous to Health 1988. When planning and developing a coaching plan, safety is always high on the checklist of priorities; this has been illustrated throughout Elements 13.1 to 13.3

A checklist is recommended when inspecting safety factors. A checklist ensures that you can address these aspects succinctly and helps to minimise the likelihood of overlooking any relevant issues. Checklists are by no means exhaustive and any safety planning should be double checked by at least two authorities at the particular sport.

Facility safety checklist

- Are the facilities suitable for the sport and the session?
- Is there sufficient provision for your students' needs, such as disabled people or children?
- Is the facility well lit and secure for personal safety and that of belongings?
- Is the facility suitably insured for your session and any accident that may occur?
- Can the emergency services be contacted quickly?
- Are there appropriate emergency procedures at the facility?
- Is the equipment in working condition?
- Is any equipment damaged?
- Are all surfaces appropriate to the sport and the session? For example, a slippery surface is not suitable for badminton, which involves sudden movement, as this could increase the probability of injury.

Requirements for coaching safely

Coaching safety checklist

- Does the coach hold an appropriate qualification to take charge of the session? For example, to take an aerobics session, the coach must be RSA qualified.
- How experienced is the coach in respect of both the sport and the student group? For example, a javelin coach has to be aware of the dangers of the javelin itself.
- Have any references been secured regarding the coach and are they suitable for the student group being coached?
- Can the coach communicate effectively, particularly in relation to equal opportunities?
- Can the coach minimise the possibility of injury through correct warm up and cool down, both general and specific?

Factors affecting participants' safety

Participants' safety checklist

The more relevant information that the coach can gather about and give to the participants before a session, the more likely the coach is to match supply to demand and so to meet the needs of the participants.

- Are there any medical details the coach should be aware of?
- Has a health declaration been signed by all the participants?
- How experienced are the participants?
- Is the grouping of the participants conducive to maximum learning?
- Are the participants correctly prepared for the activity? For example are they wearing suitable clothing and footwear? Has jewellery been removed? Are laces tied?
- If using their own equipment, is it suitable?
- Are the participants physiologically prepared for the activity? For example are they fit enough to participate in strenuous exercise?
- Have they eaten directly before the activity?
- If the exercise is strenuous, has sufficient fluid been consumed?

Written guidelines for safe practice when conducting a coaching session

All of the checklists discussed will now form the basis of your written guidelines for planning safety during coaching sessions. Each sport and each activity within the sport needs specific planning; your guidelines should address all safety issues as relevant in your circumstances.

Remember you are morally and legally responsible for the safety of yourself and your participants. Comprehensively cover all the relevant safety issues and keep an open mind and eye prior to, during and after your sessions in order to improve your service to your clients.

Assignment 13.4

Your local authority is building a Centre of Excellence in your chosen sport and has asked you to compile a report on a consultancy basis regarding a new coaching programme.

They are interested in what safety aspects must be considered in the following areas:

- At the Centre of Excellence itself
- When considering appointing a coach
- When considering recruiting participants for the programme

Unit 14
TECHNIQUES OF SPORTS COACHING

Element 14.1	Examine ways in which psychological factors affect sports performance
Element 14.2	Investigate movement in sport
Element 14.3	Examine physical fitness training for sports
Element 14.4	Investigate the special factors associated with coaching people with disabilities

Element 14.1 Examine ways in which psychological factors affect sports performance

Performance criteria

1 Explain how internal and external pressures affect the participant's performance.
2 Explain how personal characteristics affect the participant's performance
3 Describe the mental skills that assist sports performance.
4 Describe the main features of a good performance goal.

Introduction

This unit examines the factors that affect sports performance. It looks at the need to be both physically and mentally prepared for participation and how physical fitness can be developed through suitable fitness training programmes. The unit also investigates participation in sport by people with disabilities.

Improved excellence in sport has often been seen as a case of developing physical fitness and improving practical skills and technique. The development of a person's mental skills is just as important, as this element will explain. It examines how internal and external pressures, as well as personal characteristics, affect a participant's performance. In addition it develops this psychological approach to performance by looking at the type of mental skills, such as goal setting, that can assist performance.

How internal and external pressures affect the participant's performance

In all areas of life, whether it be at work, school, college or at home, there is always some degree of pressure, for example

- Pressure at work to complete tasks on time, increase sales, reduce costs
- Pressure at school to achieve good examination grades
- Pressure at home to pay the bills, provide for the family

These pressures can be either internal or external. Internal pressures are those over which an individual can exert certain control, and include

- Anxiety
- Motivation
- Personality
- Self-confidence
- The challenge of a goal

External pressures, however, are ones which individuals have little control over, such as parents, peer groups, teachers, colleagues, opposition, coaches and the press (see Figure 14.1).

Fig. 14.1 Someone facing external pressures

Activity

Make a list of some of the pressures you feel that you are under at the present time. By each one indicate whether it is an internal or external pressure. Once complete, discuss the list with classmates or friends and see if there are any common problems. You may want to suggest ways of dealing with these issues.

Internal pressures

Internal pressures are those over which an individual can exert considerable control. How individuals cope with these pressures is often determined by their personalities, and as is often stated 'no two people are the same'. It is important therefore for a coach to develop an understanding of each individual performer in order to build up a psychological profile of them.

One of the internal pressures we listed is anxiety. Anxiety is closely linked to stress; although it is widely acknowledged that some stress is necessary for ambitious performers, too much stress causes worry, waste and under-achievement. Again, how this stress is dealt with is often determined by the performer's personality, and the support received from team-mates, family and coach. The coach can help improve the performer's mental skills, thereby helping the performer to cope with all types of pressure. This area is expanded upon later in this unit.

Another internal pressure is motivation. People participate in sport for a variety of reasons and can 'put pressure on themselves' if they are not achieving their aims. This is most noticeable in highly competitive performers who participate primarily to win. People who play for the fun or recreational aspect are not as susceptible to this type of pressure.

Activity

Look at the list of internal pressures earlier in this element and apply them to
- A competitive performer you know
- A recreational competitor you know

Ask them how these factors affect their performance, if at all, and then draw your own conclusions from your findings.

How will you try and minimise the effects of these pressures with any people you may coach in the future?

External pressures

External pressures, by their very nature, are much harder to control. Outside factors such as parents or peer groups can have a tremendous effect on the performance of a competitor. There is a fine line between parents who encourage their children to achieve and those who exert considerable pressure on them to achieve success. The child put under pressure in this way has the added burden of trying to please parents as well as team-mates and coaches.

Peer-group pressure or pressure exerted by colleagues and team-mates should not be underestimated. A newcomer to a team is often keen to impress and is therefore subject to pressure; an established 'star', joining a new team has similar pressures but for different reasons.

As sportspeople become more successful, especially at national or international level, the pressures on them increase. The media, in particular the press, demand instant or continued success, often becoming vitriolic if failure occurs. Examples of this are the England football team who are expected to win every game they play. You may recall the terrible treatment Graham Taylor received when England failed to qualify for the World Cup in the United States.

A similar type of experience happens every year at Wimbledon. The nation, starved of British success for so many years, joins forces to encourage any British competitor who makes progress in the tournament. This sudden burden of expectation can place intolerable pressure on the player to succeed – not the ideal preparation for an important game of tennis.

Activity

There are many examples of external pressures in sport, from coaches who demand success (as their job often depends on it), to opposition teams or players who decry their opponents' ability to perform or compete.

See if you can identify some of these examples from television or the press and see if they actually do affect the performance of a team or individual. You may have to wait a while to monitor the effect, say after a big match or important competition.

How personal characteristics affect the participant's performance

It is undoubtedly true that the personal characteristics of participants greatly affect their performance. The personality traits, motivation level and degree of mental skill all contribute to the overall performance of many participants. This section will concentrate on two of these aspects, personality and motivation, with direct reference to examples from the world of sport.

Personality

The word 'personality' refers to the mental and emotional qualities that distinguish an individual. Many famous (and infamous) sports-stars are often as well known for their personality as for their sporting prowess.

The exploits of the footballer Eric Cantona have been well documented. He is widely acclaimed as a footballing 'genius' but is also known to have a 'suspect' temperament. Before moving to English football he had numerous run-ins with the French football authorities and is seen to have a very complex personality. Away from football he lists among his hobbies painting and poetry – not the normal pursuits of the average footballer! He would appear to be a very emotional person, with a short fuse. This side to his personality culminated in his attack on a Crystal Palace supporter at a match early in 1995. This incident resulted in Cantona receiving a lengthy ban and hefty fine from his club, Manchester United. Without this passion, it is argued that Cantona would not be the player he is, although he should learn to control his emotions if the problems mentioned above are not to be repeated.

Another talented sportsman, Nick Faldo, is well known for his personality, although he appears to be totally opposite to Eric Cantona. Faldo is often criticised for his lack of emotion or 'cold' approach to golf, a criticism made not only by the media but also by fellow professionals. Faldo rebuts this criticism but does admit to having great powers of concentration and mental toughness, qualities that have brought him much success over the years.

Motivation

Top sports performers, by the nature of their status, tend to be well motivated. Their will to win, and keep winning, often distinguishes them from performers of similar ability. Motivation can be 'inspired' by different things. For example, Wigan Rugby League Club are the most successful club in the history of the English game, repeatedly winning all the major honours. Their motivation comes from the desire to keep winning. Each new crop of players do not want to be associated with failure, so their motivation to succeed is maintained.

Other examples of athletes with different 'types' of motivation are

- *Sally Gunnell* – battled back after serious injury to try and regain her world 400 m hurdles record
- *Diane Modahl* – successfully fought a ban after she failed a drugs test
- *Frank Bruno* – wanted to be world boxing champion even after three previous unsuccessful attempts
- *Chris Eubank* – motivated by money in a sport he often describes as 'barbaric'

Activity

What personal characteristics do you possess? Are you a passionate person like Eric Cantona or unemotional like Nick Faldo? Look more closely at your personality and what motivates you. Get your classmates to do the same and then feed back your findings to one another. Is there a 'mix' in the group or are you all very similar?

The mental skills that assist sports performance

As with practical skills, mental skills can be improved with practice. Four important areas for development are

- The ability to set goals
- The ability to build confidence
- The ability to control emotion
- The ability to concentrate

Ability to set goals

All performers need to set goals. They need targets to aim for in order to progress and improve. Goal setting should be a joint effort between coach and competitor and must incorporate certain features to be effective. Goals need to be realistic, acceptable and measurable.

Realistic goals

It is necessary to set realistic goals, whether they be immediate, short term or long term. If they are not realistic, the chances are they will not be achieved, a situation that often leads to de-motivation.

Acceptable goals

Performers need to see the relevance of the goals and see them as appropriate to their overall aims. One way to accomplish this is to make them exciting, so the athlete sees them as a way of achieving future success.

Measurable goals

It is important that all goals are measurable, in order to recognise success. It is therefore necessary to be able to measure and record results. Any achievements or targets should be recorded for future reference.

Additional features of good target setting are discussed later in this unit.

Ability to build confidence

One of the most used phrases in sport is 'success breeds success'. How often do teams or individuals keep on winning when their confidence is high, or, on the other hand, embark on a losing streak when their confidence is low? A good coach, however, will place more emphasis on athletes doing their best rather than actually winning – the objective being to improve on the athlete's performance.

Confidence is a very fragile thing, but there are ways in which it can be developed. One of them is through persuasion, whether by the coach or the athletes themselves. Coaches can convince performers that they can succeed if it is done with conviction and belief – with reinforcement when goals or targets are attained. Performers can use a technique called 'self-talk', a method of urging themselves on during difficult periods in a match or race.

Activity

One method of confidence building is rehearsal. Try and find someone who uses this method and ask them to explain it to you. Once you understand it, try it on yourself – you never know it just might work!

Ability to control emotion

Eric Cantona excluded, how many other top performers can you think of who have had difficulty in controlling their emotions? One who immediately springs to mind is John McEnroe; there are others who, despite their volatile nature, have been successful, but the key to consistent success lies in the performer's ability to control emotion.

There are many causes of emotional problems, and a coach needs to be aware of them. Some of these factors are linked very closely to the external pressures discussed earlier and are therefore difficult to control. One way to help is by trying to empathise with the performer, displaying understanding and consideration when things are not always working out. This reinforces the importance of getting to know performers and trying to understand what makes them 'tick'.

A coach can also help as performers develop during their 'impressionable' stage – usually the younger years. Coaches should not underestimate the influence they have on young people, who often adopt them as a role model for the future.

Remember, performers who are in control of their emotions will have far more chance of success. Outbursts of anger or frustration, although essential in the psychological make-up of some athletes, more often than not have a detrimental effect on many performers, not least on their ability to concentrate or focus on the task in hand (see Figure 14.2).

Fig. 14.2 An irate coach

Ability to concentrate

The word 'concentration' means the focusing of the mind on something; this is very relevant in a sporting context. Competitors who can focus all their attention on the next task, and not be distracted by their opponents or by a previous error, will be able to maintain concentration and therefore remain focused on the goals they have set.

The main features of a good performance goal

Goal setting, and the importance of it, has already been described. A good performance goal should be

- Specific
- Measurable
- Acceptable
- Realistic
- Time-phased
- Exciting
- Recorded

Psychological factors affect sports performance in many ways. It is vital that you, as a coach, develop the mental skills of your performers at every opportunity, using some of the ideas mentioned. As with physical skills, people progress at different rates – but everyone can improve with practice and dedication.

Assignment 14.1

In conjunction with your tutor or coach, set yourself some performance goals linked closely to the features listed above. Make sure that the goals are challenging, with success dependent on your performance, not the performance of others.

Element 14.2 **Investigate movement in sport**

Performance criteria

1 Explain the principles of movement.
2 Describe the different movements used in sport.
3 Describe the components of movement control.
4 Analyse the movement of a participant in a selected sport, recorded on videotape.

Introduction

Understanding how the parts of the body are used, and move, when in action is important if deficiencies in technique are to be observed and corrections made. This element not only explains the principles of movement but also describes the range of different movements associated with sport. It concludes by describing the components of movement control, fundamental to success in whatever activity is being undertaken.

One facet of successful coaching is the ability of the coach to enhance and develop effective movement. Top-class performers who display almost effortless technique and graceful movement have reached that level through hard work, practice and the support of a coach with an understanding of the principles contained in this element.

Principles of movement

There can be no finer sight than the perfect execution of a particular technique or skill within a game or competition you may be watching. The advances made by television coverage of sport, such as the slow motion replay, give the viewer a fascinating insight into the movements that work towards the perfect cover drive in cricket or the powerful overhead smash in tennis.

Using joints in the correct order

In every discipline the joints of the body need to be controlled so as to work in the correct sequence. Take for example the forehand drive in squash (Figure 14.3). From the ready position the left foot steps forward and across the body and, with a bent elbow, the racket-head is thrown down and out to the side of the body to make contact with the ball. The wrist is then snapped through, the movement concluding with the follow-through.

Fig. 14.3 Forehand drive in squash

Activity

Choose three sports you enjoy watching or participating in and observe how the joints of the body move in a variety of ways within each sport. Note them down as this information will be invaluable when recognising problems with technique. Try and relate your observations to incorrect or ineffective joint movement.

Direction and application of force

As the joints move, in whatever direction, there is going to be an opposite and equal reaction; this well-known theory was put into practice many times during science lessons at school. Coaches should always take it into account. For example, a swimmer who consistently lacks power when pushing off from a tumble-turn may have flaws in technique or there may be a lack of force applied to the swimming pool wall during the push-off phase – a force necessary to give that vital 'thrust'.

Stability

An essential ingredient in applying force is the initial stability of the athlete prior to application. Some sports, such as boxing, do not only have to apply force (when throwing a punch) but also have to resist a force (when receiving a punch). How often have you seen a boxer knocked to the floor, not by the power of a punch, but by the fact he was off-balance when the punch connected?

There are two major factors affecting stability. The first is the stance of the athlete, the second is the athlete's centre of gravity, which is usually around the mid-point of the body.

Stability can be improved in two ways:

- By increasing the size of the stance
- By lowering the centre of gravity

Activity

Think of sports that rely on a high degree of stability for success and then watch how participants within them maintain a stable position. Do they incorporate the ideas discussed above? It is worth remembering that the more stable a body is, the harder it will be to initiate movement. For this reason actions that require rapid and sudden movement tend to have a more unstable starting position. Can you think of any examples?

Different movements used in sport

Within most sports there are a series of movements, some easy to recognise, others not so easy. Here are examples of the main movements used in sport:

- Kicking
- Throwing
- Hitting
- Jumping
- Catching
- Running
- Lifting

Some sports involve only one or two of these, for example the long jump in athletics. Others, such as cricket, may incorporate most of them.

In isolation, the basic concept of say kicking a football seems very simple. In reality, if performed correctly, a series of movements will have been carried out.

As a coach you need to be aware of the technical aspects associated with the different movements used in sport. An effective method of improving technique is by breaking the movement down into easy-to-follow steps. Once mastered, these steps can be performed in their correct sequence with the end result being success.

This method is used in the example below – improving the 'push-pass' in football (Figure 14.4). In all cases the complete action needs to be demonstrated beforehand in order to provide a visual image for the person being coached.

1. Demonstration of push pass.
2. Correct placement of non-kicking foot, by the side of the ball, pointing at intended target
3. Contact made with mid-point of the ball with the inside of the kicking foot; body positioned over the ball.
4. Maintain body position and follow through with kicking foot.

Fig. 14.4 The push-pass in football

This method of breaking down movements into smaller components can be used for all the movements in sport.

Activity

From the list of movements detailed choose one technique and then break the complete action down into more manageable components. You may want to combine movements, for example a football goalkeeper jumping and catching a high cross.

Components of movement control

As performers gain experience the movements they make become almost automatic. A similar thing happens when learning to drive a car. Initially, actions like changing gear or checking the rear view mirror need considerable thought and concentration. As the driver becomes more proficient these actions are performed with little thought and as a matter of course.

The same occurs in sport. For a participant to reach a level of performance whereby their actions and movement appear instinctive, a great deal of practice will have been undertaken to reach this position. As with improving technique, a coach can break down the components of movement control. The four main stages are

- Perception
- Decision making
- Organising the response
- Feedback

Perception

Perception is the ability to recognise instinctively what is happening. In sporting terms it is often referred to as 'reading the game'. An excellent example of someone who excelled at this is the footballer Gary Lineker. He always appeared to find space in a normally congested penalty box by reading the game and predicting where the ball would eventually arrive.

Decision making

As soon as it has been perceived what is happening, a decision has to be made as to the response. In the majority of competitive sports the time allowed to do this is very small. How many times can you recall a commentator remarking on a performer getting caught in two minds? These split-second decisions can often make the difference between failure and success. The tennis player who attacks the net at the correct time stands far more chance of making a winning volley than one who does not.

Organising the response

Once a decision has been taken a suitable action or response needs to be made. Put yourself in the position of a goalkeeper faced by an onrushing attacker. You have perceived what is happening, have made the decision to leave your line but what do you do now? Do you

- Commit yourself to trying to take the ball?
- Stand up as long as possible trying to delay the striker?
- Try and force the player out wide thereby narrowing the angle?

Once you have decided the next thing to do is make the movements required to implement your decision – all in a split second!

Feedback

After completing the first three stages it is time for action. Let us hope that correct decisions have been made and necessary steps taken to respond accordingly.

It is important for a coach, and a performer, to reflect on decisions made in order to evaluate their success or otherwise. The correct decisions will not be made every time but a coach can help a performer become more decisive and effective in responding to situations or events.

Analysing the movement of a participant, recorded on video

The purpose of this element is to enhance the coach's understanding of the range of movements associated with a particular sport. In isolation, this knowledge is of little value unless it can be used in identifying faults and, more importantly, making corrections. To the naked eye and at normal speed, it is relatively easy to recognise a problem, but far more difficult actually to pinpoint the cause of the problem (unless it is obvious).

Use of the camcorder

A vital tool being used by many coaches today is the camcorder. Recording someone's performance in this way not only allows the coach (and participant) to review action over and over again, but also enables specific movements to be viewed in slow motion or in a still frame.

Identifying components

It is important not only to identify poor technique and errors but also to highlight and emphasise good technique. Doing this will improve the confidence of the performer, encouraging the self-belief to correct any faults that may be evident in some other area of play.

Observation checklist

An effective way of collating information on performance is by recording observation on a checklist. The example below is one way in which such a list can be used.

OBSERVATION CHECKLIST

NAME:
Janice Smith

TECHNIQUE:
Forehand drive – Squash

PROBLEM(S):
1 Player off balance when playing the shot
2 Lack of power/distance

REASON:
1 Feet in wrong position, head drops
2 Shot finishes too soon, aiming too low

CORRECTION:
1 Step forwards and across, keep head up and watch the ball
2 Higher follow-through, aim higher on front wall

ADDITIONAL COMMENT:
Consistent failing on forehand drive. Movement and foot position on backhand drive much more effective.

PRACTICE:
Solo – back-wall drives aiming for slight overhit
Pair – one player boast/one player drive – alternate forehand/backhand

Assignment 14.2

Using this format, or one of your own design, record and then analyse the various movements of classmates participating in a range of activities. Concentrate on the issues discussed in this element with particular reference to the principles of movement and the components of movement control.

Element 14.3 Examine physical fitness training for sports

```
Performance criteria

1  Explain the components of physical fitness.
2  Explain the principles of training.
3  Describe the main parts of the human body which affect sports performance.
4  Describe types of fitness training.
5  Devise a suitable fitness training programme for a participant in a selected
   sport.
```

Introduction

This element examines physical fitness training for sports. As a coach your education in this area will help you prepare both safe and effective training programmes. It is essential though to remain up-to-date with current practice as well as striving to improve your own knowledge of training techniques and how the human body works.

As far as sport is concerned, the fitter that competitors are, the better, and more successful they will be. Everybody needs a minimal level of fitness to exist, whereas sportsmen and sportswomen need a far higher degree of physical fitness in order to compete in their chosen activity.

Fitness is a combination of a number of physical qualities, all enhanced by exercise. This element examines the components of physical fitness by describing the parts of the human body affecting sports performance. It looks at a variety of types of fitness training and gives pointers as to suitable training programmes in a range of sports.

Components of physical fitness

There are four components of physical fitness:

- Endurance
- Strength
- Flexibility
- Speed

All are required, in varying degrees, in most sports, so time needs to be taken to understand them more fully.

Endurance

Endurance is the capacity of the body to maintain continued physical activity of low intensity. It is often referred to as stamina and can be divided into aerobic endurance and muscular endurance.

Aerobic endurance

Aerobic fitness relies on the ability of the heart, lungs and circulatory system to supply the muscles of the body with the energy they require to work for long periods. The muscles used for aerobic activity will be explained later in the section.

Muscular endurance

Muscular endurance relates to the ability of a small number of muscles to sustain activity over a long period. To achieve this, muscles need to be able to retain the ability to remove waste products produced during use.

Strength

Strength can be defined as the ability of one or more muscles to apply force. There are three types of strength: static, explosive and dynamic strength.

- *Static strength* – strength applied to an opposing force (e.g. scrummage in rugby)
- *Explosive strength* – energy used in one explosive act (e.g. shot putt – Figure 14.5)
- *Dynamic strength* (endurance) – effort required for an extended period of time (e.g. sprint swimmer)

Fig. 14.5 Explosive strength in the shot putt

Flexibility

Flexibility refers to the range of limb movement around the joints of the body. Increased flexibility will enhance both mobility and agility and lessen the risk of strains and tears in muscles and cartilage (connective tissue).

Speed

Speed is an important part of most sports and can be described as the time taken to co-ordinate the movement of the body or individual joints. It can relate to the rapidity of motion, for example the speed a goalkeeper leaves the line to deny an attacker time and space (Figure 14.6) or the rapidity of action when the recipient of a bouncer bowled in cricket ducks out of the way.

Fig. 14.6 A goalkeeper needs to move quickly

Principles of training

Being involved in training, from a coaching point of view, can be a very rewarding experience. It is important though to understand some basic facts before designing a programme for the people you intend to coach.

Individual differences

No two people are the same. When designing a training programme you should bear in mind the individual differences people have, such as their

- Motivation for participating
- Ability to participate
- Level of fitness
- Commitments outside of the sport
- Age and maturity
- Previous experience

Activity

This list is by no means comprehensive. Try and find out the individual differences that exist within your class or club where you play – using the list as a starting-point. Add to the list as necessary. You should soon be in a position to compile a questionnaire that could be issued to all new participants before you design their training programme.

Adaptation

As training progresses, the body will adapt to the demands made upon it. There may be improvements in strength, flexibility, endurance and speed. The coach needs a good knowledge of how these changes occur so as not to either rush the processes or continue with training that is not effective.

Overload

The muscles of the body will become stronger or more effective only if they are forced to work harder than they are used to. This can be achieved by increasing the intensity of the exercise, such as using heavier weights, or the duration of the exercise, by making the muscles work for longer periods of time.

Progression

The best way to improve the performance of the body is through steady progress. The muscles and ligaments need time to adapt to the increased pressures put upon them, and if this is done too quickly injury may result. As a consequence, overload should be gradual.

Specificity

Different sports have different demands. The training programme you devise needs to be linked to the physical demands of the sport for which your performer is training. It is important therefore to have an in-depth knowledge of the physical requirements of the sport you are coaching.

Variation

It is often said that variety is the spice of life. This need for variety can also be applied to training programmes as predictability can lead to boredom and ultimately lack of progress. Coaches need to utilise a range of exercises and routines in order to maintain interest and enjoyment in training.

Long-term planning

Success does not happen overnight. Athletes spend years striving towards excellence and this point needs to be stressed to people starting out in a sport. The technique of goal-setting (previously discussed) should be used to set short and medium-term targets in addition to more long-term or ultimate aims.

Reversibility

Exercise and training result in improved physical fitness, but the body will also adapt to lack of use. Endurance, strength and flexibility will all decline if training is neglected or curtailed. It is unrealistic therefore to expect athletes who have missed training over a period of time, to be in the same condition as they were prior to the absence.

Main parts of the human body which affect sports performance

The human body is very complex. It has a range of systems, many of which affect sports performance. This section will describe how the skeleton, muscular system, energy systems and circulatory system are involved in physical activity.

Skeleton

The skeleton has four main functions:

- It supports the body, giving it shape
- It protects the delicate parts of the body, such as the heart
- It allows the body to make a wide range of movement
- It produces blood cells in the marrow of larger bones

The skeleton is made mainly of bone, a hard tissue comprised of large amounts of calcium. It is divided into two main parts, the axial skeleton and the appendicular skeleton.

The axial skeleton consists of the skull, vertebral column, ribs and sternum. It is this part that supports the body.

The appendicular skeleton consists of the arms and shoulder girdle and the legs and hip girdle. This part allows movement of the limbs.

To enable the skeleton to move it is jointed. These joints, with the help of muscles, cartilage, ligaments and a liquid called synovial fluid, allow movement throughout the skeleton.

Muscular system

Like the skeleton, muscles have more than one function. Muscles assist movement, help with the circulation of blood and give us our own individual shape. The body has two types of muscle, voluntary muscles which (as their name suggests) we have control over (e.g. those used in walking), and involuntary muscles, which operate automatically. These muscles operate such things as bowel movement; the major involuntary muscle is the heart.

What is a muscle?

A muscle is a collection of fibres enclosed by a layer of tissue. This fibre is linked to the central nervous system which stimulates the muscle to contract or shorten as required. All muscles have a partner that produces an opposite movement, so that as one muscle contracts the other relaxes and stretches.

To do this the muscles need energy, which comes from the food we eat. These energy systems are mentioned later.

The fibres which make up muscles can be of the 'fast-twitch' variety – the type which produce powerful movement over a short period – or the 'slow-twitch' variety, the ones which allow movement over longer periods.

Energy systems

As we know already, muscles in the body require energy to work. There are basically three types of energy systems in operation in the body. They all require a substance called adenosine triphosphate (ATP) which is made in the body's cells and helps muscles to contract. To find out more about these systems carry out the activity below.

Activity

All sportsmen and sportswomen use the systems outlined in differing proportions. Two of the systems produce anaerobic energy, the other aerobic energy. Research all three making notes on how each one works. You should then be in a position to identify the types of sports that use each system, or combination of systems.

Circulatory system

As you should have discovered by now, the energy supplies in muscles will be quickly used up unless oxygen is available. This is where the circulatory system comes in. This system delivers oxygen, as well as food and hormones, to the body cells through blood, pumped around the body by the heart. Blood not only delivers vital 'supplies', but also removes waste products such as carbon dioxide, heat and lactic acid.

The heart is vital to the circulatory system. During exercise it beats much faster and more powerfully than when at rest, responding to the increased demands made upon it by the body.

Respiratory system

The circulatory system is closely linked to the respiratory system, the process by which oxygen is taken from the air we breathe and delivered to the cells of the body. Breathing takes place when the lungs increase in size (through muscle action) and draw in air through the mouth and nose. Oxygen in this air is then transferred to the blood stream via small air sacs in the lungs called alveoli. At the same time carbon dioxide is passed from the blood to the lungs and is exhaled as the lungs decrease in size.

Types of fitness training

Whatever sport you coach, and training routines you deploy, it is important to have an understanding of the different training methods available. Fundamental to any fitness training is a warm up and cool down.

A warm up is essential as it prepares the body for the increased demands to be made upon it, as well as helping to guard against injury once strenuous activity begins.

A cool down, although often neglected, is just as important. It helps the body return to its normal state, in particular preventing muscle stiffness or soreness.

We consider various types of fitness training:

- Aerobic training
- Plyometrics
- Speed drills
- Resistance training
- Sprint training
- Stretching, warm up and cool down

Aerobic training

Aerobic training conditions the body to exercise over a long continuous period of time. One way of achieving this is by continuous training; as the name suggests, this is exercise without rest periods. This type of training increases lung efficiency and improves the work capacity of the heart.

Continuous training should be built up slowly, aiming initially to work at approximately 75 per cent of the maximum heart rate. (Depending on age, maximum heart rate can be 220 beats per minute.) This can be increased slightly as fitness improves.

Another way to train aerobically is by using the Fartlek method. This involves running over long distances, at low intensity, interspersed with short bursts of more intense activity. More prolonged intense activity and less low intense activity will improve the anaerobic capacity of the athlete.

Plyometrics

Plyometrics is a training method used to increase power. It involves stretching a muscle before it contracts which stores elastic energy in the muscle. Plyometrics conditions the muscles to permit faster and more powerful movement which in turn increases speed and power. Plyometrics places strain on joints and therefore requires close supervision and a high degree of expertise and preparation.

Speed drills

Speed training needs to concentrate on strength, endurance and power, remembering to maintain technique at all times. It needs to involve practising movement at a speed faster than it would normally be performed.

Resistance training

Resistance work, linked to weight training, can be used to either increase strength by using heavier resistance (heavier weights) with fewer repetitions or to improve endurance by increasing the repetitions and reducing the resistance (lighter weights).

Sprint training

Spring training will be of real benefit only if technique is maintained throughout. Training of this type includes acceleration sprints where the athlete gradually increases pace up to maximum and repetition sprints where the recovery time allowed encourages sound technique.

Stretching, warm up and cool down

The importance of warming up and cooling down has already been stressed, as has the need for flexibility. An ideal way to improve the latter is by stretching, in particular static stretching.

Static stretching involves lengthening a muscle and then holding it in that position for a few seconds (approx. 30 seconds). Stretching should be incorporated in every warm up session once the muscles are warm and, just as importantly, during the cool down.

Devising a suitable fitness training programme for a participant in a selected sport

The information contained in this element outlines the major ingredients of fitness training for sport. Although many sports have similar characteristics, with respect to physical performance (e.g. football and rugby), there are differences which need to be reflected in the type of training that participants undertake.

When planning a fitness training programme, it is important to look in depth at the requirements of the sport in question in order to prepare a programme that specifically addresses its key issues.

Aims and objectives

Any fitness programme should have clear aims and objectives. The aim of the programme will focus attention on what is to be improved (e.g. endurance, strength, flexibility and speed), while the objectives will detail how the aims will be achieved through the type of exercise (e.g. stretching, muscle building, weight training, running or circuit training).

Duration

When preparing a programme it is also important to decide upon its duration. This could be short term (to address a current problem or need) or long term (aimed at a particular event or future ambitions).

Assignment 14.3

Prepare a fitness training programme for two participants in contrasting sports. Think carefully about the requirements of each before committing your thoughts to paper. Try to incorporate a variety of different training methods in your programme to achieve the aims you have stated.

Use the information in this element as a starting-point. Build on it with additional reading and research.

Element 14.4 Investigate the special factors associated with coaching people with disabilities

Performance criteria

1 Describe types of impairment.
2 Explain barriers to participation.
3 Describe appropriate means of communication with people with disabilities.
4 Explain how sports can be adapted for people with disabilities.
5 Produce safety guidelines for coaching people with disabilities.
6 Describe organisations with expertise in working with sports participants with disabilities.

Introduction

This element should dispel many of the myths associated with disability and sports participation. It aims to develop confidence in students, enabling them to actively participate in helping people with disabilities partake in a range of sports and physical activities. However, it is important to remember that additional and more comprehensive information, available from some of the organisations mentioned in this element, should be sought *before* undertaking any coaching with people with disabilities.

Many very good and committed coaches are apprehensive when it comes to coaching people with disabilities. In addition to addressing many key issues relating to disability, this element will allay apprehension and give practical advice on how to adapt and ultimately provide access to a range of activities.

Types of impairment

There are many varied types of disabilities, so to list and describe them all would be almost impossible. The types of impairments expanded upon below are just a small example of some of the terms you may come across during your coaching.

- *Amputee* – Someone who has lost one or more limbs or part of a limb
- *Hidden impairment* – A hidden impairment is one which is not obvious to the eye, including conditions such as diabetes
- *Paraplegic* – A person who has lost the use of both legs
- *Quadriplegic* – Someone suffering from paralysis of all four limbs

- *Physical disability* – Disability affecting the movements of the body
- *Sensory disability* – Disability affecting sight or hearing
- *Learning difficulty* – Terminology given to conditions affecting a person's ability to absorb and implement information, such as autism
- *Les autres* – Term covering disability that does not fit into other categories

When coaching, or during normal conversation with physically impaired people, offence can easily be caused if thought is not given to the type of language used to describe their condition. In order not to fall into this trap, carry out this activity.

Activity

Disabled people like to be classed as individuals. The way they are addressed (often put into generalised groups) can cause anger and frustration. As incorrect terminology is often used through lack of knowledge, spend some time talking to a range of people with disabilities, finding out how they prefer to be addressed.

If possible, ask your fellow students to do the same. In this way a comprehensive list can be prepared and made available for use by everyone.

Barriers to participation

Perceptions

It is thought, quite wrongly, that people with disabilities are reluctant to participate in physical activity. It is believed that they are fragile or that they like to participate in a sport only with people of similar disabilities to themselves.

Many of these so-called 'barriers' are problems perceived by able-bodied people who do not fully understand that with help, planning and with a change in attitude, many of the obstacles put in the way of participation can be removed.

Negative attitudes

Many disabled people often become disheartened with the general public's misperceptions. As a consequence they may lack self-esteem or confidence, so you, as a coach, may have to spend some time addressing this.

Not all barriers are the result of negative attitudes. Some of them are very real, but with increased awareness, many can be overcome.

Access

A great many of the sports facilities in Britain were built with little or no consideration for people with disabilities. Fortunately, after strong representation by organisations committed to improving access for disabled groups and with a general increase in awareness, buildings constructed today tend to be much more 'user-friendly'.

Successful coaching of disabled people can be greatly enhanced by ensuring that any access problems be kept to a minimum. For this reason all facilities need to be carefully checked for appropriateness well in advance of an event or coaching programme (see Figures 14.7 and 14.8).

Fig. 14.7 Designated parking space for disabled users of a sports facility

Fig. 14.8 Suitable toilet facilities for disabled people
(Photos: P. Kleesman, reproduced by kind permission of South East Derbyshire College)

Areas of access to be considered should include:

- Designated (and wide) parking bays
- Ramps
- Lifts to different levels

Activity

Visit your local sports centre and investigate whether the access it provides is suitable for disabled people. If problems do exist, note down ways that they could be overcome. Discuss your findings with other members of the group to see if many of the issues are common to a number of facilities.

Pricing

When facilities are good for disabled people, there is also the need to ensure they are affordable. Many disabled people are on low incomes and have additional costs such as special transport and equipment needs. A sympathetic pricing structure will encourage participation by people with disabilities.

Transport

Transport to and from facilities and events can be a problem. Volunteers are always very welcome in helping with transport and with general logistical problems when disabled people are participating in activities.

Competition opportunities

As the number of disabled people participating in sport grows, so does the opportunity for them to compete in competitions. Many people have heard of the Paralympics, but there is also a network of international, national and regional competitions which are not so well known. To ensure that participants compete against people of similar ability, they are placed into categories that relate to their type of disability or to what is known as their 'performance profile'.

Activity

The British Sports Association for the Disabled (BSAD) have information on the profile system. Write to them requesting this information, explaining your interest in coaching people with disabilities. You may get other information to help with this element of your studies.
BSAD
Sole Cast House
13–27 Brunswick Place
London N1 6DX
Tel. 0171 490 4919

Appropriate means of communication with people with disabilities

Effective communication is one of the key elements in successful coaching. To be effective communication should be 'two way', allowing for feedback from the person being coached. Asking for their ideas/input will enhance their confidence and self esteem. When dealing with people with disabilities far more thought and planning needs to be given in how to 'get your message across'. Good coach practice such as making explanations clear and relevant still apply but many other factors need to be considered. The three major means of communication are

- Visual
- Verbal
- Tactile

Visual communication

Visual communication is vitally important when coaching athletes with either hearing or visual impairment. Many people with visual impairment have some vision, so when using demonstrations or written materials, it is important that the coach

- Ensures that any written material is produced in large type
- Faces the athletes when addressing them
- Stands facing the light and in a place where all the athletes can see and hear
- Uses brightly coloured equipment

Verbal communication

Both visually and hearing impaired athletes will benefit greatly if the coach follows some simple guidelines when using verbal communication. It is important that the coach

- Speaks slowly and pronounces words clearly
- Minimises external noise or distractions
- Is prepared to repeat instructions

Tactile communication

The use of touch is often neglected as a means of communication, but can be an effective way to communicate with disabled sportspeople. Touch can be used to

- Guide athletes around an area, following familiarisation with the training environment
- Aid body positioning or movement
- Attract attention
- Establish communication

The activity on page 224 offers an opportunity to implement some of the ideas mentioned. Coaches who work with people with disabilities will need the ability to adjust their methods of communication to suit individuals or groups, and, as with most things, this skill will improve with practice.

How different sports can be adapted for people with disabilities

It is now widely acknowledged in the sporting world that many activities have to be adapted to the needs of particular groups if successful or meaningful participation is to be achieved. Junior sport provides good examples of this, in tennis, basketball and football. In all of these activities, adaptations have been made to allow easier skill acquisition or more enjoyment and involvement. In tennis, short tennis has been introduced with a smaller court, lower net and lighter equipment. In basketball and football, similar changes have been made with the equipment and the dimensions of the court or pitch.

Sports competitors with disabilities often require similar adaptations, many of which can be easily implemented.

The following ideas are just some you may want to use. See if you can add to the list:

- Limit the area of play to reduce the need for mobility
- Use larger or smaller balls
- Widen the goals
- Lower the net
- Use softer balls to reduce bounce
- Give players defined areas of play to limit interference from other players
- Use bright coloured equipment

Activity

Choose a sport or activity that you think could be adapted for disabled people and prepare a 20 minute session for delivery within your own group. To make the exercise realistic the group will need to simulate a form of disability. For example, hearing impairment could be simulated by wearing ear muffs. You will need to plan carefully how the sport or activity will be adapted and how you intend to communicate with the group.

Once the session has been delivered, ask for feedback from the group on what went well or badly.

Try and incorporate any suggestions for improvements in future sessions.

Safety guidelines for coaching people with disabilities

When coaching any sport, the safety of participants and coaching staff should be of paramount importance. Before taking any session, coaches need to make sure that

- They have insurance cover for personal liability
- They know the location of first aid equipment and trained assistance

- They have access to a telephone in case of emergencies
- They are familiar with evacuation routes and procedures in case of fire

Additional considerations need to be taken into account when working with disabled sportspeople.

Medical conditions

Many disabled people suffer from medical conditions that are not always evident, such as epilepsy and heart conditions. It is always advisable to ask participants well in advance if they have any medical conditions you need to be aware of. Guidance should also be sought from any appropriate national bodies or organisations such as MIND or the British Amputee Sports Federation.

Lifting and carrying

It may be necessary to lift and carry some participants, which is a potentially hazardous procedure, both for the disabled person and the people who are lifting and carrying. If carrying someone is necessary, you should

- Check that the person being lifted is agreeable
- Ask how the person would like to be lifted
- Always lift and lower with a straight back and bent knees
- Be clear on what you are going to do *before* you start
- Get help if at all possible
- Make sure the person is comfortable at all times

Accidents

Accidents will happen, but coaches with a good awareness of safety will be in a position to make sure they occur as little as possible. Planning, preparation, alertness, consideration and knowledge of your sport will all reduce the opportunities for unsafe practice. Coaches are advised to have some form of accident insurance.

Organisations with expertise in working with sports participants with disabilities

Throughout the UK there is a network of organisations with expertise in working with sports participants with disabilities. Of these, two organisations, UK Sports Association for People with Mental Handicap (UKSAPMH) and the British Sports Association for the Disabled (BSAD), are known as national development organisations. Others (mentioned later) are known as national disability sports organisations.

CASE STUDY

British Sports Association for the Disabled

The British Sports Association for the Disabled (BSAD) was founded in 1961 by Sir Ludwig Guttman, to provide and develop sport and physical recreation for people with disabilities. It has a wide membership throughout the UK, with regional offices, and works very closely with Sports Associations for the Disabled in Northern Ireland, Scotland and Wales. It provides recreational activities in a range of sports as well as many opportunities for competitive sport at local, regional, national and international level.

The BSAD takes great pride in its provision of coach training for people working with disabled people. This includes coaching and development days and disability awareness training. It also provides information and advice to leisure providers and local authorities in such areas as access and integration, and has helped to raise the profile of sport for people with disabilities throughout the UK.

As a charity, the BSAD relies very heavily on personal donations and commercial sponsorship for financial support. It also relies on the good will of an army of volunteers who help with administration and general logistical problems.

The BSAD has ten main aims and objectives:

1 To provide opportunities for people with any type of disability to enjoy and compete in physical recreation and sport in accordance with an individual's own wishes
2 To promote the benefits of physical recreation and sport to all people with disabilities and to encourage participation
3 To develop opportunities for the interaction of people with disabilities and able-bodied people in physical recreation and sport, in particular through liaison with the national governing bodies of sport
4 To assist with the establishment and development of physical recreation and sports clubs and organisations for people with disabilities
5 To support clubs and local groups in their provision of recreational and sporting opportunities for people with disabilities and to help to introduce new sports
6 To maintain a comprehensive information and advice service on all aspects of sport for people with disabilities
7 To co-ordinate and ensure the provision and improvement of opportunities for coaching and training in sport for and by people with disabilities
8 To encourage people with disabilities to take an active role in the organisation and development of sport at all levels
9 To educate the general public, the sporting world and the media to be aware of the sporting abilities and achievements of people with disabilities in a step towards total interaction
10 To enhance the image and self-image of sport for people with disabilities through a professional approach to the provision of support

(The aims and objectives are reproduced with the permission of the BSAD.)

National disability sports organisations

In addition to the national development organisations, there are a range of more specific national disability sports organisations. They include

- British Blind Sport (BBS)
- British Wheelchair Sports Federation (BWSF)
- British Amputee Sports Federation (BASF)
- British Les Autres Sports Association (BLASA)
- Cerebral Palsy Sport (CP Sport)
- British Deaf Sports Council (BDSC)

Assignment 14.4

Research one of the organisations listed above and prepare a short factsheet on it for use by the rest of your group. Other members of the group should do the same, but for alternative organisations and by doing so a valuable and informative resource could be produced.

Unit 15
HUMAN PHYSIOLOGY

Element 15.1   Describe the skeletal and muscular systems of the human body

Element 15.2   Describe the cardiovascular and respiratory systems

Element 15.3   Explain the digestive system and the nutritional requirements of the human body

Element 15.1   Describe the skeletal and muscular systems of the human body

---

Performance criteria

1   Describe the main functions of the human skeletal system.
2   Use an annotated diagram to describe the macroscopic appearance and organisation of the major bones and joints of the skeleton.
3   Use diagrams to describe the characteristic microscopic features of the three types of muscle.
4   Explain the arrangement of the muscle groups and their attachment to bones.
5   Relate the macroscopic and microscopic structure of the muscle groups to function.
6   Explain the relationship between the muscle groups, joints and bones in movement.

Introduction

The aim of this unit is to introduce you to the major structures and systems of the human body. In addition nutritional requirements and the effects of different life stages are described. Units 12, 13 and 14 will also be found helpful.

The information within this unit is limited; it is seen only as an introduction to human physiology with no application; this application comes in Unit 12 on Health Related Fitness.

The details of this unit are also factual and give little scope for individual flexibility; as a consequence not all of the performance criteria are developed fully as students would merely have to copy these notes and present them as evidence for their portfolio. Although many students would appreciate this, it is not acceptable for the accurate assessment of GNVQ.

We usually take our bodies for granted; they function automatically and we rarely have to give them a second thought. This balanced state is easily disrupted by illness or injury and it is only then that we tend to pay our bodies the attention they deserve.

In order to develop our fitness programmes and achieve the optimum benefits and performance, we must understand the basic details of human physiology and apply our knowledge of sport to these details to produce a superior programme for performance.

In order to understand the functions of the human body we must look at the structure first; this includes the skeleton, muscles and joints and their relationship to produce movement.

Main functions of the human skeletal system

There are four main functions of the human skeleton:
- Protection
- Support
- Movement and attachment
- Blood production

Protection

The skeleton is designed in such a way that the delicate parts of the body are protected. The delicate parts are the major organs, for example the rib cage protects the heart and lungs, while the cranium protects the brain.

Support

The skeleton gives the human body structure. It supports the organs and tissues and gives us our form. Without it we would collapse under our own body weight. The bones are also used to suspend the vital organs.

Movement and attachment

The skeleton is jointed to allow movement. A joint is the articulation of two or more connecting bones. The joint provides either stability or mobility depending on its structure. A stable joint provides little movement, whereas an unstable joint provides a wide range of movement. Muscles are attached to bones by tendons.

Blood production

Both red and white blood cells are produced in the bone marrow; the bones also store minerals for other body functions.

Major bones and joints of the skeleton

Figure 15.1 labels the major bones in the body. The joints of the skeleton are explained at the end of this element.

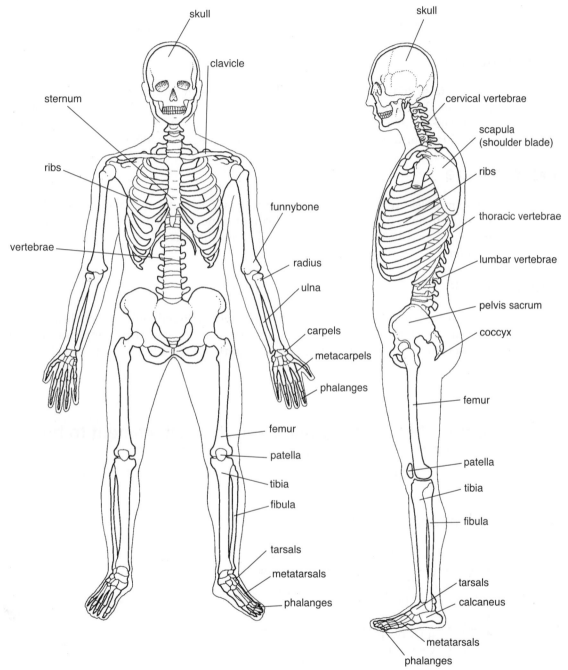

Fig. 15.1 Major bones in the body

Microscopic features of the three types of muscle

Muscles are primarily concerned with movement but with over 600 voluntary muscles we do have some control over our form; through muscle building we can develop the muscles to their maximum potential and thus effecting our individual shape.

There are three muscle groups: striated, smooth and cardiac muscle.

Striated muscle

Striated (also known as striped or skeletal) muscles are voluntary muscles; we call on these muscles by nerve stimuli, for instance when we are simply walking or playing sport. The voluntary muscles make up 40 per cent of our body weight and there are over 150 in our head and neck. The voluntary muscles are identified in Figure 15.2.

Smooth muscle

These muscles are involuntary, in other words they will contract and relax whether we want them to or not. They are made up of spindle shaped cells. Examples include muscles found in the blood vessels and those that operate the bowel, uterus and bladder.

Cardiac muscle

The cardiac muscle is highly specialised and is found only in the heart. It is involuntary and is made up of branched fibres, giving it a striped appearance. The rate of contraction of the cardiac muscle is part of a complex nervous and chemical system.

Arrangement of the muscle groups and their attachment to bone

Figure 15.2 identifies various muscle groups; they are all striated or voluntary muscles.

Examples of muscle groups

- *Trunk* – latissimus dorsi, trapezius, erector spinae
- *Abdomen* – obliques, rectus abdominus
- *Shoulders* – deltoids
- *Upper arm* – biceps, triceps
- *Hip* – hip flexors
- *Thigh* – quadriceps, hamstrings
- *Lower leg* – gastrocnemius, soleus, tibialis anterior

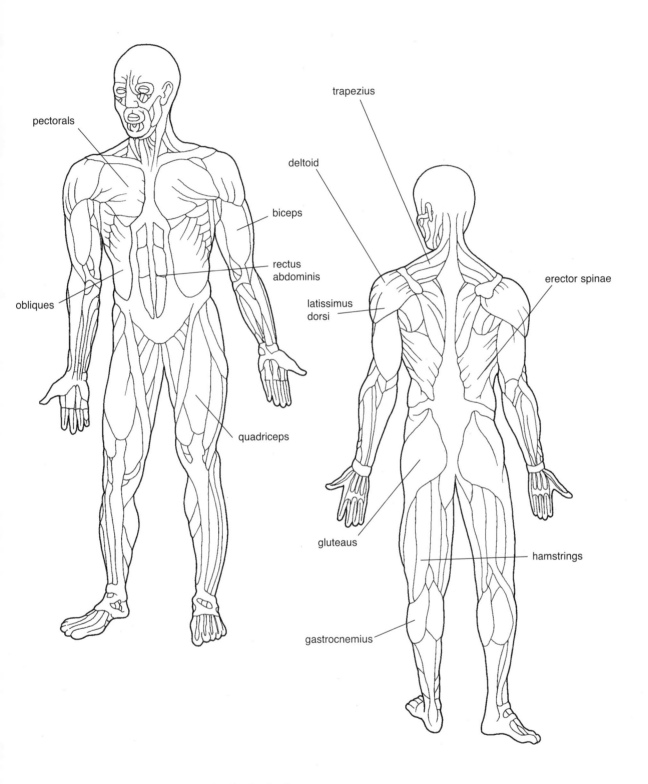

Fig. 15.2 Major voluntary muscles in the body

Attachment to bone

Muscles are attached to bones by tendons; these act as buffers to sharp movement and help prevent injury.

Strong bands of fibre called ligaments attach bone to bone; these add stability to our joints.

Function of muscle groups

Muscle action produces movement; there are various types of muscle action depending on the joints involved. They are

- *Abduction* – movement of the bone away from the body mid-line, either in a horizontal or vertical plane
- *Adduction* – movement of the bone towards the body mid-line, either in a horizontal or vertical plane
- *Extension* – the increasing of an angle between bones
- *Flexion* – the decreasing of an angle between bones
- *Rotation* – movement of the bone around a central axis, for example the arm rotates at the shoulder

Examples are identified in Figure 15.3.

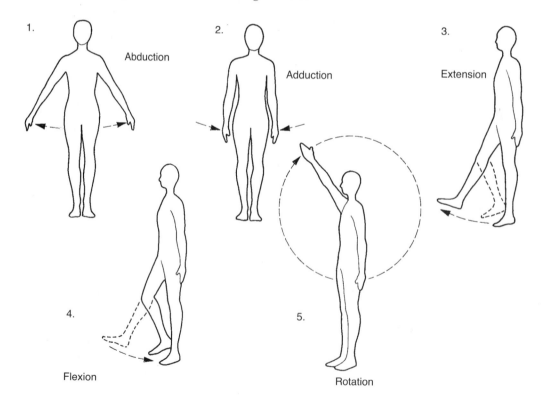

Fig. 15.3 Measurement through muscle action

Relationship between muscles, joints and bones in movement

The muscle types and groups have now been clearly explained; however, it is the relationship between the joints, the muscle and the bone that produces a specific movement and it is this relationship that allows the human body to be so precise and accurate.

Synovial joints

Accurate and smooth movement relies on one particular type of joint – the synovial joint. All synovial joints have the following characteristics:

- The bones are covered with articular (hyaline) cartilage which is tough, yet smooth and shiny. This reduces friction between bones.
- Within the joint there is a liquid which is yellow and oily. This is called synovial fluid, which also reduces friction; it provides a medium between the bones which can absorb any debris and also feeds the hyaline cartilage.
- The synovial fluid is produced by the synovial membrane which surrounds the joint.
- The bones are held together by strong fibrous bands called ligaments. These add stability to the joints.

There are four types of synovial joints:

- Ball and socket (e.g. the hip)
- Hinge (e.g. the knee)
- Condyloid (e.g. the wrist)
- Saddle (e.g. the thumb)

Figure 15.4 provides further information

The hip

The elbow

Ball and socket joint
Movement is free and easy as the ball of the femur fits the depression of the pelvis

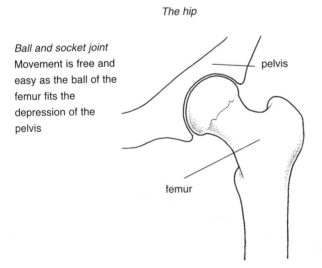

pelvis

femur

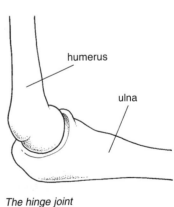

humerus

ulna

The hinge joint
Movement is in one plane only; movement is free but stable

Fig. 15.4 Four types of synovial joints (continued on following page)

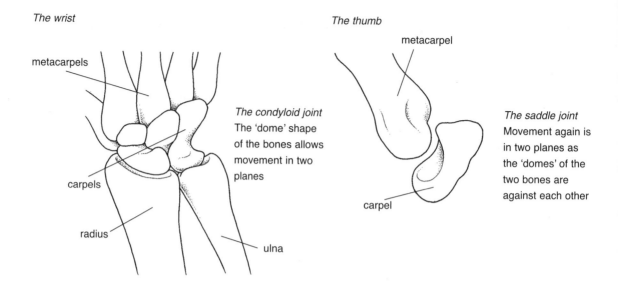

The wrist

metacarpels

carpels

radius

ulna

The condyloid joint
The 'dome' shape
of the bones allows
movement in two
planes

The thumb

metacarpel

carpel

The saddle joint
Movement again is
in two planes as
the 'domes' of the
two bones are
against each other

Fig. 15.4 Four types of synovial joints (continued from previous page)

Levers

Body movement actually occurs when the striated muscle pulls hard enough on the bones. The muscles use the bones as levers. Levers are rigid; they comprise a pivot (the point which is hinged) and two points of force, one of which is an object or weight, the other is effort or energy. There are three different types of levers depending on the positioning of the pivot, force and effort; the body uses all three (see Figure 15.5).

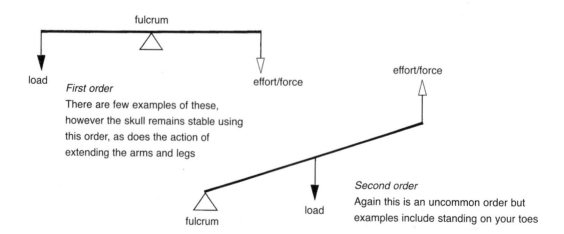

Levers
The bones of the body use levers to produce movement
There are three orders of levers

fulcrum

load

First order
There are few examples of these,
however the skull remains stable using
this order, as does the action of
extending the arms and legs

effort/force

effort/force

fulcrum

load

Second order
Again this is an uncommon order but
examples include standing on your toes

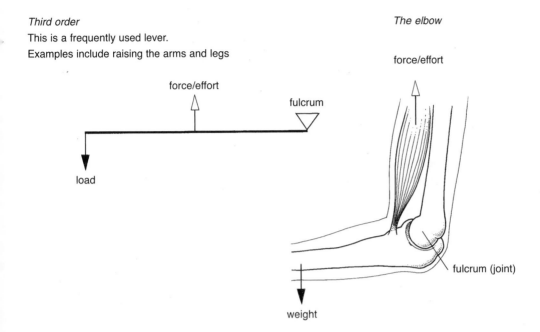

Third order
This is a frequently used lever.
Examples include raising the arms and legs

force/effort

fulcrum

load

The elbow

force/effort

fulcrum (joint)

weight

Fig. 15.5 The three types of lever

Pair principle

If a muscle acts across a joint and pulls two bones closer together, then another muscle is needed to pull them apart. Therefore every contracting muscle known as an agonist also needs an extending muscle in order to produce movement. The opposing muscles are called antagonists. This is known as the pair principle.

The main muscles used to produce movement are called prime movers; as these contract the antagonist must relax.

Synergists

Muscles that assist agonists and antagonists are known as synergists. These provide stability, as does a fixator muscle. For example, during elbow flexion the agonist is the biceps, the antagonist is the triceps, while the synergists are the brachioradialis and the brachialis.

Contraction

When the muscle contracts and shortens (for example the biceps in a biceps curl) this is called concentric contraction. When the muscle lengthens (for example during a triceps extension, the biceps lengthen), this is known as eccentric contraction.

The human body produces fine, skilled movements as a result of bones, muscles and joints acting in harmony. Every individual and all sports use this relationship but with differing priorities. For example skiing relies mostly on the lower body, swimming relies mostly on the upper body and aerobics relies on both equally. This element is introductory to allow you to understand the basics of human physiology. Unit 12 Health Related Fitness enables you to apply this knowledge in your chosen area.

Assignment 15.1

You are a coach taking a group of students for a coaching qualification. As part of this qualification you have to be aware of basic human physiology. Prepare some revision notes for your students that discuss the function of the skeleton, the major bones in the body, muscle types, groups and actions and their relationship to produce movement. Use a skeleton to illustrate your points and a flip chart to record major points.

Describe the cardiovascular and respiratory systems

Performance criteria

1 Describe the structure and action of the heart by means of annotated diagrams.
2 Explain the functions of the cardiovascular system.
3 Explain the effect of exercise on the cardiovascular system.
4 Describe the structure and functions of the respiratory system.
5 Explain the effect of exercise on the respiratory system.

Structure and action of the heart and functions of the cardiovascular system

Cardiovascular system

The two main components of the cardiovascular or circulatory system are

- The blood
- The heart

Our bodies require oxygen to be supplied to all our cells in order to survive; this includes the muscles. Oxygen is carried to the muscles by blood. Blood is pumped around the body by the heart and is transported in blood vessels of varying sizes. The circulatory system is a delivery and disposal service which supplies our bodies with their needs and then transports waste products to elimination sites.

Functions of the blood

- Delivers food and oxygen to the cells via the digestive system and lungs
- Transports waste products to the lungs and urinary systems
- Transports hormones
- Regulates the body's temperature; heat can be dissipated or conserved by the action of the blood vessels
- Regulates normal pH
- Fights infection as an integral part of the immune system

Blood vessels

Transportation of blood is via blood vessels; these carry blood from the heart, distribute it and then return the blood to the heart. These can vary in size from 1 cm to 0.001 cm.

Arteries

Blood vessels that take blood away from the heart are called arteries. They lie deep in the body and at the surface. If one is severed it will result in significant blood loss. The largest artery in the body is the aorta, which transports oxygenated blood from the heart to the rest of the body. These branch off and divide into smaller vessels called arterioles and then even smaller vessels called capillaries. The capillaries are microscopic (only one cell thick) and semi-permeable. This allows nutrients to pass through the body tissues and at the same time waste products to be passed back into the blood.

Veins

Capillaries, which function in a network, then start the passage back of blood to the heart via venules and then larger vessels called veins. The largest vein in the body is the vena cava, which transports deoxygenated blood from the body to the heart.

The heart

The heart is a hollow muscular organ about the size of a closed fist; it contains four chambers (see Figure 15.6).

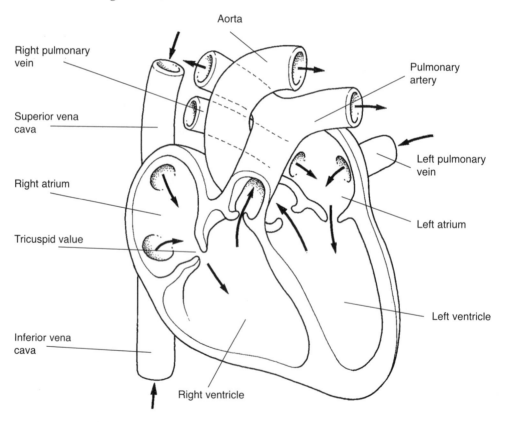

Fig. 15.6 The heart

Two thin-walled chambers at the top of the heart are called atria. The blood flows in one direction only, in to the heart.

Two thick-walled chambers at the bottom of the heart are called ventricles. The blood flows out of the heart from the ventricles.

The heart is situated in the thorax between the lungs and the diaphragm. It is a finely tuned organ; it transports blood around the body at a rate of 45 litres per minute when required, such as when exercising. At rest it beats 45–80 beats per minute rising to 180 beats per minute during exercise.

The action of the heart

When the cardiac muscle contracts, it squeezes blood out of the heart into the arteries (systole). When the cardiac muscle relaxes it fills with blood from the veins (diastole). The action of the heart can be described in six stages:

1 Deoxygenated blood arrives at the right atrium via the vena cava; it is a dull red and contains waste products. The blood has little oxygen left in it; this has been used during the blood's travels around the body.
2 The atrium contracts to pump the blood through the tricuspid valve into the right ventricle.
3 The blood is now transported to the lungs via the pulmonary artery in order to be stripped of carbon dioxide and to be supplied with oxygen. It then returns to the heart via the pulmonary vein.
4 The oxygenated blood, now bright red in colour, enters the left atrium.
5 The ventricle muscles contract, forcing the blood out of the heart via the aorta.
6 The blood is transported around the body via the arterioles and capillaries as the cycle starts again.

Effect of exercise on the cardiovascular system

Aerobic exercise will increase the efficiency of the heart; blood is pumped around the body with minimal effort as the coronary arteries are smooth and the levels of fat in the blood are reduced. Cardiac capacity is increased by exercise although only by a maximum of 20 per cent. We are all born with varying cardiac capacities and so pulse rates, etc. Training can improve our efficiency but not improve the overall capacity of the heart. Our fitness programmes must aim to maximise the efficiency of the cardiovascular system. (Please see Unit 12 Health Related Fitness.)

Structure and functions of the respiratory system

The function of the respiratory system is to take in air from the atmosphere, delivery oxygen to the blood, and return carbon dioxide to the atmosphere. Our bodies need oxygen for aerobic energy production and for life to continue.

Lungs

The organs involved in respiration are the lungs. The lungs are sited in the thorax which is separated from the abdomen by the diaphragm. The lungs are protected by the rib cage. We have two lungs; the right lung is slightly larger than the left.

Breathing cycle

We breathe in air containing oxygen from the atmosphere via the nose. From the nasal cavity the air is transported to the pharynx, by the epiglottis and to the larynx or the voice box (see Figure 15.7). It is then transported down the trachea or windpipe to two main branches of the respiratory system at the entrance to the lungs; these are called the left and right bronchus. The air then moves through each bronchus to smaller rubes called the bronchi and then even smaller tubes called bronchioles.

At the end of each tiny branch or bronchiole are alveolar ducts which are attached to alveolar sacs which contain alveoli. The alveoli are covered in capillaries.

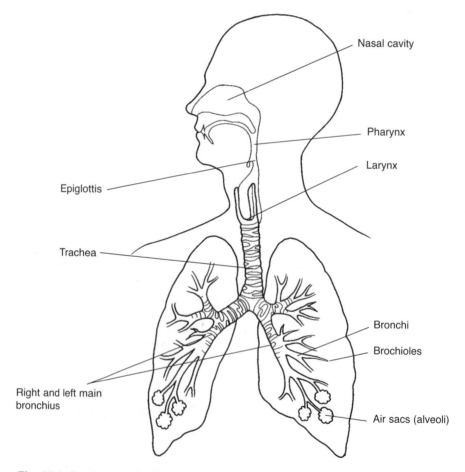

Fig. 15.7 Repiration and the breathing cycle

Gaseous exchange

It is at the capillaries that the deoxygenated blood, sent from the heart, is reoxygenated and carbon dioxide is discharged. The blood at the capillaries is low in oxygen and high in carbon dioxide. The opposite can be said of the air we have breathed in, which is high in oxygen and low in carbon dioxide. Therefore the oxygen is transferred to the blood by diffusion and the carbon dioxide moves from the capillaries into the alveolis for discharge. The blood is then transported back to the heart.

Effect of exercise on the respiratory system

The capacity of the lungs changes as a result of exercise; exercise has a beneficial effect on the respiratory system and is indeed one of the reasons we are encouraged to exercise.

Lung capacity

The tidal volume of the lungs, that is the volume of air inspired or expired per breath, increases during exercise.

The inspiratory reserve volume, that is the maximum volume of air we can breath in after quiet inspiration, decreases during exercise.

The expiratory reserve volume, that is the maximum volume of air we can breathe out after quiet expiration, decreases during exercise.

The vital capacity, that is the maximal volume of air that can be forcibly expired after maximal expiration, slightly decreases during exercise.

The residual volume, that is the volume of air remaining in the lungs at the end of a maximal expiration, slightly increases during exercise.

Stamina

As mentioned with respect to the cardiovascular system, exercise encourages our bodies to perform more efficiently and so allows us to exercise or perform everyday tasks for longer with reduced levels of effort. This is as a result of increased aerobic efficiency and stamina. (See also Unit 12.)

Assignment 15.2

This unit only needs to be covered briefly; in order to gain sufficient evidence for your portfolio, you need to describe both the cardiovascular and respiratory systems of the body, in detail but only as an introduction. You do not need to be a biochemist for example! Use diagrams to supplement your descriptions.

Performance criteria

1 Describe the structure and function of the digestive system and its associated organs.
2 Describe the nutritional requirements of the human body.
3 Explain the factors contributing to a healthy diet.
4 Explain the different amounts of nutrients required at different life stages and by individuals with different lifestyles

Structure and function of the digestive system

'We are what we eat' is a common phrase for discussing our individual nutritional requirements; these depend on our individual physiological make-up and also our lifestyles. A simple analogy is if we do not put the correct fuel in a car it fails to run efficiently; without fuel the car stops. The same can be said of our diets; we need certain nutrients in order to function and without food we would die.

Nutrition is the study of the food we eat and how the body uses it. Nutrients are those essential elements in food that we need for life and growth, but which our bodies cannot manufacture.

This element illustrates the varying nutritional needs of different categories and lifestyles.

Structure of the digestive system

Food is our fuel and without it we would cease to exist; however, the food we eat has to be broken down so to be useful to our bodies; this is the process of digestion (see Figure 15.8).

The structure of the digestive system includes the following organs and parts of the body: mouth, oesophagus, stomach, duodenum, ileum, caesium, colon, rectum, liver and pancreas.

Function of the digestive system

There are five main functions:

- Ingestion
- Digestion

- Absorption
- Assimilation
- Egestion

Figure 15.8 illustrates the digestive process, whereby food is broken down into molecules small enough to be digested into the bloodstream. The body is then provided with nutrients to

- Build new tissues
- Repair damaged tissues
- Provide energy

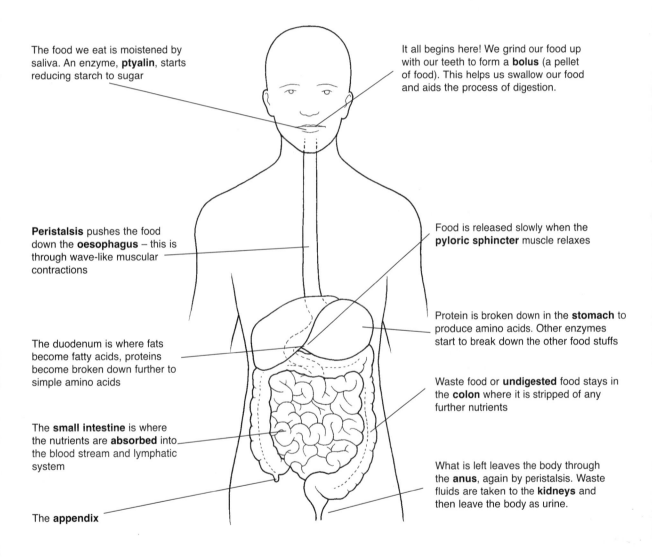

The food we eat is moistened by saliva. An enzyme, **ptyalin**, starts reducing starch to sugar

It all begins here! We grind our food up with our teeth to form a **bolus** (a pellet of food). This helps us swallow our food and aids the process of digestion.

Peristalsis pushes the food down the **oesophagus** – this is through wave-like muscular contractions

Food is released slowly when the **pyloric sphincter** muscle relaxes

The duodenum is where fats become fatty acids, proteins become broken down further to simple amino acids

Protein is broken down in the **stomach** to produce amino acids. Other enzymes start to break down the other food stuffs

The **small intestine** is where the nutrients are **absorbed** into the blood stream and lymphatic system

Waste food or **undigested** food stays in the **colon** where it is stripped of any further nutrients

What is left leaves the body through the **anus**, again by peristalsis. Waste fluids are taken to the **kidneys** and then leave the body as urine.

The **appendix**

Fig. 15.8 The digestive system

Nutritional requirements of the human body

There are six groups of nutrients that our bodies must consume for efficient functioning:

- Carbohydrates
- Fats
- Proteins
- Vitamins
- Mineral salts
- Water

Each group has a recommended level of consumption and each plays a vital role in the 'balanced diet' and general well-being.

Carbohydrates

Carbohydrates are composed of carbon, oxygen and hydrogen and are the primary source of energy in the body. They provide energy for exercise, for transmitting impulses through nerves and for the formation of new compounds in the body. There are two types of carbohydrates

- *Starch* – major sources include potatoes, bread, flour, pasta, rice
- *Sugars* – major sources include fruits, honey, confectionery, jams, table sugar

Carbohydrates in the form of sugars are in reality 'empty calories', although they do provide energy, the are also a cause of tooth decay and obesity. We should aim to take 80 per cent of our carbohydrates in the form of starch as these foods also tend to be rich in vitamins, minerals and dietary fibre. The simplest form of carbohydrates is the monosaccharide, which is a sugar such as that found in fruit (fructose) and in honey (glucose). The process of digestion breaks down disaccharides (for example lactose found in milk and sucrose which is table sugar) and polysaccharides (which are starch carbohydrates) to monsaccharides, which are then ready to be used by the body as energy.

Fats

Although it is recommended in the developed world that we decrease our fat intake, fat is not 'bad for us'; it does serve a vital purpose within the body. It is excess fat intake that is unhealthy.

We need fat to keep us warm, to act as a buffer against injury, to protect vital organs and as a secondary source of energy for muscular activity.

There are two types of fat: saturated and unsaturated.

Saturated fats

Major sources of saturated fats include milk, cheese, butter and red meat. It is recognised that this type of fat increases cholesterol levels in the blood and so should account for only 10 per cent of our fat intake.

Unsaturated fats

Major sources of unsaturated fats include oil, margarine, fish and nuts. It is argued by some that this type of fat actually helps reduce cholesterol levels in the blood and so our fat intake should be mainly made up of unsaturated fats. There are two essential fatty acids that we have to consume through the diet: these are linoleic and linolenic fatty acids, which are both provided by unsaturated fats.

Cholesterol

Cholesterol is a fatty substance found mainly in animal produce. It is actually produced naturally by the body but any excess gained from the diet tends to line the walls of blood vessels and prevent efficient circulation of the blood thus increasing the risk of heart disease.

Proteins

Proteins are made up of amino acids, the building blocks of all tissues in the body. An adult person needs twenty-one amino acids, of which nine need to be consumed from our diet; these are known as essential amino acids. Proteins can be obtained from both animal and vegetable sources; animal proteins, for example meat, fish and cheese, contain all these essential amino acids. Protein is used by the body to build cells and tissues and so is particularly important during periods of growth such as childhood, adolescence and during pregnancy; it is never the primary source of energy and so the theory of a 'steak before a fight' is actually of little value to an athlete.

Vegetarians have to ensure they supplement their diets in order to consume all the essential amino acids as these are not provided in all vegetable protein. Vegetables usually provide one or two essential amino acids and so a broad range must be consumed to ensure the body receives an adequate supply of all nine.

Vitamins

Vitamins are organic compounds that are needed for the efficient functioning of muscles and nerves, the growth of body tissue and for the release of energy from foods. They are required only in small amounts and are not stored in the body, so it is essential that our diet supplies all of these vitamins. Table 15.1 (on the following page) lists specific sources and details of vitamins needed in the diet, and the effects that deficiencies cause.

Vitamins are divided into two groups:

- Fat soluble vitamins
- Water soluble vitamins

Mineral salts

Minerals are basic elements that account for 4 per cent of our body weight; they assist in many body functions, for example calcium aids the formation of healthy bones and teeth. There are fourteen minerals we need in minute quantities called trace minerals and seven we need in larger quantities called macrominerals. Table 15.2 gives sources and details of minerals needed in the diet, and the effects that deficiencies cause.

Table 15.1 Vitamins needed in the diet

Vitamin	Source	Functions	Effects of deficiency
Vitamin A (retinol) Fat soluble	Animal: butter, eggs, cheese Vegetable: carrots, greens, tomatoes	• Necessary for the health of mucous membranes of the throat, digestive and excretory tracts • Resistance to infection • Growth of bones and teeth • Helps vision	• Blindness – ulcerated cornea
Vitamin D (cholecalciferol) Fat soluble	Animal: fish liver oils, fish, eggs, dairy fat Sunlight	• Formation of bones and teeth (+ calcium + phosphorous)	• Rickets • Dental decay
Vitamin E (tocopherol) Fat soluble	Wheatgerm oil, eggs, milk	• Used to treat women who have had miscarriages	
Vitamin K	Obtained sufficiently in well-balanced diet, including green vegetables	• Enables blood to clot	
Vitamin B_1 (thiamine) Water soluble	Wheatgerm, yeast, oatmeal, nuts	• Liberation of energy to form glucose (enzyme system) • Growth and good health	• Arrested growth in children • Loss of appetite, nausea, fatigue, constipation, nervous irritability • Beri-beri
Vitamin B_2 (riboflavin) Water soluble	Yeast, liver, cheese, cereal goods	• Release of energy from goods by oxidation (enzyme system) • Utilisation of food fats and amino acids	• Arrested growth in children • Inflammation of mouth and tongue • Nervous depression, unhealthy skin and digestive tract (disturbances) • Cornea misted and vision impaired
Vitamin B_{12} (nicotinic acid) Water soluble	Yeast, peanuts, liver, beef	• Release of energy from carbohydrate foods	• Arrested growth in children • Diarrhoea, digestive trouble • Rough, red, raw skin • Mental disorders – pellagra

Vitamin	Source	Functions	Effects of deficiency
Vitamin C (ascorbic acid) Water soluble	Fruit: blackcurrants, lemons, oranges, apples Vegetable: parsley, peppers, cauliflower, cabbage	• Healthy body tissues • Helps heal wounds • Healthy teeth and gums • Formation of connective tissue • Absorption of iron	• Bad skin • Teeth and gum decay • Slow healing of wounds • Arrested growth in children • Laziness, instability • Scurvy–severe

Table 15.2 Minerals needed in the diet

Mineral	Source	Functions	Effects of deficiency
Calcium	Cheese, milk, bread, oily fish	• Development of bones and teeth • Clotting of blood • Functioning of muscles	• Rickets • Badly formed bones and teeth
Phosphorus	Found in all living cells so is present in most foods	• Energy production • Regulate acid balance in body • Development of bones and teeth	
Iron	Liver, kidney, egg yolk, meat, wholemeal bread, fruit, vegetables	• Formation of haemoglobin • Transporting oxygen in blood	• Poor health • Anaemia
Iodine	Seawater fish, water	• Sufficient amount of hormone produced by thyroid gland in neck • Babies born with mothers who have serious deficiency problems may be mentally handicapped	• Derbyshire neck (goitre)
Sodium (+ chlorine)	Salt	• Correct composition of body fluids	• Muscular cramps
Fluorine	Drinking water, fish	• Healthy formation of bones and teeth • Prevent dental decay	• Excess causes mottling on teeth

Water

Water is an essential nutrient; it is second only to oxygen in importance for the body. It transports nutrients; it removes waste and regulates body temperature. We would all survive a number of weeks without food but only a number of days without water. Water accounts for two-thirds of an adult's body weight.

Factors contributing to a healthy diet

The diet we consume affects our overall well-being and performance. Current guidelines recommend that our diet is balanced; all the nutrients listed in the previous section are essential; we all need them in differing quantities and it is only when they are consumed in either insufficient or excessive amounts that our diet becomes unbalanced and our bodies do not perform maximally.

In a balanced diet, it is important to consider the quantities of fat, salt, sugar and fibre that we eat.

Generally we are recommended to

- Reduce our intake of fat, particularly saturated fats, as this is linked to obesity and heart disease
- Reduce our consumption of salt, as this is linked to an increase in blood pressure and heart disease
- Reduce our intake of sugar, as this is linked to problems of excess weight gain and to tooth decay
- Increase our consumption of fibre, as this aids digestion, controls blood sugar levels, reduces blood cholesterol levels and promotes a general feeling of well-being

Nutrients required at different life stages and by individuals with different lifestyles

The amount of energy and the different nutritional requirements we need depend on our lifestyle, our life stage or age, and whether we are male or female.

Calorie

The calorie is used to measure energy production in the body; this is defined as the heat required to raise one gram of water by one degree centigrade. Measurements are usually made in kilocalories as the calorie unit is too small for any practical use (1 kilocalorie = 1000 calories). A more recent measure of energy production is the joule, which is the energy expended when one kilogram is moved by a force of one newton.

Basal metabolic rate

The more energetic we are, the more energy we need and so the more calories we use. However, whatever our lifestyle, we all need a certain amount of energy to maintain the life processes. This is called the basal metabolic rate (BMR). This is normally 50–70 per cent of our daily caloric expenditure. It is influenced by size and composition of the body, for instance a muscular person uses more energy than a fat person. Age is known to lower the BMR.

In order to calculate your daily caloric expenditure, you need to add the caloric costs of the activities of your day. This is measured by the amount of oxygen used to perform the activity. Energy expenditure is only an estimate as it will depend on such factors as skill and body weight.

Lifestyle

Lifestyle affects an individual's energy requirements. A sedentary lifestyle has few extra activities and generally involves a 'sit down' office job. An active lifestyle includes regular exercise and perhaps a manual or labour-intensive job.

Other influences on energy expenditure include pregnancy, lactation and other medical conditions.

Life stage or age

Energy requirements change, depending on age. Energy requirements are shown in Table 15.3. Peak requirements are during the ages of 15–18, due largely to rapid growth through puberty. After this time energy requirements fall. This can account for 'middle age spread' where people continue with the same diet but tend to acquire a few unwanted pounds in weight.

Table 15.3 Energy requirements by age and sex

| Age | Estimated average requirements | |
| | MJ/day (Kcal/day) | |
	Males	Females
Months		
0–3	2.28 (545)	2.16 (515)
10–12	3.85 (920)	3.61 (865)
Years		
1–3	5.15 (1230)	4.86 (1165)
4–6	7.16 (1715)	6.46 (1545)
7–10	8.24 (1970)	7.28 (1740)
11–14	9.27 (2220)	7.91 (1845)
15–18	11.51 (2755)	8.83 (2110)
19–50	10.60 (2550)	8.10 (1940)
51–59	10.60 (2550)	8.00 (1900)
60–64	9.93 (2380)	7.99 (1900)
65–74	9.71 (2330)	7.96 (1900)
75+	8.77 (2100)	7.61 (1810)

(*Source:* Statistics from COMA: Committee on Medical Aspects of Food Policy)

Sex

The BMR of a man is higher than that of a woman because of the differing body compositions; men have more muscle and women have more fat. The BMR for a man weighing 65 kg is 7560 kJ/day and the BMR for a woman weighing 55 kg is 5960 kJ/day.

Obesity

You often read in the newspapers about a number of eating disorders and the health of the nation. It is claimed that in the developed world, the number of obese people, that is those carrying excess body fat, is ever increasing. Obesity causes high blood pressure, which is associated with an increase in the risk of heart disease. The cause of obesity is generally social. Our society encourages overeating, often rewarding success with high calorie/low nutrition snacks. Obesity can be caused by the malfunctioning of the thyroid gland but this is extremely rare.

Anorexia nervosa

There is also a general raising of awareness of the disease of anorexia nervosa. This is an eating disorder where the victim refuses to eat to the point of starvation as a result of the fear of being fat. The extreme result is death. This condition tends to affect young women but is not limited to this group. Anorexics need medical help in order to return their diet and lifestyle to the accepted norm for their age and weight.

Conversion of food into energy

Carbohydrate, fat and protein are all energy providers; our primary source is carbohydrate, followed by fat and protein is never our most immediate source of energy. Carbohydrate provides 17.1 kJ; fat provides 38.9 kJ and protein provides 18.2 kJ of energy. So how can a potato become the fuel that allows our bodies to perform everyday and elite activities? The process of digestion and absorption ensures that our food provides sufficient energy to keep us warm and to provide movement.

This process takes place in the mitochondria of every cell and by a process of oxidation, a chemical compound called adenosine triphosphate (ATP) is produced. This is the energy currency of the body and supplies energy for muscular contraction.

Carbohydrate, fat and protein are burned in the presence of oxygen and adenosine diphosphate to produce ATP; other bi-products include carbon dioxide and water. Any surplus energy is given off as heat.

Creatine phosphate is another high energy substance stored in the muscles; this allows muscular contractions to take place without the presence of oxygen. (This is discussed further in Unit 12 Health Related Fitness.)

Healthy living

Our ability to perform depends greatly on our lifestyle; we all have the option to pursue healthy living yet a great number of people abuse their bodies. This abuse includes excess alcohol consumption, smoking, drug dependency, overeating, undereating and malnutrition.

Our life stage affects our demand for nutrients: the fitter and (more importantly) more active we are, the more energy we expend, therefore the more calories and nutrients we need. An active lifestyle will require more fluid intake due to increased loss of fluid through sweating; this can include a manual or active occupation as well as exercise. The diet of a child is different from that of an adult; a child has to sustain growth and so too does a woman's body during pregnancy.

Pregnant women

It is important that the diet of a pregnant woman should be nutritionally sound, so that she produces a healthy baby and at the same time maintains her own health.

Even before pregnancy, it is vital that a woman of childbearing age has a balanced diet so that she is able to cope with the demands of pregnancy, once this occurs.

There used to be a popular saying that a pregnant woman should 'eat for two'; in one sense this is true, but it does not mean that she should double her daily amount of food. This is unnecessary and can lead to excessive weight gain. What it does mean is that her diet should provide sufficient nutrients to cope with the demands of the growing baby as well as the needs of her own body. The increased requirements for the individual nutrients are shown in Table 15.4

Table 15.4 Nutritional requirements during pregnancy

	Non-pregnant	Pregnant	Lactating
Energy (kj/kcal)	9,000/2,150	10,000/2,400	11,500/2,750
Protein (g)	54	60	69
Vitamin A (µg)	750	750	1,200
Thiamin (mg)	0.9	1.0	1.1
Riboflavin (mg)	1.3	1.6	1.8
Nicotinic acid (mg)	15	18	21
Vitamin C (mg)	30	60	60

The foetus receives nutrients from the mother; these nutrients are carried from the mother's bloodstream through the placenta and umbilical cord into the baby's bloodstream.

Nature ensures that if a particular nutrient is in short supply, it is the foetus who receives the nutrient, not the mother.

If the mother's diet lacks some nutrients, here are the possible effects.

Lack of calcium

If the diet is deficient in calcium or vitamin D, then some of the calcium from the mother's bones and teeth will be removed and passed on to the foetus. This will weaken the mother's bones and teeth and she may develop adult's rickets.

Lack of vitamin A

If the diet is deficient in vitamin A, then any that is stored in the mother's liver will go to the foetus. This may result in the symptoms of vitamin A deficiency. Often the foetus' store of vitamin A does not build up sufficiently; once born many babies develop a vitamin A deficiency which in extreme cases can lead to blindness in these babies.

Lack of iron

A deficiency of iron can lead to anaemia in the mother and a failure to build up a store of iron in the foetus. This store is important because both breast milk and cow's milk are poor sources of iron, and the newborn baby has to rely on the store of iron that it builds up as a foetus for the first three months of life. In the UK most pregnant women are prescribed iron tablets.

General advice during pregnancy

In the UK a careful check is kept on both the mother and her developing baby in order to ensure that an adequate diet is maintained; low-incomed families can get statutory help with this. During antenatal clinics, mothers are given plenty of advice on diet and well-being during pregnancy.

It is generally recommended that the following nutrients should be increased in the daily diet:

- Vitamin D
- The minerals iron and calcium
- Folic acid
- Dietary fibre as constipation is an unpleasant side-effect of pregnancy

It is important not to increase the consumption of energy through high calorie foods such as chocolate and biscuits, as this can lead to excess weight gain.

After the birth the mother's nutrient requirements increase to enable the body to cope with breastfeeding and also the increased activity associated with rearing a baby; fluid intake during breastfeeding should also be increased.

Infancy (up to one year)

An infant's diet for the first few weeks of life consists solely of milk. Human breast milk is specifically designed to feed human beings and it follows that is therefore more suitable than other milks for consumption. The reasons for this are

- The correct composition and proportion of nutrients are provided automatically
- The milk is at the correct temperature and consistency
- Virtually all the milk is digested by the baby
- The baby takes only what is needed and is therefore less likely to become overweight
- Immunity from some diseases is passed to the baby from the mother
- There is a reduction in gastric infections as the milk is sterile

Bottle-fed babies do also thrive; however, they do not benefit from the advantages above. Bottle milk is manufactured as closely to breast milk as is possible.

Children

When babies have been weaned on to solid food they can enjoy the wide range of foods on offer. A broad-based diet should be followed; children do tend to grow quickly and the following nutrients should be increased to supply this extra demand for energy:

- Protein for body growth
- Calcium for bones and teeth
- Fluoride for teeth
- Iron for red blood cells

Children should be limited in the amount of sugary foods they eat as these serve little nutritional benefit and do cause tooth decay. Babies and young children should not be given nuts, which can cause them to choke, and they should not eat foods containing nuts, as these can lead to severe allergies when they are older.

Adolescents

Adolescence is a period of rapid growth and body development; consequently nutrient requirements increase at this stage of development.

The hormones for adulthood are produced at this stage and this may cause skin disturbances. It is important for adolescents to eat plenty of fresh fruit and vegetables and avoid eating fatty foods that may aggravate these conditions. The diet should provide plenty of protein. Girls particularly need sufficient iron to avoid the symptoms of anaemia, which may develop with the onset of menstruation.

Adults

Once body growth has declined in adulthood, food is required to maintain and repair the body and keep it healthy. Nutrient requirements will to some extent be determined by the body size of the individual and the amount of daily activity.

Women need less food than men in general.

The type of job will affect the balance of the nutrients required:

Very active jobs

Sufficient energy must be provided for this sort of occupation but in the form of carbohydrate, not fat, as this can increase the risk of heart disease. Fluid intake must increase, particularly if the job is in a warm atmosphere.

Sedentary jobs

Careful attention should be paid to the energy intake of meals for this type of worker, as it is easy to exceed energy output and therefore lead to weight gain. Meals should be kept simple and less bulky as these are more comfortable to digest during inactive periods.

Old age

As age increases, activity slows down, especially after retirement from an active job. Food is required to maintain the health and state of the body as in the younger age group but there is an increased requirement for calcium and vitamin D to prevent decalcification of the bones and teeth, and for iron to prevent anaemia.

The size of meal should decrease with levels of activity but the quality should not. Often the diet of elderly people is affected for social reasons, such as a reduction in income. The death of a partner can mean that there is no motivation to cook meals for one person, or possibly the bereaved partner lacks the domestic skills required.

Advice on diet

For each of the life stages there are huge amounts of literature regarding diet. Advice given can conflict, both currently and over time as research increases knowledge and opinions change.

Diet is a specific aspect of a fitness programme and is totally individual, through social, physiological and environmental causes. When discussing a specific diet, all facts must be noted first and preferably referred to a qualified dietician or doctor.

Assignment 15.3

Now is the time to be truthful! Take a long, hard look at your diet. For a week log your activities and your diet; at the end of this week relate your findings to the recommended nutritional requirements. Discuss your lifestyle and the effects it may have on your nutritional needs and how this may affect performance. What could you do to improve your diet? Now study a different category of person and discuss their diet and the differences between it and your own.

Index